FAST AND FREE

Pete Livesey

STORIES OF A ROCK CLIMBING LEGEND

Compiled and produced by
John Sheard and Mark Radtke

2QT Limited (Publishing)

First Edition published 2014 by
2QT Limited (Publishing)
Lancaster, Lancashire. LA2 8RE

Grateful acknowledgement is made for the permission by contributing authors
for inclusion of their work and photographs. All rights reserved and used with
permission.

Cover design: Hilary Pitt, Robbie Associates Ltd.

Front cover image: Livesey Portrait by John Cleare 1974.
Rear Cover Image: Pete Livesey soloing New Diversions
5.10a. Yosemite 1976 by Geoff Birtles.
Inside flap image: Livesey on Wellington Crack
Ilkley Quarry 1974 by John Cleare.

Although every precaution has been taken in the preparation of this book, the
publisher and authors assume no responsibility for errors or omissions. Neither
is any liability assumed for damages resulting from the use of this information
contained herein.

Printed in Malta on behalf of Latitude Press Limited.

A CIP catalogue record for this book is available from the British Library.
ISBN 978-1-910077-01-6

This shot by Geoff Birtles accompanied Pete's article '*You Too Can Have a Body Like Mine*' first published in *High Magazine*. The article is reproduced in the appendix of this book under the title '*A Short Treatise on Training*'. This was one of Livesey's more academic essays, but if there was a joke to be had Pete would have it.

Acknowledgements

Soma and Tai, who gave this project their approval. All the contributors who put pen to paper and who get special mention in the appendix of this book, without you this project was a non-starter. They include; John Barker, John Barraclough, Martin Berzins, Geoff Birtles (thanks Geoff for the encouragement and technical advice on the book), Andy Cave, John Cleare, Ian Cooksey, Graham Desroy, Jean-Claude Droyer, the late Jim Eyre, Ron Fawcett, Peter Gomersall, Dennis Gray, Frank Kew, Jill Lawrence, Alison Livesey (for giving us permission to use the letter sent to her from her uncle Pete), John Long, Nicho Mailänder, Rob Matheson (for sharing some of his memories of events during Lakes development in the 1970s), Dan Morgan, Bernard Newman (for permissions to include extracts from Extreme Rock), Janine Newman, Sid Perou (for suggesting the inclusion of his recorded interview with the late Ray Stoyles and for making video recordings at Pete's eulogy, which enabled us to turn some of the readings into text), Tom Price (who gave permission for us to use the Bingley College chapter from his book shortly before his death), John Stanger, Tony Thornley, and Johnny Walker. Everyone who donated their photographs, with special thanks to John Barker, Geoff Birtles, John Cleare, Ron Fawcett, Pete Gomersall, Adrian Ledgway, Bernard Newman, Ian Smith and John Stanger, who took the time to trawl through their archives and pull out the excellent historical shots. Also to Alan Carne for supplying the contemporary photographs of the Verdon. In times past, friends often shared their photographs with each other and it was commonplace to have photographs that were of personal relevance in one's own private collection. We have included a few shots that fall into this category taken from the Birtles and Sheard archives and would like to thank Dave Croaker, Brian Cropper, Bob Dearman, Al Evans, Bonny Masson, Chris Tullis and John Woodhouse, whose work appears in the plated sections. In the spirit of climbing camaraderie we trust that you appreciate the inclusion of your fine shots in this publication. Special thanks go to Sharon Horry for translating the Jean-Claude Droyer piece and to Carol Sheard for her support and assistance. Thanks to all the team at 2QT Limited Publishing, including, Robert Auty, Catherine Cousins, Gerry Keenan and Ian Smith, and Hilary Pitt for her design work on the cover, end papers and plate sections. John Coefield and Vertibrate Publishing, who now own the rights of the Diadem publications *Games Climbers Play* and *Mirrors in the Cliffs* in which some of Pete's writings appear. Mark Radtke supplied the images and design concepts for the end papers.

Contents

Part 2. – The Original Rock Athlete

Part 3 – Game On

Part 4 - Astroman

Appendix

I had cause to reflect less upon the meaning of death than upon the nature of life and how wonderful and mysterious it was. There seemed to me nothing mysterious about death; it was just negation, emptiness, a void. What was miraculous, and strange, and passing all understanding, was life. It was at once precarious and enduring. One walked a tightrope between oblivion and the inestimable riches of being in the land of the living.

Travail So Gladly Spent - Tom Price.

Preface

By John Sheard

December 2013

Way, way back in time, when Cloggy was a mere forty minute stroll from the farm buildings at the end of the road up from Llanberis, and that with a ten minute stop for homemade lemonade at the half-way house, two youngish climbers were making their way towards a frequent destination, Clogwyn du'r Arddu, the Black Cliff. One very athletic, rangy and a little goofy in appearance, slightly scruffy and clad in steel toe capped work boots. The other smoother looking, in Norwegian sweater, Alpine salopettes and climbing boots; keeper of new ropes and the latest equipment – alloy chocks, moacs and new-fangled wire things. An observer might have been confused as to the respective roles of this partnership; that was until they hit the rock! Livesey, the rangy one, and most unlikely of the two, was a force to be reckoned with but didn't know it yet, a man completely at one with the crag before him, unfazed by the past performance of others and eager for adventure. Aware of his worth in the more familiar world of caving, he was coming to realise that he could also make a major impact in rock climbing. No one knew it just then but, *'The times they were a changing.'*

The big route of the crag was *The Boldest*; ads in the magazines showed Cliff Philips on the crux, with a caption to the effect that a fall from this point would be fatal – serious stuff and, as it emerged, Pete's plan for later in the day.

A Lakeland star of Nepalese extraction, or so we naively deduced from an overheard conversation, was retreating from the lower wall, with tales of lack of protection and impossible conditions. His audience was suitably impressed with the attempt, and even more so as Pete elbowed his way to the front and proceeded to lead the route with obvious ease. The point was forcibly made. He had arrived!

Over the next decade Pete became a dominant force in British rock climbing, leading an escalation of grades, instigating a different approach to new routing and creating a change in so called ethics; revolutionary at the time but eventually accepted as natural and common place. He was ahead of the game and, with few exceptions, remained that way until the time came to leave the stage. Some of his routes and his refusal to conform attracted a degree of criticism which lingered after his departure, but, in the words of Pete Whillance, a man well qualified to express a valid opinion, '*Quite a few in the Lakes say that Livesey never instigated any new move in the 1970s and there was no real increase in the grade and there were a lot of people climbing about the same standard. But I was there and I know differently … he brought a new approach. It might have been ruthless and professional, but he had that urge within himself that he was going to do things; he was going to push standards, go for the hard lines – and he stood on his own and went for them.*'

Pete Livesey didn't just raise standards; he brought a zany humour, controversy and a degree of common sense to an anarchic game, which could have been in danger of taking itself seriously.

When compared with some of his contemporaries, his output of new routes, if viewed only in terms of quantity, was relatively modest. What is impressive is their quality. At the time they provided a step change in commitment and difficulty, and looking back we can see that, as with the routes of Brown and Whillans in the 1950s, Livesey's contribution marks another standout milestone in the history of rock climbing. These routes were put out not only in the UK, but in every popular climbing area that existed in the 1970s. Some were of epic proportions and, given the prevailing standards and mind-set of those times, required not only exceptional physical ability but also vision, and an inner mental strength. It was this 'cool' which allowed him to venture into serious situations whilst maintaining control and for a time this set him apart from his peers. His achievements in 1974 which produced the likes of *Footless Crow* and *Right Wall* were extraordinary and, whilst not unexpected by those who knew him well, came as something of a shock to the establishment in Wales and the Lakes. It would be two or three years before the competition caught up and much more than that before his standards were surpassed and assimilated by the wider climbing community.

At a time in the 1970s, when it was unusual for UK rock climbers to venture far beyond the European Alps or the Vercors, Pete led a series of local experts and mates to destinations in the USA, Germany, Austria, Canada, Italian Dolomites, Greece and France, to explore and, in most cases, introduce a uniquely British style of rock climbing, which would become accepted as the norm and form the basis of what was to become known as 'sport climbing'; the latter development unplanned and ultimately contrary to the traditions to which he subscribed.

But Pete was far more than a Rock Climber. He had a love of wild and rugged countryside; embracing the many outdoor activities associated with such places and forming many lasting friendships along the way. His death from pancreatic cancer at his home in Malham, amidst the Yorkshire Dales, where he had spent a significant part of his life, was felt by all who had shared a part of his adventures; it was February 1998, he was only 54 years old. In his final year he had, on several occasions, commented on the importance of the quality of life, compounding the tragedy of a premature end to an extraordinary record of achievement. For a man who had always been strong and self-contained, keenly aware of his position at the top of the many games he chose to adopt, and self-reliant within those games, his ultimate dependence on the care of others and loss of control of his destiny, must have been particularly hard to bear. That he was able to do so with dignity, strength and even occasional humour bore testimony to the power of the man. After his death, friend and mentor Tom Price, who must have greatly influenced Pete in the field of effective adventure based education, and who was to enjoy a long, active life lasting 94 years, posed the simple, mountaineers' question, 'Did he suffer?' Well, he must have done as he felt the life force slowly deserting him, but throughout that final year he never appeared to complain or to rail against the unfairness of it all. Rather, as in his climbing life, he set an example of how to lead for those who must inevitably follow.

His abilities, both in his many adventure activities and in his academic world, were exceptional and unique. Often single minded and driven by a vital need to achieve self-imposed goals, he was, never the less, fascinating company and seldom scornful of those incapable of meeting his standards. Having set himself a project he would go to any ends to achieve its completion. Time had to be found, transport had to be made available, a companion had to be recruited. Whilst this might give the impression of a ruthless, self-centred man, driven to succeed at any cost, and if necessary at the expense of others, the truth is that he was at his best when sharing his dreams with like -minded friends who knew his real value both on and off the rock. His perception of the absurdities of life gave rise to a piercing humour and a casual image, at least to the uninitiated, which was incompatible with his position, for a time, as one of the world's most accomplished climbers and a worthy, if sometimes closeted, academic.

His life was celebrated by friends and colleagues at a gathering in Skipton Town Hall; there was much laughter in the normally austere room as a full house of climbers, cavers, orienteers, fellow teachers and family recalled stories of happier times shared together, and not only of derring-do; only Pete could turn up wearing a 'Buy British Beef' T-shirt at a dinner party provided by vegetarian hosts. There might have been the occasional lump in many a throat but grief was kept well hidden; it was not his way.

In the last week of his life I asked the question, *'Did you write it all down.'* His simple reply was, *'No, and it's too late now.'* Sometimes seen as a self-publicist, the truth is Pete had a talent and love for writing, which started long before his prominence as a rock climber, his often self-deprecating pieces appearing in many earlier caving journals and local newspapers. What a book it would have been! Though it must inevitably fall short of what he would have left for us, what follows is simply an attempt to leave an authentic, if possibly unusual, record about the life and climbs of Peter Livesey, presented through the words of those who knew him best or who had the good fortune to have had the experience of his company. If we have been successful then profits arising from the publication of this book are to be donated to Take Heart, the registered charity of The Yorkshire Heart Centre administered from The Leeds General Infirmary.

Self actualisation is not the end of the journey. The human spirit gives us the power to transcend ourselves. At its best leadership touches and releases this spirit in us.

David McClelland.

Introduction

By Mark Radtke

We are acutely aware that Pete was far more than a rock athlete, but took the view that to produce a comprehensive biography of Pete as the complete outdoor pursuits activist would be a mammoth task and beyond our resources. From the outset, we decided to focus on Pete Livesey the rock climber, since this is where we feel he has left his greatest legacy.

When we embarked on this project we were unsure of the reception we would receive, indeed whether people would wish to contribute to a work that would be clearly a 'labour of love'. In the event we were not disappointed, virtually everyone we approached accepted the task unfalteringly and enthusiastically, and we are eternally grateful to all those who helped, no matter how great or small their efforts. Perhaps this is testimony enough to the respect that people have for Pete as one of our all-time greats. We understood at the outset that the final body of work eventually assembled would, in all likelihood represent a disparate array of subject matter and writing styles. We were also sympathetic to the fact that putting pen to paper would be quite daunting to a number of key contributors. With this in mind we kept our project brief broad in order to encourage contribution and creativity. This approach proved a success in that the diversity of subject matter and the unique range of 'authors' voices' brings a quality to this work that we think transcends 'the take' on Livesey that a single biographer might present.

Inevitably some of the essays stray into his early caving exploits, but these set the scene for his development as a rock climber and give insight into what came to have personal meaning for him. One of our key objectives was that what was produced would provide some understanding of the man himself, not just what he achieved. We hope that what we have brought to the reader is a body of work that conveys aspects of Pete's unorthodox approach to life, his inner values, his drive, his achievements, his influence, and his legacy.

In order to give the book form and structure, we have assembled essays under four generic themes ordered into four distinct sections. We think this brings a sense of evolution to Livesey the rock climber. There is also a logical, though not precise chronology to the ordering of chapters.

We have positioned John Long's essay, *Haunted House*, as the prologue because it sets the scene for what follows, *Fast and Free*, perfectly.

Part 1 Birth of a Rock Climber – Provides some insight into Pete's early motives, his personal drives and values. It gives the reader the opportunity to gain an understanding of what shaped him as a pioneering explorer and how he was able to apply these personal qualities to rock climbing with such great effect. Aspects of Pete's professional life are also covered here.

Part 2 The Original Rock Athlete – Illustrates how and why Pete became a catalyst in pushing climbing standards and raising the game nationally. Essays provide objective commentary on some of his more controversial methods, but above all we gain an appreciation of the quality of rock climbs that Livesey established across the UK.

Part 3 Game On – Looks at 'the inner game' of Livesey, focussing on his approach to competition, training and how he loved to break with convention and bend the rules. This section contains some of the more quirky pieces in the book, allowing a little peek at what made him tick and what made him such a stand out character.

Part 4 *Astroman* – Enables the reader to gain an appreciation of Pete's Impact on the global stage. How he changed attitudes and approaches to free climbing both at home and abroad. It also seeks to highlight how influential Livesey was in shaping free climbing as it exists today and answer the question, 'Does Livesey deserve a place in the pantheon of climbing Greats?'

As well as his athletic prowess, Pete was a gifted writer with a wonderful and humorous turn of phrase indicative of his character. Some of Pete's essays such as, *Travels with a Donkey*, are fantastic and timeless ripping yarns, whilst others such as, *The Grades of Things to Come*, *Jonathan Livingstone Steelfingers*, and, *Castaway on a Gritstone Island*, were quite visionary when written, yet should still resonate with today's contemporary rock climber. We are pleased that we have been able to reproduce them here and hopefully reintroduce some of his previously published work to a new generation of climber. Pete's work now can live for posterity where it should belong, in one volume.

At the end of the narrative we have included an appendix containing further information that might be of interest to the reader, including a chronology of events which highlight some of Pete's more significant achievements. Hopefully this will help put some of the essays in their historical context. In true guidebook style, and as a tribute to Livesey the pragmatist, we have compiled a 'tick list' of his great classic UK routes. Go out and climb them all and really appreciate and enjoy what he's left for us.

We should brush nothing aside, set no restrictions. We should experience hunger and thirst, be able to go fast, but also know how to go slowly and to contemplate.

Starlight and Storm - Gaston Rébuffat (1956).

Prologue

Haunted House

by John Long

Nobody knew which one was hotter, Yosemite in the summer, or the middle of the sun. This heat is the main reason I met and climbed with so many Englishmen.

All the way into my mid-20s I was marooned in college and couldn't escape for summer vacation till June, when most of the Yosemite hardcore had migrated to the sissy slabs up in Tuolumne Meadows, or went mountain climbing in the High Sierra, or sailed for Europe if they had the dough, or worked some dead-end job if they didn't. Valley journeyman, Hank Dubois, must have landed the best of these gigs when he worked the summer as a night watchman in a Fresno mattress factory. No shit.

British climbers with Yosemite aspirations usually waited till June, when the valley caught fire, to invade Camp 4 (Yosemite's traditional climber's campground, and now a Historical Site in the national registry). Most had fooled away another desultory UK winter scratching up the grit, slumming around pubs and drinking warm beer, pestering girls and watching *Dr Who*. The California heat was a boon to this gang, who often arrived looking gaunt and as pale as corpses. Right into the mid 1970s, most of the time, it was just me, some mad dogs, and a few Englishmen who actively climbed Valley walls in July and August.

Of course, this is not literally true. A handful of California and Colorado climbers, plus a smattering of French and Germans, were also so keen on Yosemite glory, you couldn't have dragged them from 'The Ditch' with a 20-mule team. There was loads of new ground to prospect and we tried laying claim to it all. Young maniacs fall in together much as water pools. I'd barely finished shaking hands with Ron Fawcett when we stuffed a few things into a mail sack and started up El Capitan, an event in every rock-climber's career. I think we were both 18 years old and, like sharks, had to keep moving or die. We climbed at roughly the same level, and might have made the first one-day ascent of *The Nose*, had we not gotten fried alive by high noon temps and no wind, leaving us to huddle under our sleeping pads on the ledges below The Great Roof. Ron had never done any aid climbing and had no clue about the techniques, which I hadn't bothered explaining and which he'd faked and bungled all the way up. We spent the remains of the day panting and going over the basics, 1,500 feet up The Captain. Ron also mentioned another climber named Pete Livesey, reigning Lord of British rock, who he especially admired and who'd brought modern training techniques to the work.

The next season I met Pete Livesey at Arch Rock. The other Brits I'd climbed and caroused around with, like Jerry 'Steel Fingers' Peel, Chris 'I love French birds' Gibb, Doug 'Bugger Off' Scott, and Nick 'Got a smoke?' Estcourt, to mention a few, all seemed like Limey imprints of a Stonemaster, always seeking novelty, havoc and brotherhood. Pete Livesey was different — thin, with oversized glasses, a rowdy blond mop and one of those faces Rockwell never painted.

Most everything Pete did was his own idea, and he did a lot wherever he went. This made it almost unique when he agreed to join me on one of my projects; the first free ascent of the North Face of Sentinel, via the classic *Chouinard-Herbert* Route. Pete, who was ten or so years older than me, was maybe the only other climber in camp just then who seemed up to the task. I'd never roped up with Pete but

Ron called him a great technician and I'd read about his routes like *Footless Crow* in the Lakes, and the *Right Wall* on Dinas Cromlech, which my hometown partner Rick Accomazzo came screaming off while attempting to dick the on-sight. Anyhow, Pete and I got the gear together and hiked up to the base of Sentinel early one morning.

At that time, the *Chouinard-Herbert* was a trade route, a cobblestone on the road towards El Cap, Mount Watkins, and the other valley mega walls. Most every pitch involved some direct aid. Parties normally took two days, with a bivouac at the base to avert the bar and cultivate an Alpine start. Pete and I took a single 9mm rope that seemed a half-mile long, a daypack with chocolate and a little water, fags for me, since Pete didn't smoke, and a skeleton rack of gear. I didn't even wear a shirt. By the time we'd hiked across the meadow and started up the switchbacks for Sentinel, we'd exchanged little more than grunts.

The first complete sentence I said to Pete was to slow the fuck down. The guy hiked like an antelope. 'Better throttle it back and save it for the route,' I said. He picked up the pace. Then we were racing for real, a contest that nearly killed me because Pete, as I later learned, had been a national level middle-distance runner, in the mould of Sebastian Coe. If Pete had slowed in the meantime, it wasn't by much. We raced all the way to the base, where bushy terraces jag up right to the start of the climb. We didn't break stride and kept blazing, snot flying, wheezing like horses, over crumbly rock and through the green stuff, where I nearly pitched off, lunging for roots and hummocks, trying to reel Pete in. Never could.

From Camp 4, directly across the Valley, Sentinel resembles a huge grey tombstone blocking the sun. From rock bottom, the upper wall rears into ancient shade, neither friendly nor benign, but wholly other. It sobers you right up. I informed Pete that this initial section followed an infernal Valley wide crack. And since what most Englishmen don't know about 'the wide' I could almost squeeze into the Grand Canyon,

I'd be leading the first block of a dozen or so pitches. Ignoring me, Pete had already flaked out the cord and was leading off, sans belay. I told him I'd have him on in a moment and he said whenever I got around to it was fine. At the belay I reminded Pete that I'd followed the pitch in half the time he'd taken to lead it, and he promised me the same at the end of the next pitch.

And so it went as we swung leads over the next 1,200 feet. Besides a pesky slanting crack down low, which Pete followed in no time, the rest went free and quickly. Then the wall jacked up to vertical. Pete stemmed up a corner God must have polished with jeweller's rouge, and rigged a belay from slings at the start of the 'Afro-Cuban Flakes' pitch. Most Yosemite big walls feature some passage of trouser-filling exposure, and this was that place, in spades, us pasted right out on the bald face a few hundred feet below the summit.

We paused, dangling side by side off a cluster of bolts and old pitons, hammered straight up into a roof crack, drank a little water and wondered out loud where 'Afro Cuban Flakes' came from. I suggested that to some eyes, one of the dark, gong-like flakes scabbed on the wall described a rough outline of Cuba. Pete didn't know Cuba from Mars and figured the name came from nothing in particular. Climbers were always ascribing fly titles to features and routes, said Pete, and they didn't have to signify jack shit so long as they sounded cool or brainy. Pete also said that since I outweighed him by fifty pounds, belaying me out on the sharp end felt like being strapped to a bomb. I said I wasn't there for his opinion and to just drink the Kool Aid and throw me on belay. And where the hell did he think I should go?

The normal route traversed dead right past a line of old bolts and a few rusted fixed pegs, meeting a fingertip roof crack maybe twenty-five feet away. None of this looked easy. Unfortunately, the only holds were down below the fixed gear, and I wasn't sure what, if any, protection I might arrange. Then Pete changed his tune, swearing this was light lifting for a climber of my magnitude, who he'd seen bouldering with that pint-sized Hercules, Jerry Peel. I could check off Cuba and Africa and half of Europe in nothing flat because we'd free climbed *Astroman* the previous year, and this was the next legitimate big wall to go, if I could just bust past these flakes, which I owed Pete since we both wanted this thing bad, cha cha cha. So there was no sense in pissing in his ear about protection and shitty holds because I knew the sound of thunder. I needed to chalk up and get it done. I told Pete that such a blinkered, Pollyanna-ish opinion might mitigate me into an ass fucking. I went anyhow since Pete was older and canny and could talk a cat off a tuna boat when he needed to. Plus I wanted the First Free Ascent like mad.

The traverse do-si-doe'd out across side-pulls and barnacles and went swimmingly except for the bouldering move I cranked just after clipping a rusty, good for nothing bolt from the Bronze Age. Climbing slightly down and right from there, sadly beneath the bolts and fixed pins, I had to run out the rest of the traverse, all the way to the ceiling.

I hadn't taken any small wires, which is what I needed to protect the crux thin crack moves over the ceiling, so I thieved past looking at a great pendulum fall. In fact, I'd pretty much botched the lead in every way bar pitching off. (Subsequent ascents followed an easier, smarter, and slightly higher line, with the thin jamming over the ceiling remaining the crux.) Above the ceiling the angle lessened and I chugged to a stance and the end of the hard stuff. One more easy pitch and the *Chouinard-Herbert* was ours.

Then Pete yelled up that there was no need for him to follow my lead, since the hard part was over. And because if he pinged off that boulder move, at the start of the run-out, he'd log a horrific sideways whipper, into the sweet by-and-by. So I was free to abseil down and back clean the lead, then we would rap the route from there. Pete hadn't brought his plimsolls and didn't want to hike down in tight

EBs. The hell you say, I yelled down, but I'd set Pete up for a hellish task following this lead. So I pulled up the cord, doubled it and started down, hanging miles above the Valley floor on that skinny 9mm rope, swinging sideways and twirling in midair, lunging in to unclip bolts, finally pulling myself horizontally and hand over hand, over to Pete's hanging stance. We started down, Pete first.

Since the climb followed a fairly direct line, descending went quickly on the one long rope. While the lead rack comprised an Anglo-American medley of our personal tackle, it wasn't till near the bottom that I appreciated Pete's diligence in rigging each anchor with slings, nuts and krabs belonging exclusively to my person. By the time we touched down on those ramps at the base, my rack consisted of a few sun-bleached runners I'd nicked off other routes and a couple of wired Stoppers. But we'd bagged the first free ascent of another Yosemite big wall, so who cared? Of course we weren't done. We still had to contend with the infernal heat, and the moment we coiled the line and got into our hiking shoes and saddled up, we started racing down those ramps and down the switchbacks, across the meadow and we both just dove into goddam Merced River with our packs and shoes still on.

Several years ago I co-hosted an episode of the popular American news show, *60 Minutes*, where soloing prodigy, Alex Honnold, climbed the *Chouinard-Herbert* with no rope. I couldn't tear my eyes off of him, a red pixel on a black face, pulling through the anxious silence. Decades later at the juncture of back then and not yet, Alex booted up and soloed the wall right now. Riding old routes into the future. Following the line of phantoms whose bones might well be dust. As I watched the TV monitor, where an enormous lens had pulled Alex close and personal as he floated over the roof, I wondered if the collected astonishment, engrained in the rock, murmured to him about a day 25 years earlier, before anyone cared but us, when the late, great Pete Livesey and I raced and harangued, rattled and wheezed up the trail, up the wall and down all over again, feeling like Alex Honnold.

Every route is an enchantment. Every crag is a haunted house.

PART ONE

BIRTH OF A ROCK CLIMBER

Polymath

by Dennis Gray

ichael Peter Livesey was, I believe, the most outstanding all-round outdoor pursuit performer of his, or any other, generation. He excelled at so many disciplines that perhaps the title of a polymath is best used to describe him: an athlete, a fell runner, a canoeist, a caver, a climber, and in his later years, a veterans' champion at orienteering. This is to say nothing of his talents as a teacher, a writer, an instructor, and in the field in which he earned his living, a college lecturer. But there were also so many other sides to Pete's character such as his maverick wit, his roguish sense of fun, his love at tilting at establishment windmills, where even on occasion, he finished by demolishing them.

I first met Pete at Harden Moss cross country races in 1957. These were held on an open moor, above Huddersfield. There was none of your modern namby pamby park-like courses in those days and the winner of the youth race was an unknown 14-year old Michael Livesey, beating by a large margin, and to our chagrin, several of our Leeds Athletic Club kids of a supposed more proven pedigree. Pete was at that time welcomed into the bosom of the Longwood Harriers, Huddersfield's best, in the town where he was born in 1943. In the early 50s, just like climbing, there were clubs in the athletics world that really did breed character. Groups like the Bramley Harriers, Hare Hills, which by the way was Arthur Dolphin's Club, and Longwood. You knew when you went there for an interclub event that it was

1

muck or nettles. You changed in a draughty, unheated hut and washed afterwards in buckets of cold water, and anyone who complained was dismissed as a big jessie. It really was 'Tough of the Track' stuff and Michael Peter Livesey revelled in it. During this time, and by pure fortune, Michael Livesey fell under the tutelage of Derek Ibbotson (a.k.a. Ibbo) who was the world mile record holder and a Longwood man to his razor sharp spikes. With Ibbo as a mentor, and as he put on years, Mike ran from success to success, setting a new national junior record for the mile of just over four minutes. Winning the Northern Junior Steeplechase two years on the trot, and coming, in his last year as a junior, third in the senior race in the Three A's, which are the national championships.

Besides his interest in athletics, Pete had, from a young age, been going down caves in the Dales and climbing out on the grit in the quarries and outcrops around Huddersfield and West Yorkshire. His abilities and natural interest in outdoor pursuits suggested a career in that direction, so he decided to train as an outdoor pursuits teacher and entered Bingley College in 1966. Over the next few years Bingley College, under the benevolent influence of its Dean, Tom Price, and senior tutor, Wally Keay, became, it seemed, the alma mater for half of the then British outdoor pursuits world, and Pete revelled in the new challenges and fresh competition, particularly canoeing. Within a short while, he became a First Division slalom canoeist winning several important white water events, results that even drew him to the attention of the selection committee for the 1968 Mexico Olympics.

His caving exploits during this period were also earning him the reputation of being a bit of a hard man. I well remember Jimmy Fullalove, alias Daniel Boone, a junior member of the legendary Rock and Ice Club, returning from a caving trip one weekend, sometime in the mid-60s, with stories of *'the hardest physical specimen I've ever met'*. He told me that he'd first observed Pete in action in Gordale, on a bitterly cold day, and had been impressed by Pete's ability to withstand the cold and also his climbing, particularly the way *'he ran it out without any equipment'*. On this occasion Pete had persuaded Jimmy to join him on a caving trip. Jim recalled how this, his first real cave outing, was in the depths of midwinter and typically down a super severe pot. The leader of the group was Livesey himself and he was wearing the same garb that he'd worn climbing in Gordale – no more than an open neck shirt and ripped jeans, (wetsuits hadn't been adopted by cavers at that point). After abseiling down into the pot, Pete, wearing Alpine boots, had led some horrendous pitches, climbing free up white greasy limestone and through waterfalls to get them back out of the cave. As Jim recalled the tale to me he kept repeating, *'He was bloody incredible, he never feels the bloody cold.'* I remember as Jim told me this story 'the penny dropped'. This Pete who was being described to me was the same person as Michael Peter of Longwood, who I'd met when he was just a junior several years earlier. I knew then that I would be hearing a lot more about the exploits of Peter Livesey.

After finishing at Bingley College, Pete opted for a career as an outdoor pursuits instructor. He worked at Bewerley Park in Nidderdale, and then at Humphrey Head on the southern side of the Lakes, and whilst this gave him the means of combining his love of outdoor pursuits with a career, he didn't complete his probationary year as a teacher, failing to gain his formal teaching qualification. This proved to be an Achilles heel when later his personal drive and ambition saw him wanting to progress from outdoor instructing into the more challenging field of outdoor education and lecturing. The only place he could find to re-do this probationary year was in Lincolnshire. As we all know Lincolnshire is one of the flattest counties in the UK and about as far away from fast-flowing rivers, caves and crags as you can get, but Pete took it on the chin and went to a school in Scunthorpe.

However, as usual, he was ahead of the game and selected this particular school because it had a climbing wall. It was there that he started applying a new set of rules to his climbing, devising a rigorous regime of climbing-specific training, using traversing circuits and weights, which was pretty revolutionary in those days. Having finished his year as a probationary teacher successfully, he was able to pursue his career in outdoor education. The job he wanted and coveted more than any other was that of Lecturer in Outdoor Pursuits at his old college of Bingley and in 1974 he managed to get it.

Over the next 10 years, working at Bingley, and then later at Ilkley College, he became one of the UK's leading authorities in many things to do with outdoor education, but in particular the field of mountain safety. So much so, that when I was at the British Mountaineering Council, if we wanted an opinion about any rock-climbing technical matter, we would consult with Pete. He later became a valued member of the BMC's Training Committee and helped to reform the Mountaineering Instructor scheme. He was also on the Mountain Leadership Training Board and the Plas y Brenin Management Committee. The Single Pitch Supervisors Award (SPSA) scheme (now the Single Pitch Award, SPA) was another of Pete's initiatives. After witnessing bad safety practices both at the crags and on indoor climbing walls, Pete had the foresight to recognise that there would likely be a massive increase in climbing activities by school parties and organised groups at outdoor climbing centres. He proposed the SPSA scheme to promote best practice and safety standards. Although initially the BMC only accepted this as an advisory scheme, following a string of accidents, the SPA, as Pete had originally proposed it, was accepted as the nationally recognised qualification.

Above all, however, he continued to be a leader in the field of rock-climbing, pushing the standards ever higher and inspiring those who fell under his own tutelage. Young climbers like Ron Fawcett,

Pete Gomersall and Jill Lawrence were taken under his wing, 'shown what was possible' and went on to push the boundaries of the sport themselves and in turn inspire those around them.

Even when Pete retired from climbing he still had to fuel his competitive drive and returned to his passion for fell running and orienteering. As a Veteran he rose to the top of the pack in competitive orienteering. In a short space of time he became leader of the M45 and over class, and managed top ten places in four Karrimor International Mountain Marathons. It was only the illness that eventually took his life that got the better of him.

Jamaica 1965

by Sid Perou and the late Ray Stoyles

In 1965 a four-man expedition consisting of Mike Boon, Pete Livesey, Tich Morris and Ray Stoyles left the UK to explore the cave systems of Jamaica. The Karst Hydrology Expedition was the first of its kind to leave the shores of the UK. During the six month trip the team explored and mapped 29km of cave passage, much of it previously unknown, including the Quashies River System.

Here, Raymond (Farmer) Stoyles (1945 – 2012) recollects the trip in an interview with Sid Perou, first recorded at the Bradford Pothole Club Winch Meet at Gaping Ghyll in 2009.

Sid Perou: Two of the larger than life characters in the caving world who you were involved with in the 1960s were Pete Livesey and Mike Boon and you went on the Jamaica trip with them. Can you tell me about that?

Ray Stoyles: Well, I was dragged in at the last minute really. I was working at the Ingleborough show cave then and was in the New Inn one night when I got a phone call from Mike Boon, 'Can you come to Jamaica with us?' he asked. Yes, I said instantly. One of the original team had got a diving job in the Med, preferred that and had pulled out. So I was in, youngest member of the team. I was only 19 then and it all sort of went on from there. We sailed out on a boat, it took us two weeks on a Royal Mail Line ship, you know, a cargo boat. That was quite good because we were treated as passengers, although we were classed as supernumerary crew. We were literally dining at the captain's table, four huge meals a day, and we all put on about half a stone going across there. There was no way to exercise properly, apart from a 30-foot ladder down to the emergency steering gear at the back. So we used to spend half a day climbing up and down this steel ladder trying to keep fit.

SP: So what about Jamaica when you got there? Describe the sort of country it was and what the caving opportunities were there.

RS: The caves had been looked at by Leeds University in 1963. They'd had a small recce over there because one of their lads was related to this guy who owned this huge sugar estate. They'd gone out and looked at some of the caves near the coast. But the sugar estate was right in the middle of the country and we'd got all the maps and stuff from the Leeds Uni lads and looking at them, found this huge area called the cockpit country, which from an aerial photograph looked like a giant egg box covered in trees. We realised there was a lot of potential there. So we got all the large scale maps out and looked and found where all these rivers were and where they suddenly stopped we knew it must be a sink.

Once we got there, the first place we went was the Institute of Jamaica, just to find out about dangerous creepy crawlies and things and we found out that there weren't any. They don't even have any poisonous snakes on Jamaica, unlike the rest of the Caribbean which has snakes that are totally deadly. There's nothing on Jamaica like that, apart from these centipedes which we never came across, but evidently if they bite you, you're flat on your back for three days, yeah they're really nasty. We'd just spent three weeks caving in Norway before we sailed out, so Jamaica was quite a contrast, but we got used to it and we started looking around. The first cave we looked at was one called Quashies River Sink. It's an enormous shake hole with vertical sides, and we had to climb down the narrowest bit on lianas and things like that to get to the bottom, which was big enough to house a banana plantation. The river came down a very, very narrow cleft at the top, ran down, and then straight into this big cave mouth, which is about 70-foot wide and about 50-60-foot high, and then from there it just went in a succession of whacking great big pitches for about 400 feet.

SP: Nowadays, with places like the Mulu system known, and the new stuff in Vietnam, and some of these big river caves throughout the world, the Jamaica systems are not particularly unusual, but putting your expedition back in perspective for its time … what year was it, 1965? That's ten years before we went to New Guinea! Most caving clubs were just going off to places like Spain or somewhere like that, so your trip was extraordinary really. It was something completely unique in early expeditions.

RS: Yeah, ours was probably the longest, you know, because, we were there for six months and caving literally every day. Well, we used to go out for a fortnight into the bush, camp at the particular cave we were exploring and then come back to base for a week to do all the surveys and plan the next expedition to wherever. We just carried on like that for six months and just got harder and faster as we went along, caving literally 24/7.

SP: Livesey and Boon have become legends in their own ways since then. I remember the pictures of Livesey from the expedition; he looked really young with glasses.

RS: Yeah, that's right. He was tall and very thin with this mop of curly blonde hair and wire-rimmed glasses. But he was extremely fit, so we'd just send him down first and he used to go running off ahead exploring, while we followed doing all the surveying,

SP: Tell me a bit about the characters of Livesey and Boon, because both of them were very individualistic and became well-known.

RS: I think Boon was the weirdest. The first time I met him was down at the old dump at Clapham, (the dump was the building where local cavers stored their kit). I'd hitched up from Bradford, I couldn't afford buses in those days, I was only an apprentice. I got to the old dump, opened the door, the place was in darkness and this little voice from upstairs said, 'Have you got a shilling?' The electric meter had run out and he had no money. He's the only bloke I know who could come up on a weekend with nothing and go back with a rucksack full of food at the end of the weekend. He was a born con man. He could con people out of anything and he did that as long as we knew him. I think that's why the expedition to Jamaica was such a success. He managed to convince all these firms to give us food and stuff like that. We went out with nine huge packing cases each about nine-foot long by about five-foot square, mostly full of tinned food and things like that, one full of caving gear and two big drums of carbide which were lashed on deck in case we got a really rough seas and we had to throw them overboard before they exploded. All in all, we had two and a half tons of gear when we went out.

SP: I'll butt in with a story about Boon. We were on a trip in 1973, I think it was. Boon turned up out of the blue with nothing, as you say and blamed the pigs for stealing food from the tents. Someone, who will be nameless, fed the pigs with bread loaded with carbide towards the end of the trip and they died. Obviously the farmer wasn't best pleased, but as you say Boon came with nothing and managed to live quite well while he was out there and then left with nothing.

RS: Yes, he was an amazing character.

SP: Was there just the three of you?

RS: No, Tich Morris was with us as well. He was Chelsea Caving Club, you know, but Boon knew him. He was like our quartermaster. He was a teacher. Issued everything out very grudgingly and kept an eye on Boon, who was always pinching food and things like that. Tich was an amazing character, but I lost touch with him completely because at the end of the expedition, he and Livesey had enough money in the kitty to leap across to Florida and get one of those $99 Greyhound bus tickets to ride around America. They went up to Canada, to McMaster University, because we'd had a lot of help from them with dye testing stuff and things like that. Tich got a job at the University straight away. Livesey came back, and me, Livesey and Boon sailed home to England and then Boon got this offer with a job in the Speleological Department there and I haven't seen him since.

SP: I heard he was living for a while in the heating system, in McMaster University in the basement.

RS: That sounds about right with Boon, because I've known him sleep in some very strange places, with his plastic bag full of gear.

SP: What about Livesey?

RS: Livesey was a one-off; no two ways about it, an extremely capable caver, and of course, a very, very famous climber. I think a lot of his fame came from the fact that he wrote about everything he did and bulled himself up. Everybody thought, oh the great Pete Livesey, but it was only because he'd written about the great Pete Livesey. Otherwise, I think he'd just have been another one of the crowd.

SP: Except that, you know, he was in turn a top canoeist, and a top caver, and a top climber and a top orienteer – everything he went into he was top. He was very, very competitive.

RS: Yes, he was and you're right. I mean the last time I met him was actually up here and he literally came running across the fell said hello and disappeared up Ingleborough, and that was the last time I saw him. Then the next thing we heard he'd died of stomach cancer. So it was a sad end really, because he wasn't all that old when he died , certainly younger than I am now.

SP: And to think he'd been fell running just a little earlier.

RS: Yeah, it all happened very suddenly. You know what I mean? Getting shuffled off his mortal coil so to speak. I suppose in a way it might have been better for him if he'd have carried on and sort of died gracefully of old age, but I don't think Livesey was like that. I don't think he could've done it.

Transcript from the original recording by Sid Perou, 27th May 2009. Previously published in the audio archive of the British Caving Library and reproduced here with the kind consent of Sid Perou; transcribed and edited by Mark Radtke.

On Organising Expeditions

by the late Jim Eyre

I first heard of Pete Livesey as a novice caver, barely a teenager, who'd just been to the end of Mossdale Caverns and back. This really frightened me; it was a vicious sort of place and we used to keep well away from such dangerous caves. After that Pete quickly made his mark in the caving world and I caved with him quite a bit. I soon realised he was quite different from the rest of us. He didn't train in pubs and he was full of bright ideas. Who in the 1960s would have dreamed up the idea of scrounging a lift on a banana boat to Jamaica to spend a year exploring miles of virgin river caves, and then get paid for it? Who else but Pete Livesey would go to Greece with a bandit who was carrying a shotgun and gelignite, and then volunteer to be lowered down a 1,300-foot chasm on a winch, which, in Pete's own words, *'Was built by a crazy Irish mechanic who could improvise a winch from three empty tins of SAS spam, a bayonet and a donkey.'*

Pete Livesey was obviously a man before his time. I recall his ideas for getting an early expedition to Greece together, which revolved around recruiting nubile female students as Sherpas. *'After all,'* he explained to me, *'women, pound-for-pound, are fairly strong and they don't weigh much, they don't eat much, and they don't smell as bad as men, so they should be ideal on an expedition.'* With this in mind, Pete drew up an impressive brochure for his next Greek expedition to Epos in the Pindus Mountains. It read, *Visit the magic land of Greece, very cheap holiday, subsidised travel, see the glorious Aegean, see the ruins, pleasant walking tours and beaches.* Pete stuck this up on the notice board at Bingley College. He omitted to mention that the luxurious coach was two Transit vans, which had been modified for carrying bread. They consisted of two large alloy boxes, which had been bolted to the chassis behind the cab, and at the back was a roll-up blind. He'd stuck some Union Jacks on the sides to make them look good. We piled inside these things with all the gear, but had to lift the roller blinds up so we could see out. We found that every time we went uphill somebody fell out of the back and we couldn't stop the driver because we had no communication. So we devised this method of banging on the side of the tin box until somebody stopped. We improvised some pieces of wood across the back as slats, so we could pull the roller blind down halfway and leave the slats there just to stop us sliding out on the hills. The only problem was when we did this the exhaust fumes sucked into the tin box, nearly poisoning us all. Thanks to Pete's ingenuity we opened some tins of beans and used the bean tins to extend the exhaust pipe, which proved effective in taking the deadly fumes away.

Anyway, we're galloping across Europe in our two vans with Sid Perou swinging off the back of one of them in a harness making an expedition film, which we intended selling to the BBC on our return. As we drove through Bulgaria, Sid almost got arrested by the secret police for illicit filming, but they decided to let him off – such was our motley appearance. Needless to say, some of our female crew members weren't too happy with the whole arrangement, as they bounced around in the back of these tin cans, particularly after what Pete had said in his recruitment brochure. Things took a turn for the worse when we arrived at Epos and they found out that the pleasant walking tour involved lugging heavy rucksacks full of caving gear up a mountain. After some hard caving down the shafts of Epos the only ruins that the girls saw was us. For the whole trip we'd been living

13

on curry, and life was grim, until we discovered Pete's secret horde of lemonade powder and chocolate bars, which were hidden away in his tent. *'For the underground camps,'* Pete said, *'I'd forgotten about them.'*

The magic of Greece soon began to fade, when we were bombarded by thunder bolts, washed out by torrential rain and attacked by wild dogs. One of which nearly did a 'Bobbitt' on Tom Wiggly, a wild Australian caver, who chased after a large ferocious beast when it ran off with Sid Perou in its mouth. The fact that Tom was naked didn't deter him and he hit the dog with a boot; it let go of Sid and ran off. The trouble with mad Australians is they don't know when to stop. And Tom galloped after the dog again and threw his other boot and missed. Have you ever seen a dog smile? This dog stopped, gave a crafty leer over its shoulder and then turned and chased after Tom. He was clutching his willy as he ran like a Pink Panther on speed, completely naked with this dog after him.

Now our Sherpas were anxious to see a beach and we really felt that we owed them that, but unfortunately we'd run out of money. So Mr Livesey, as resourceful as ever, suggested that we sell our blood in Thessalonica. *'At £3 a pint,'* he said. The problem was we were foreigners in a strange land, trying to sell our bodies, with not an ounce of Greek language between us. Eventually we managed to figure out what the system for selling blood was, which went something like this; stand outside the hospital, wait until some distraught Greek comes flying out and pinches your skin to test whether you're full enough. If you pass the test you're taken inside and drained of your blood. We had a member of the team who was fairly expendable, a lad called Jim Farnworth, who we used to call Oxfam because he was always hungry and broke. So we pushed Jim forward and this old lady came out, grabbed him and took him inside. He emerged a bit later looking very pale and translucent, but smiling and clutching a fistful of money.

We escorted him to the nearest bar to see if he filled up again before the rest of us tried it out. It was a great success and soon we were all flogging our blood. One bloke's blood type was so rare we had him emptied. And then Pete went in and came out shortly afterwards in a complete rage: '*Bloody Greeks!*' he shouted. We just cracked out laughing, Peter Livesey, our gallant leader and super human, had been rejected. '*Your blood must be too strong for 'em Pete,*' was all I could say.

Written and orated by the late Jim Eyre at Pete Livesey's eulogy and recorded by Sid Perou in 1998. Transcribed and edited by Mark Radtke.

Abseiling

101 Golden Rules

by Pete Livesey

The first whistling noise made a sharp crack on a boulder a few feet away and I was showered in shattered bits of Jumar. I moved slowly, not knowing where in the darkness my lamp was, it was probably the second whistle and crash, followed seconds later by others. Descendeur, krabs and, finally, with a great 'vroomsh', came the transmitter, a beautiful and expensive squashed mass of bits.

I sat down again and groped around on the floor for something, anything – any piece or gadget, modern and reassuring, that would save me. My fingers lighted on a dead bird, and another, then a smashed microphone with no lead.

'*Livesey calling Wallamboola base, Livesey calling Wallamboola base, come in, please.*' Silence, not even the chirping of dead choughs. Silence!

As I sat there I pondered – quite logically I thought – the chain of events that had got me into this position. But first I decided to retire, give it up, get married.

It had all started about three years before, this fatal fascination of mine with sliding down ropes; now here I was 2,000 miles from home sitting on a rock 1,300 feet underground, in a dark icy cathedral, staring up at a pinpoint of light that was the surface of a mountain somewhere in a military zone on the Albanian border. How ridiculous.

Twelve months ago abseiling had seemed the obvious way to descend this unexplored shaft in Northern Greece. Expeditions were rushing out in the summer to attempt a descent, so I tried to persuade John Sheard to come with me on a 'phantom' trip a month or so earlier. We would tie all our climbing ropes together and abseil down, then learn how to jumar to get out. Unfortunately for me he wouldn't come, and I was forced into joining the only team heading for the hole that was short of men. Kelly's Heroes, a group of brigands and mercenaries from Whaley Bridge, led by a fugitive from the SAS, who'd run off with a whole year's supply of the Regiment's dope.

The plan was beautifully simple, hire a big van for a day in Manchester, pick up a *Daily Express* reporter in London, drive to Greece, borrowing money from the reporter for petrol on the way, go to the blood bank in Thessaloniki and sell eight pints of this reporter's blood, which would pay him back for the petrol, keep him out of the way and finance the rest of the expedition. I felt a bit sorry for the reporter as he was wheeled out of the clinic by a doctor in mechanic's overalls who was giggling, '*We meek ee leetle meestake.*'

The rest of the plan, which they hadn't told me about, was to bribe the Greek Army with a crate of whisky, steal a fleet of donkeys, pack into the hole and then lower me down it on a 2,000-foot length of something akin to barbed wire (the surfeit of straying sheep in Castleton around that time could well be coincidence). They were then either to leave me down there and collect a load of money from the *Daily Express*, or get me out and sell all my blood in Thessaloniki for the journey back.

As I sat there on my boulder pondering which plan the loonies above were about to adopt, a great avalanche came rumbling down the shaft – yes, avalanche! – and there, 700 feet above, was Shaun, the Irish mechanic, leaping about on a 50 degree icefield stuck to the wall of the shaft, having just cleared it of snow to make a ledge for himself. Like the rest, Shaun was crazy, but he could improvise a winch from three empty tins of SAS spam, a bayonet and a donkey. And, in fact, he just had done.

You see, when I'd been lowered down and had reached the bottom, I hung all my gear on a krab on the end of the barbed wire as I wandered around letting my eyes get used to the dark. The radio wouldn't work and the tension was off the barbed wire, so the team on top had naturally assumed I was dead (as this would bring in more money from the *Daily Express* anyway) and begun to haul the wire back up.

I had turned round in time to see my 'sack just leaving the ground and had run for it, leaping up just far enough to grab the trailing waist strap of the 'sack. At about 15 feet I had begun to ponder the wisdom of this course of action, and by 17 foot six inches (five metres 37 centimetres) I had let go and dropped back down. My 'sack and harness had snagged on the way up, shredding on the rock and spraying me with the contents. When the tattered remnants arrived on the surface their hopes were confirmed, and the Irish mechanic descended for a souvenir – an arm or a leg or something.

Well, I was rescued, and so began the journey back, with the blood bank and the American nymphomaniac – but that's all in another story. In fact, a whole novel that may never be told.

Now I suppose you're all wondering what all this has got to do with rules for abseiling. Obvious. Here we have the first and probably the most important rule.

- *Never go abseiling with the army, SAS, or Marines. And never abseil in a style that looks as though you've been with them. You'll end up stuck on The Guns of Navarone.*

You see, when I wrote a book on rock-climbing the other day (*Rock Climbing* by Peter Livesey, EP Sports Series) I was very careful not to introduce any climbing safety rules, knowing how you, the climbers, object to rules. On the other hand, people who read books on how to climb expect a rule or two, so I compromised and stuck a long list of

Norway 1967

Right: Pete in camp looking up at the Karlskratind.

Below:
Left: Pete in action demonstrating his classic bridge on Mongenura.
Right: Pete approaching the Kongen.
Photographs by John Stanger.

Livesey making the second ascent of the Jack Street test piece *Adjudicator Wall*
E3 5c, Dovedale in 1973.
Photograph by Bob Dearman.

Above: John Sheard and Pete Livesey during a photo shoot at Ilkley in1974.

Right: Livesey on pitch 2 of *Jenny Wren* E5 6a, Gordale Scar in1974.
Photographs by John Cleare.

Another shot of Livesey on *Jenny Wren* in 1974.
Photograph by John Cleare.

The Livesey classic *Face Route* E3 6a. In 1971, the YMC refused
to believe that Livesey had been able to climb it free – after all
some of their best had tried and failed. Climber Mark Radtke.
Photograph by Adrian Ledgway.

Austria 1972

Left: The Fleischbank, home to some big wall routes that received early British ascents by parties including Alan Richard McHardy and Geoff Douglas as well as Livesey and Sheard.

Below:
Pete on the South East Diedre of the Fleischbank.
Photographs by John Sheard.

The Sentinel Yosemite Valley.
The setting of John Long and Livesey's first free ascent of the *Chouinard-Herbert* 5.11c. The route follows the line of corners up the right-hand side of the face.
Photograph by John Sheard.

Pete Livesey making an early repeat of *Twikker* E3 5c, Millstone Edge, Derbyshire.
Photograph by Geoff Birtles.

20 golden rules for abseilers in at the end. After publication, however, it struck both myself and *Crags* (Magazine) that, while the book was excellent for teaching *Crags* readers to learn how to climb properly, it wasn't quite right for the kind of abseiling loonies who use rolled-up magazines as brake bars on their karabiners. So here I am explaining the amended set of rules.

- *Never go abseiling without your bayonet or carving knife or a dagger down your sock.*

Consider the case of Phil Webb (known to everyone as Gordale Gob) and Paul Trower (known to everyone) who were having their weekly epic at Gordale one day a few years ago. They were high up on *Hangman*, below the crucial roof section, when it got dark, like it does most evenings. Phil decided to abseil the 100 foot or so to the ground, rather than jump (it's rational decisions like this that have made Yorkshire climbers famous the world over for their fast bowling).

Phil disappeared down into the darkness and eventually reached not the ground, but a big knot in the rope. There he was hanging in space in the darkness with a big tangle in the rope below him – what would you do? Yes, that's right, whip out your dagger and cut the rope above! Which he did – real sharp finking. Then he was flying through the night to end up with a broken ankle on Gordale's rocky floor. Quick as a flash he shouted up to his partner: '*Okay Paul, I'm down,*' and Shagger, who always abseils in a press-up position, also found himself flying through the night, to break both wrists on impact. What a pair they must have made, limping and moaning into Malham to be rescued.

- *Make sure the normal procedure for abseiling is followed in the correct order.*

It is obvious that a little bit of clear thinking and organisation is necessary for abseiling. I was caving again – with Dave Cording, who was fresh out of Leeds University and president of their climbing club. (It is an unbroken tradition at Leeds that the president does not finish his course of study at the university). Dave knew all there was to know about rappelling and we knew nothing. Potholing was much easier if we rappelled, he said, just fix up the rope, throw the rest of the gear down the pitch and ab down to join it, and so on down the cave. So, barely convinced, we arrived at Juniper Gulf's awesome entrance pitch, 70 feet deep, with a great river roaring across the bottom. Dave was in control, calm, cool and impressive, as he slung all the gear over the edge. Yes, all the gear, including the rope for the first abseil. Five faces peered over the edge watching their precious tackle being washed away down the next pitch.

- *Descending is not the easiest way to melt ropes, but it does work.*

An American climber is stuck at a sling on a chockstone at the crux of *Rixon's Pinnacle East Chimney* in Yosemite. He is 60 feet up with a full-length rope trailing behind him. He ponders how to get down. Now, 'rappelling off', as they say over there, is far too simple for the technocrats of the Western world. Clint (as we shall call him) unties his rope, passes it through the sling and then ties on again. He begins to lower himself down by paying out the long end. When the Yanks paid a record transfer fee for Einstein, part of the deal was to forget about Newton (who was British and, therefore, should be forgotten). Clint had obviously never heard of Newton, and by the time I'd got round to explaining the conservation of energy laws to him, the sling had melted. He wasn't interested in the slightest when I pointed out that his dent in the ground and his broken leg were also excellent examples of Newton's same law. Never learn, these cowboys.

- *Do not abseil upside down with a woman dangling from your neck.*

Jack is evacuating his gripped-up female partner from a tree halfway up the crag. He abseils down to her and tells her to jump on his back. She does, clutching tightly, and down goes Jack. After a few feet Jack begins to realise that things are taking a turn for the worse and a few seconds later Jack is hanging upside down, harness round his knees, with his partner dangling in space clutched tightly to Jack's neck. And so the whole choking, screaming, dangling mass of arms, legs and descendeurs has to continue downwards in that manner until stopped by the ground. As I am a firm believer in learning through experience, a point which I make quite clearly in my book *Rock Climb...* the reader is left to make the other 96 mistakes himself and so discover the remaining rules. In conclusion the author wishes to thank Bonny Gossip for telling him about many of these incidents.

First published in Crags No 16 (1979).

Troll Wall

by John Stanger

The Phoenix Climbing Club was formed in 1959 by half a dozen or so discontented members of an older more established and less ambitious club. These new Phoenix climbers were young and keen to push themselves towards the harder rock-climbs of the day; keen, in fact, to rise above the ashes of what they saw as a stagnant Yorkshire scene. I joined in 1962 to find a degree of association between the Phoenix and a group of cavers, or potholers as they were then known, one of whom was a local lad by the name of Pete Livesey.

By 1964 I could lead 'Extreme' and it was apparent that Pete was also becoming rather handy. By 1965 we were doing routes like *White Slab* on Cloggy, and later that year I teamed up with the potholer to attempt an early repeat of Joe Brown's *Vector* on Craig Bwlch y Moch at Tremadog. The climb had been put up five years before and, like the rest of the Rock and Ice Club's routes, had acquired a fearsome reputation. After the atmospheric Cloggy, I felt quietly confident and Pete was clearly up for anything since, in his eyes, no climb could be as serious as his regular potholing activities. Our confidence even increased as we approached the foot of the route. A party was just completing *Vector* and the leader seemed to move effortlessly up the last pitch, making it look ridiculously easy. We later discovered this was Pete Crew, one of the country's best rock-climbers.

I remember belaying in the cave above the Ochre Slab whilst Pete had disappeared above to lead that 'easy' last pitch. All at once I was being gently pulled out of the cave by a very tight lead rope. It was then that Pete appeared in the void, dangling like a spider on its thread and a great cheer went up from the spectators on the road below.

Someone was good enough to give me a top rope, so after lowering him to the ground I finished the route getting the gear off. A slightly subdued Livesey later reported:

'With fingers and arms now aching I looked up at the last awe-inspiring section of the climb, a wicked looking overlapping flake on the overhanging wall above, curving upwards out of sight. Time was important now and I moved quickly up the underside of the flake, laying out from the rock on occasional holds. Close to the top now, still no footholds – no handholds either, just a small fingerhold on the left. Both hands on the fingerhold, I search for a hold high up at the top of the climb but can't find it. Fingers start to uncurl from the hold – suddenly everything flashes past and I bounce to a halt on the rope, swinging in space 40 feet down. The piton at the bottom of the flake must have held – but next time perhaps.'

Other routes climbed with Pete followed, until March 1967 found us with John Barraclough, a brilliant climber from a club in Bradford, at Malham Cove intent on a new route. In those days the most exposed, daring route was *The Dalesman*, which started from the right-hand end of the terrace below the upper central wall. We decided to push a line further right still and even more exposed and daring, casually ignoring the state of the rock at that point. I did the first pitch, which was mainly grassy ledges, to a possible belay ledge about 50 feet up, but with no possible anchor point. I decided to come down, take the rope to the top of the crag, abseil to the ledge and belay directly onto the descent rope. That rope was 300 foot of Number 2 (i.e. thin) laid nylon, used double. Pete tied on the other end and up he came. The top pitch was a steep hanging corner above a wall of loose holds. He led through up to the steep section for about 20 feet, where he started to exert his physique. Inevitably a hold came away and he spun round into free space. As luck would have it his arm caught the rope and he fell clutching it, to land on top of me. We both shot out into the Malham void and, with the rope stretch, swung back onto the terrace where John Barraclough came out with the classic comment:

'*I don't think I'll bother doing this route, kid.*'

At the second attempt Pete led it without mishap and so was born Pete's first route at Malham, the mighty *Douk*.

Despite air time and these temporary setbacks, it was obvious that Pete was made of the right stuff. I'd been thinking of making an attempt on Norway's then unclimbed Troll Wall back in 1965, but had been beaten to it by Tony Howard and his mates from the Rimmon Club. I mentioned to Pete the possibility of a second ascent in the summer of 1967 and he immediately took the bait. Pete knew Norway quite well from previous potholing trips and, forewarned about the cheap price of diesel (and the formidable price of beer), we set out in his old Land Rover on what was intended to be a lightweight trip. On arrival we did a classic climb on the nearby island of Svayer before returning to Romsdal for bigger things. We also found there were teams of four different nationalities in the area, all with their eyes set on the second ascent. Fortunately, Pete and I were first there, but we baulked as the weather turned to rain and snow after two weeks of good conditions.

Pete was later to write about our coming project with great enthusiasm and respect not often openly displayed:

'*At the head of one of Norway's most beautiful fjords lies the Romsdal Valley, a deep cleft cut through 7,000 feet of solid rock by the Rauma River and its preceding glacier. On either side soar stupendous walls of rock, higher and steeper than most Alpine faces. The highest and most forbidding of these is the dark overhanging mass of the northward-facing Trolltind Wall, a one mile high sweep of black featureless rock, rising to a sharp jagged peak.*'

The wall had been admired by climbers for many years, but from a safe distance. It was not until the summer of 1965 that climbers had dared attack its sunless outlook. When the attack did come it was a two-pronged affair, which developed into a race between British and Norwegian parties.

The Norwegians had unluckily chosen a bad line, which led them off the wall and onto the East Ridge to join Hoibakk's *Trollryggen Route*, which they finished direct. The British team under Tony Howard had better luck, their route following a tremendous natural line directly to the top. They reached the top, after five and a half days, on their second attempt.

The route was mostly free with two long and impressive artificial pitches in the middle, with just over 5,000 feet of climbing in all. Their feat in overcoming the great psychological barrier in pioneering a route up such a wall should not be under-estimated, though the actual climbing is probably not as hard as was first thought. The first ascent did nothing to sweep away the air of impregnability that hung over the wall and it was two years before climbers once again scrambled up the 2,000 foot of scree to the foot of the wall'.

On our first day the weather was still bad so we walked up the scree to try to get a closer view of the face. The rain was pelting down in the cold cirque that enclosed the wall and we were soon soaked, stood amidst the birch scrub covering the lower part of the scree. The wall was in terrible condition, streams of water cascading down it bringing loose stones and slivers of ice whistling down from above. The Troll Wall, when occasionally seen through breaks in the cloud was huge, more than living up to the impressive reports we had from the first ascent. We kept well away from the 'Introductory Wall' as we could hear rocks whistling through the mist and the pitted snow slope served as a definite warning to stay clear. In its present condition the climb was lethal.

On the next day, 27th June, the weather was beautiful and we hurriedly, and excitedly, got ready in the hope that conditions on the wall would have improved. We had the word from Tony Howard that they had left all the pegs in place so we knew a fast ascent could be possible if we travelled light and fast, a style that was to become familiar on future Livesey climbs. Unfortunately, 'light' in those days involved the use of mountaineering boots, heavy bivvy gear, old fashioned climbing gear and 30 steel karabiners. This was to be Pete's first big route on a big mountain and the experience of climbing with such a weight was to shape his future minimalist attitude on multi-pitch routes in America, the limestone Alps, and the Verdon.

We left the valley and all went smoothly up through the birch woods, up the 2,000 feet of scree and across snowfields. The Trolls seemed unaware of our intrusion and the 'Introductory Wall', 800 feet of steep, slimy slabs, was now reasonably quiet and hastily climbed in long run-outs on our 300-foot single rope. Pete led to the bergschrund below the overhanging start of the wall proper and, finally, we were onto the sombre Troll Wall itself, where the real sustained climbing began. Conditions were much better once we had started on the 4,000 foot sweep of rock above us, large overhangs 2,500 feet above kept the cascades clear of the rock and we soon dried out. By eight in the evening we were 600 feet up and just starting the first pegging pitch, a green cleft known as The Nick. The pegs were all in place and we were easily up within an hour and a half. Leading through, we reached snow-covered ledges below The Great Wall where we made our first bivouac. The wall above was sheer and monolithic and would require hanging belays throughout its 400 feet. We dug sleeping platforms in the snow with bare hands and by midnight the sun was disappearing behind the Arctic mountains for its brief sojourn.

Next morning, Pete tensioned down into the crack-line containing the Rimmon's *in situ* pegs in the narrow hairline crack running the full height of the wall. Halfway up the wall I was about 10 feet above Pete using the pegs as handholds when I grabbed a loose one, which promptly came out and I fell back down onto the hanging stance. After this scary mishap all went smoothly again and five hours later we had completed The Great Wall. Above us The Black Cleft and Flake Crack gave 1,000 feet of free climbing up soaring flakes and cracks that was a welcome relief after the long artificial pitches below. By three o'clock we had reached the Central Basin which Pete described as:

'Like sitting on the inside of a 3,000-foot high milk bottle, the walls nearly closing up and shutting out the sky.'

Here we took an airy lunch break and admired the huge overhanging wall directly above. This was cut through by The Narrow Slab leading to the bottomless entry into the long Exit Chimneys, which gave access through the overhangs above.

In September 1998, this entire huge upper wall collapsed causing a great explosion as it hit the 'Introductory Wall' and effectively destroyed the route. The resulting earth tremor registered 2 on the Richter Scale. Fortunately, in 1967, we were blissfully unaware of what the future held in store and happily started up the pegs of the 300 foot Narrow Slab. The following overhanging Exit Chimneys would now give us access into the summit gully, but we were only halfway up when a freezing mist descended and soon the air was full of hail and wet snow. The effect of a sudden soaking after more than 20 hours of continuous climbing was soon felt and we decided to bivvy at the top of the chimney, where we were shocked to find that our long summer rock-climb had turned into a Scottish ice-climb.

The bivvy had to be taken on a small snow platform under space blankets, making brews with the stove sheltered in the bottom of the climbing sack. After a few uncomfortable hours we stirred into life at first light with still 1,200 feet to go. Far from being the easy 500 foot of rock work which we had expected, the next section proved to be the hardest on the route, 500 feet of faith without friction or adequate belays, followed by 300 feet of steep corners plastered with ice and soft snow. We could see the pegs beneath the ice and soon used up our meagre spare supply. Pete was now wearing lightweight climbing shoes, which by this time were looking very sad, soggy and floppy. He'd never really climbed on ice before so I set off leading all the way, cutting small nicks in the ice with the spike on my peg hammer. Once I got the measure of it I started to enjoy myself, especially when the occasional protection appeared on odd patches of bare rock. Two hardish, ice-coated rock pitches and more gully climbing led to the final rock wall, thankfully clear of snow and giving a fine pitch onto the summit ridge. Abruptly it was all over, we allowed ourselves the briefest of celebrations then made a speedy descent of an easy snowfield to endless cups of coffee and the bus back to base. Job done and now a few days rest to let it all sink in.

After the Troll Wall we did further routes on Kongen and the Romsdal Horn. Pete was intent on putting his name on the Norwegian new routes register and his pet project became a fine direct line up the top part of the south face of Bispen (the Bishop). After a successful first ascent a damp mist enveloped us near the summit and we had an argument about a crackling noise we were hearing. Pete claimed it was only the lichen absorbing water. I was sure it was static, dancing on the wet rocks; clear warning of the build-up of an electrical charge. I said I was going straight down but Pete thought it a pity not to go to the actual summit. He wasn't going to be denied by wet lichen. We parted company, Pete headed towards the summit and me towards the valley. I'd only descended about 100 metres when there was an explosion and a blue flash illuminated the surroundings. I spun around to see Pete two feet up in the air and then falling to collapse on the ground. Sprinting back up I found him dazed and concussed on the ground and had to tell him he had been struck by lightning. He was not burned and had been lucky not to receive the main discharge. He later told John Sheard that initially he thought I had hit him from behind with a large rock. We descended the mountain together without further mishap. Pete named our climb the *Phoenix Route* in celebration of the club's association with Norway, but the name could have been even more appropriate if that strike had been closer.

Other members of the Phoenix now began to arrive bringing with them the horrifying news of the Mossdale Cave flooding in the Dales, where a number of Pete's mates had died. I stayed on but Pete was understandably shaken by the tragedy, which had overtaken close friends. He decided to return home, climbing having lost its attraction for a time in the light of such a personal disaster. It was, for him, a sad end to our hitherto successful trip and one that stayed with him, to be later commemorated in his epic route *Mossdale Trip* in Gordale's wild gorge.

Bingley College

by Tom Price

Bingley College, founded in 1911, was built on an elevated site between the Aire Valley and Ilkley Moor. Its imposing gritstone buildings, including five massive halls of residence, were originally designed to accommodate 250 women students, but by the 1960s it had become co-educational with an intake of about 1,000.

I joined in 1973 as Dean of Students. At that time all freshers were required to take a three-month induction course of outdoor activities. This programme was managed very ably by a tubby, not to say spherical man, called Wally Keay, senior lecturer in the PE Department. He told me one day that one of his students, asked how he had enjoyed his summer vacation, had mentioned in an off-hand way that he had climbed a big wall in Norway. This turned out to be the second ascent of the Troll Wall, and the student in question was Peter Livesey. The first ascent had taken the Norwegians three days, but Livesey, with John Stanger, had done it in one.

Peter Livesey had been in the forefront of British kayaking, and was in line for inclusion in the Olympic slalom team, but the competitive demands of that sport were so time-consuming that he turned his attention to climbing. His academic work, in spite of the enormous amount of climbing he did, was of high standard and he completed the course with honours. A year or two later he applied for a post in the College's PE Department. The Head of Department was a woman and her chief interest was Dance. She had her own nominee for the post, and in any case had not much liked Livesey when he was a student. According to Wally Keay, she was opposing his appointment.

I have never been much inclined towards politics and lobbying but something moved me to take the Principal aside and make sure he knew that Livesey was, by this time, a top performer in the climbing world. *'To get him on our staff,'* I said, *'would be akin to getting Nureyev in one's ballet company.'* He listened to me and Livesey was appointed, though not without a struggle.

Bingley College did, in consequence, attract a number of very good climbers. Of course, it was also well-placed geographically, within reach of many gritstone outcrops and not far from the Lake District. But largely it was that birds of a feather flock together. John Sheard was never a member of the College but he was often to be seen in the Union and another rising star arrived in the elegant shape of Jill Lawrence. She was a 'mature student', in other words she came to the College not from school but from the world of low-paid work. Pleasantly hard-bitten and street-wise, she spoke with a Liverpool accent and treated pretension of any kind with withering scorn. She had style and with her tall, flat-chested figure, crowned by a mass of honey-coloured curls, she stood out in any gathering. She was elected President of the Students' Union, and though that and her rock-climbing took up much of her time, her college work was consistently excellent. She soon came to be regarded as Britain's leading woman rock-climber.

Another brilliant woman climber and a friend of Jill's was Gill Price. She was small, dark, neat, reserved and self-effacing. When some years later she and Jill Lawrence were included in Chris Bonington's series of films, tracing the development of rock-climbing in the Lake District, they tried out a climb on the flank of King's How in Borrowdale. It was *Nagasaki Grooves*, a route that Livesey had first climbed in 1972 on Great End Crag, that big rock face that had remained unnoticed until a fire burned the vegetation off it in 1940. I went with them, for Jill kept in touch with me for several years after I left Bingley. When they came to the 6b crux Gill Price got up it but Jill Lawrence could not follow, and after she had made several unsuccessful attempts they abseiled off and turned their attention to a route graded E3 on Raven Crag, Thirlmere. Jill told me later that when they were being filmed on this climb the adrenaline rush swept them up the rock face with the smooth fluidity of a dream, and they did it so quickly that the film had to include weight training sequences, in order to make up the allotted time. Gill Price qualified as a teacher but took a job with a French firm specialising in the external inspection of high buildings, using climbing techniques instead of scaffolding. So she became a steeplejack, or a 'steeplejill'.

Peter Gomersall and Andy Jones were also Bingley climbers of note. Jones worked for several years at the Sunderland Education Authority Centre, Derwent Hill at Portinscale, Cumbria. Gomersall, I remember very well as a student, as I had repeatedly hauled him over the coals on account of his absenteeism and his failures in academic work. I found myself defending him time and again against the demands of exasperated tutors to have him thrown out of the college. What I liked about him was his readiness to take the blame and admit his shortcomings. I knew he was a climber, though I did not know how good he was, and I suppose I thought 'there but for the grace of God go I'. For in my youth I too had been all but sent down from Liverpool University for putting climbing before Latin. He seemed almost to hope that he would be thrown out, but somehow he always managed to hang on by his fingernails, resitting every exam and never quite giving up. This tenacity clearly paid off in his climbing for he became one of the leading performers of his time.

A female climber very different from Jill Lawrence and Gill Price was Bonny Masson, another 'mature student'. Good looking, personable and self-assured, she gave the impression that Bingley College was fortunate in securing her as a student. In climbing, too, she was a bit of a snob, disdaining routes easier than Hard VS, and dismissive of those who climbed them. Years later, on the day following a BMC AGM, I remember doing *Hope* on the Idwal Slabs while she was still moving up and down the same few feet of *Suicide Wall* or some such desperate climb. Her dedication and persistence in hard climbing, however, led her to improve steadily, and she became a climber of note.

Peter Livesey turned out to be an excellent teacher of climbing and outdoor pursuits, showing a good understanding of ordinary people's difficulties and recognising how quickly or slowly to progress in their tuition. For some time, as a sideline, he ran evening classes for climbers at various gritstone crags in the district, recruiting me as an assistant. He encouraged people to learn by leading, and would minimise the risk by nipping smartly up the climbs, placing protection for the beginners to use.

Some years after I left Bingley, Jill Lawrence phoned me to say that she, Livesey and Gill Price were planning to climb on Great End and would I care to bring my crampons along and join them. I did so, but Livesey was late in arriving, and the short winter day was well-advanced when we at last set off, at a punishing pace, up Grains Gill. Pete arrived wearing lightweight footgear resembling trainers, and he put crampons on these. Central Gully already had two parties on it, so we took the SE Gully, I with my long ice-axe, the others with more modern ice tools. This was a far cry from the days when a winter ascent of Great End without crampons would take us all day. We were up in less than two hours and while we stopped to eat and sort out the gear before descending, Livesey went off and made two more solo ascents of the crag by different routes before it got dark.

There was a certain quiet flamboyance about Peter Livesey. One day as I was having lunch in the college refectory he joined me and after a little conversation he said he must be off now as he was climbing that afternoon on Raven. I knew of no Raven Crag anywhere near Bingley and was astonished to learn that he meant Raven Crag, Thirlmere. He was going there in his fast sports car. In this respect he was rather like Hamish MacInnes who used to sweep up to a crag in his E-type Jaguar.

Pete once told me that he was in a lay-by when another car pulled in and the driver emptied a heap of cigarette butts onto the ground and drove off. Livesey scooped them up, gave chase and signalled to speak to him. The man wound his window down and Livesey threw him the butts with the comment, '*I think you forgot these.*'

Another little story he told me was of when he was wanting to sleep out on the side of Wastwater and was persistently harried by a National Park warden. In the end he found what he described as the only place left to hide, which was over the fence and inside the official camping site.

There was one Bingley College climber whom I never got to know, and that was the one who put the Christmas tree on top of the dome of the main building's clock tower. This happened soon after I had been appointed Dean of Students. Seconded by Dennis Gray, I made the second ascent and took it down, finding the route greasy with industrial grime. I was glad to be able to prise the lightning conductor away sufficiently to get my fingers behind it, and I should certainly not have liked to do it solo, in the dark, even given the Dutch courage of a few pints of beer. I fully expected the name of the culprit to come out sooner or later over the grapevine, but it never did.

First published in Travail So Gladly Spent *by Tom Price (Ernest Press ISBN 0948153679). Reproduced here with kind permission of the late Tom Price.*

The Black and White Days

by John Barraclough

'The past is a different country, they do things differently there'. (LP Hartley).

They certainly do, and looking back from 2013 to when I first met Pete in the mid-1960s, it seems a world away. He would have been 23 and earning about £14 a week top line, about £200 now. He was still living at home so like the rest of us he had enough money to get along, but not enough money to really do anything other than go to work. Petrol was 60 old pence a gallon (240d to £1), but not many people had cars. The average price of a house was about £3,000. We were changing from nylon to perlon ropes and replacing drilled out steel nuts with custom made alloy chocks. We still had long slings in leather sleeves. Helmets were coming in, but not for many of the really hard climbers. We had about eight slings and krabs each. Because we'd moved onto more difficult climbs, we began to carry three or four pegs and a hammer. The obligatory footwear for any serious climber was a pair of PAs (Pierre Allain), but they were expensive. Pete wore RDs (Rene Desmaison). There were no mobile phones, laptops, or Internet.

Three young men came strolling along Woodhouse Scar in Halifax one evening. They turned out to be Pete Livesey and a couple of his friends, all from Huddersfield; they were not climbing. I was with a few members of the Calder Valley MC at our weekly get-together. Our club had only a handful of members and was hardly a club at all. Total membership included Edwin Leggett, Brian Crawshaw, Christine Walker, Stephen Beaumont, one or two others, John Sheard (JS) and me. Our climbing standard had risen to VS by then. JS and I had done *Central Buttress* on Scafell in 1964. Edwin was the best climber and was famous for scaling the local mill chimney to paint a massive 'ban the bomb' symbol near the top, seen by all and sundry. Pete Livesey appeared tall, lanky and quietly dressed – there were no brightly coloured clothes or climbing gear in those days. You'd have been laughed off the crag wearing some of the things they wear today. Like WW1, life was pretty much in black and white. Photos, monochrome, were just beginning to appear on the covers of new guidebooks. Prior to that, it was words and a few line drawings. There was no chalk and no 'sport climbing'. *How To Climb Outside* (BMC's *Summit* magazine, spring 2013) would have raised an eyebrow or two, as would going around the mountains with a video camera mounted on your helmet. Pete just stood around rather awkwardly, while his friends chatted to JS. Maybe he, like many of us, found it difficult meeting new people, even easy-going climbers from the same social class. I think class, or at least 'us lot versus the well-off' was an issue.

Edwin Legget, John Sheard and myself stood dripping wet in front of a roaring fire in the Fell and Rock Club Palace in Langdale one afternoon in November 1963, attempting to dry out the few clothes we possessed. Needless to say we were not supposed to be there. The door burst open and a bona fide member confronted us with the words, 'My god, Kennedy's been shot.' I'm not sure which had more impact, those words or the elegant evening dress he wore, presumably in preparation for the banquet which was shortly to be laid out; such was the class divide. I remember being below Scafell East Buttress in 1968 with a working class lad from the Bradford University Mountaineering Club. A well-known member, of what we then saw as the privileged establishment, turned up with a small entourage and started lording it.

He recognised someone leading *Great Eastern* and shouted up to ask how he was doing.

'*Struggling, actually,*' came the reply.

'*I say,*' shouted up the worthy newcomer, '*anyone who can do the* Sudgrat *can fly up* Great Eastern.'

My climbing partner looked me straight in the eye, '*If you think I'm climbing on the same crag as a pillock like that you've got another think coming!*' We went up and over Mickledore and did *Botterill's Slab* in compensation for missing out on a route on the prized East Buttress – so rarely in condition.

Rock-climbing was a bit of a cult activity. We took it very seriously, perhaps too seriously. It was all we talked and thought about. Our role models were Brown and Whillans (not that we knew them), and other top-flight climbers of the day: Moulam, Moseley, Banner, Boysen, Biven, Crew and Ingle, Edwards, Austin, *et al*. Bonington, Scott and others were in the mountaineering category. Scotland had its own heroes, MacInnes, Marshall, Smith, Cunningham, Patey and Haston. American climbers were visiting Europe, including Royal Robbins and Yvon Chouinard. There was a whole raft of up-and-coming British climbers: the Holliwells, the Barleys, Yates, Rouse, Ward-Drummond, Braithwaite, McHardy, the Burnley twins (Pete and Ian Heys) and many, many more. Then there were groups like ours.

Spurred on by *New Climbs*, published annually from 1966 by The Climbers' Club, a growing number of British climbers, from all parts of the country, were looking for new places and new lines to climb. TV climbing broadcasts were beginning and The Eiger North Wall was all over the front pages. Perhaps for some climbers their motivation, instead of simply being climbing as an end in itself, was the search for fame, notoriety, or the opportunity for some 'name dropping' in the pub. Here was a chance to see your route and your name in *New Climbs*. Naming your route was an additional attraction. Pete's *Plastic*

Iceberg came from him being affronted by the brewers of a new lager having the gall to have a plastic iceberg by the pump on the bar. *'Just look at this! A PLASTIC iceberg. Do you think these people have ever seen an iceberg?'* This wave of exploration included trying to free, or partly free aid routes, seen by most as an inferior form of climbing, perpetrated by the 'the whack and dangle brigade'. In those days bolts, rawl-plugs and golos were placed using a hand-held star drill (no electric battery drills good enough) and so, in a way, putting up *Central Wall* at Malham was no mean feat; Peck and Biven had bolted 270 feet by hand.

New routeing, whether on a traditional crag or at a newly discovered venue brought us up against one of the contentious issues of the day, so called 'climbing ethics'. Even in our small group, views differed on what was kosher. Some would consider only 'on-sight' new ascents i.e. from the bottom up, no abseiling down to inspect, clean or place protection, and no top-roping to rehearse an ascent. They would argue that although that method may result in, say, aid being used, repeated ascents would very likely 'clean' the route up and it would become just another route on the cliff. Some stoical characters would admire a hard line, perhaps where no aid could be placed or where the rock was very loose and, although abseiling, top roping and placing protection could probably make it climbable, they would leave it alone for future climbers. Others would do what was necessary to get the route done. I'd put Pete in the latter category, and this approach had been used throughout rock-climbing history: *The Collie Step* and O G Jones top-roping *Kern Knotts Crack* are just two of many, many examples.

We thought that the best lines had already been climbed. What remained would be very difficult indeed, calling for new ways at probably higher standards and where an on-sight 'clean' ascent would likely be out of the question. However, I had a lot of sympathy with those who objected to Rowland Edwards pegging the overhangs guarding Cloggy's West Buttress area, to access the free-climbing lines above. Cloggy, in my opinion is hallowed ground; a rock-climbing cathedral. This whole issue of what you should or should not do was brought to the fore in *Games Climbers Play* by Lito Tejada-Flores, in 1967, which Pete considered a very impressive, and no doubt useful, analysis.

Another contentious issue was that of competition. Back then, climbing did not lend itself to overtly competing against other climbers. There were, however, related factors present. Rivalry for the few remaining important lines, some accusations of not being truthful about how, exactly, an ascent had been made (particularly hinting at cheating) and, occasionally, some banter. I heard that Pete, climbing with 'Hot' Henry Barber at Tremadog on Henry's first visit 'across the pond', shouted up to Henry, who was taking a long time, '*I think you'd better get a move on kid, you're supposed to be really good.*'

You certainly knew who were harder climbers than you, and you strove to improve your standard, but this is totally different to, say, a race over a mile to see who is the fastest. Friends would say, 'There's so and so, he's done *Cenotaph Corner*, and he's really good', or 'Saw Harry Smith at Gogarth, setting off up *Serendipity* (VS) in his boots, in the wet', or perhaps someone would say, 'Have you heard Big Ian has done *Zero* and *Point Five* in a morning, back at the CIC in time for dinner and that's after breaking his ankle at Woodhouse Scar and never letting it heal properly'. So I guess admiration was the key word, not competition.

We competed individually against ourselves, to get stronger, to hold our nerve in bad places and we competed against the routes themselves, to be able to repeat them like they should be repeated. If we failed at a proper ascent, used aid where we shouldn't have, make no mistake, we felt bad and knew we had to do better. Read the Cloggy guide of 1963 and you'll see lots of examples where aid was used on on-sight first ascents of hard routes, even by Joe, later to be 'freed'. Climbers understood that process, but using aid where you shouldn't meant you were not good enough, and you knew it. If you managed to do a route without any accepted artificial aid, then that was a plus, but if you'd done it without, you could bet plenty of others had also.

We didn't come across the 'climbing establishment' much in the early days. I think we may have if we had been in a really important climbing club, or if any of the older climbers we knew had been of that ilk. We didn't do committees, meetings, guidebooks and that kind of thing; we just went climbing with all the carefree freedom that entailed. I remember only one occasion where a record was kept of the climbs we did. We camped in The Pass, about eight of us, and it may have been a Phoenix meet, because Stanger went around, while we were having a wash before going down to the Vaynol, to see what people had done. John Sheard, Peter and I had spent the day on Cloggy. We'd managed to do *Llithrig*, *Diglyph* and *Pinnacle Arête* without incident. This was a very successful day for us and we were very chuffed. The weather had not been great, misty at first, but it brightened up a bit and the rain stayed off. As Pete was starting out on *Llithrig*, Al Harris turned up on the path below with what very much looked like a client in tow. He shouted up, through the murk, '*What's it like? Looks greasy from here.*' Before thinking about it, we shouted back that no, it was okay. He looked a bit crestfallen and headed off towards the Far East. I think we'd let him down – maybe he wasn't in the mood, or had promised a hard route, and we could have got him off the hook.

I don't want people to think that we always had good days, simply cruising hard routes. We had plenty of bad days, and weekends. We went to St Bees and did nothing. JS and I once made an absolute arse of *Wasp* – thank God nobody saw us. And, of course, we fell off, most did, but very rarely. Alan 'Spuz' Spurrett had a fall on Dinas Mot; Terry Taylor fell retreating off *Pinnacle Flake* on Cloggy, resulting in a fatality.

We were very firmly not in the top flight of climbers. We did, however, have a couple of very good climbers who were getting even better: Pete was one; Dan Boone (Jimmy Fullalove) the other. Dan came from a very poor background in Bradford and was always broke. Asked why he went out climbing, he said that it was better than staying in and getting beaten up by your dad. He somehow got 'apprenticed' to the Rock & Ice Club. He had adventures both in and out of climbing and roped up with some of the leading climbers of the day, including Whillans. I read in his obituary that it is likely he made the second or third British ascent of the Eiger North Face, with Ray College. It was odds on that Pete, honed on years of stringent training and overt competition in athletics and with the necessary drive to be the best, was going to the very top.

The 'climbing establishment': what was it? We didn't really know. I guess we'd heard of the BMC, the Alpine Club and the other big climbing clubs with their huts and famous climbers, with their mountaineers who went to the Alps. There's no doubt in my mind that the media had a big hand in establishing the public images of famous climbers, along with the lecture tours that were taking place, tragedies that were covered in the press, and big clubs having loyalties to their top climbers. Being known and accepted helped to get you invited to join prestigious expeditions (and so gain the necessary sponsorship), and onto media productions. Being outsiders, with lots and lots of others, of course, maybe we were seen as poor, scruffy upstarts with no style and no deference towards our betters. We did not endear ourselves to the climbing establishment. In a way, somebody as good as Peter was becoming, was throwing down the gauntlet to those in the hierarchy. We did not want to kowtow, we wanted to go our own way.

In contrast, Joe Brown, over the years, had become Mr Rock-

Climbing. He was loved and admired, probably by dint of his modesty, his extremely down-to-earth nature and his working class origins. He was never, to my knowledge, involved in any controversial issues. Chris Bonington was Mr Mountaineering, with all that went with it. Pete's situation was a very different kettle of fish. I remember coming across him in a pub in Bingley one Sunday evening. He was with a few friends, nursing his usual gill of bitter. I went back to where they were 'living'. It was a rundown old stone terrace, no mod cons, cold, damp and very poorly furnished; not quite a slum, but not far off. I remarked on what they were eating when they started cooking up: 'It's free, kid, left over from a caving expedition.' I declined the powdered potato, egg and peas and was glad I had not asked the date of the trip. I took this as a sign that Pete did not really look after himself; he was very tough in that way.

At our level, we were anonymous in the world of climbing. Our friends were endearing in a personal, individual way – good reliable friends, always generous if you were in need. Some could be called 'lovable lads', because they drew people to them by their attractive nature. I'll always remember asking someone how Ian Nicholson had got on, on the Eiger. I think he went out there with Alan Fyffe and a few other Scottish lads. 'Oh, he did it, but you'll love this. The farmer's wife where they were camping, at Alpiglen, she took him in the kitchen and washed his hair for him. Typical!' This was no sex thing. He was just that sort of lad – no barriers. There were many others like him, including Tut Braithwaite and Peter Brook.

Rock climbers, by repute, wore cheap working clothes (especially jeans), were tough, lived a bit rough, were careful with what little bit of money they had (except when it came to boozing). They might not have a regular job, might even have moved away to a climbing area. They lived cheaply, but might have a bacon butty between beers for sustenance. You might well see them on noisy motorbikes or in old bangers. It helped to be from the north of England (accent, camaraderie) and, of course, climbers lived on the edge, risking a fall at any time which might kill or maim them. When asked, 'What do you do?' you were likely to get, 'I'm a climber ... oh, and I'm a bricklayer'. Of course, personal hygiene could leave a lot to be desired. Mountaineers, a different clan, might use the phrase 'crag rats' to allude to the limited horizons of rock-climbers. But rock-climbers went places and had incredible adventures too, risking all, just like mountain men. They never trained, apart from a few press-ups in the pub. We knew of no climbing walls. Anyway, how would you have got to one?

If I had to choose the single most important cause of the huge growth in climbing activity, it would be the rise of private transport. I cannot overemphasize the difference between driving to, say, Malham, and going there by public transport; bus into Bradford, another bus to Skipton and another bus to Malham. It would take half a day easy, and then the walk to the Cove. Hitching to the Lakes for the weekend was not much fun either, with all your gear, but it was done. I did not know anyone who hitched to Wales – you had to cadge a lift. It seems to me that Pete and John Stanger realized early on that somehow you had to get some 'wheels'.

Friends could be forgiven for thinking they were mean, or at least very hard on themselves. They spent very, very little on anything you saw, because they were scraping everything together to get the essential items they needed to do what they wanted to do. Somehow Stanger bought, and managed to afford to run, a Minivan. Peter, never one to compromise (Minivans were minute with only two seats) got a Land Rover; how, I will never know. If you saw Stanger out climbing, he might be in wellies or similarly poor gear, because he was saving his good stuff for the Alps, duvet jacket and all.

Climbers did not have a semi, wife and two kids, or wash the car every Sunday morning. They did not want to 'get on', or wait for the boss's job. Looking back, I wonder if, really, we were misfits. Why weren't we like other young men, interested more in girls, fashion, the Beatles, dancing, football and cricket, and other normal team sports? Sports? I never saw climbing as a sport and climbers were never referred to as athletes then, nor would they have liked it.

It became clear at Woodhouse Scar that fateful evening in the mid-1960s, that Pete was angling after going climbing with us. To climb at any real standard required a regular climbing partner. Options were limited, and existing partnerships were pretty fixed and could last years. I can't remember any teams of three. I climbed with John Sheard and that was that. There was some flexibility/swapping around, however, and Pete started climbing with me and John. When 'the climbing policeman', John Barker, wanted to join in, there was no messing about. Unlike Pete and the rest of us, he was a very direct and colourful character. First time we met him, it was, 'Look, kid, I've just had my 40th birthday and realised I've done nowt with my life and I want you to take me climbing, before it's too late.'

I should mention that 'kid' was used a lot. I remember these West Yorkshire words and phrases with much affection. Even today, nearly 40 years on, when I'm struggling to do something, I come out with one of Pete's phrases from the Norway days. We were stumbling across loose, vegetated, ankle-breaking scree, on our way to the Hoibach Chimneys. I shouted to Pete, way out in front as usual, *'Pete, this is bloody awful.'*

'Just keep going kid,' came the simple reply.

I use it a lot – you may want to try it, *'What are we going to do here Pete?', 'Just keep going kid'*. We failed on the route and I said that retreating was better than having some sort of epic.

'I want at least two epics before I go home,' he said.

Looking back on that first meeting, having got to know Pete better during the next few years before I moved away, I think, typically, he was sussing us out. There was nothing casual about him turning up at Woodhouse Scar that evening. If he liked what he saw, thought he could get along with us and that we knew what we were doing climbing-wise, then that was it. Why go to Woodhouse Scar? Why no climbing gear? I think he came with his friends because JS knew one of them, and that got the conversations started. I wish I'd have got Pete's take on his joining us. He was, I learned later, already a member of the Phoenix Club and the Bradford Pothole Club and had been on caving expeditions. Perhaps I did not ask him at the time because being in our twenties we just went places and did stuff. We reflected on very little.

Another puzzle I came across in recent reading, I understand that prior to and during the years I climbed with him Pete was participating at a very high level in two or three other outdoor activities, particularly caving and cave diving. He never mentioned any of it. I came across some info from other sources. I heard that as he built a box underwater in Malham Tarn on a cave diving test, he caught a fish and nailed it to it, to the astonishment of the examiner. Much more significantly, I learned that his bitter disappointment at coming only third in the 3 A's senior steeplechase final at the White City – competing while he was still a junior – turned him away from a very promising future in athletics. Not a word from Pete himself about all this.

Pete's casual, rather scruffy appearance, what with the hair, glasses, and rather goofy look, not only belied what was going on between his ears, it was also out of line with his strength of character. He was not a fighting man, like John Barker, but he could stand his ground and dig his heels in. JS has reminded me that Pete, once we'd found out that too many had turned up to go to Wales one Friday night, briskly chose three people and told them they were not going. Yet he was quiet socially back then, unlike one of his caving friends, Bill Frakes who was full of confidence, fluent patter, clean, smart and very good looking.

The YouTube videos show an older, worldlier Pete, with a teacher's voice for the cameras. Back then our everyday language could be crude and of course 'non PC'. Barker could do the ugly words bit very well. By all accounts, he was being inspected at a West Yorkshire Police Parade by a Police Commissioner up from London. Disappointed with Barker's uniform, boots or something, he began jabbing John in the chest with his forefinger.

'*You do that one more time and I'll tear that finger off and stick it up your fucking arse,*' Barker had said.

The Commissioner swiftly took two steps back, shouting, '*Discipline that officer!*'

The videos give you a good idea of just how impressive Pete was on the rock. Anything you could do, he came to do more quickly. I found he became too good to climb with and he assumed you were as good as he was. He might not place all the runners you'd want as he led out on a serious traverse; when bringing you up a hard pitch there could be too much slack, because he was eyeing up the next pitch or spotting a new line; you might have had enough for the day, but he wanted another. He pushed on, it seems, with all that he did. Around 1973 I bumped into him at Wallowbarrow Crag. In his lunch break from guiding his students, I saw him strung out in the overhangs on *The Plumb*. When he got down, I congratulated him on such an impressive solo ascent. '*Climbing with beginners all the time brings your standard down. You've got to do what it takes to maintain it,*' he told me.

The last time I saw him was at his café in Malham, in 1988. We had a 'long time no see' embrace for quite a few moments. '*That was nice,*' he said.

In 1998, living down in Kent, I got the phone call, from a tearful John Barker.

Into the Limestone Arena

by John Sheard

In 1961, Graham West produced the first definitive guide to climbing on the limestone crags of Derbyshire. It was to be an instrument that changed the perceptions of many climbers who had, until this point, practised their art only on the traditional gritstone edges. John Laycock had written as early as 1913 that he was satisfied that, '*mountain limestone is beyond the border line of safety... it is safe to assume that all holds are loose*'. These then, were days when many climbers of lesser vision and boldness decried the limestone crags, declaring them generally to be lethally loose and unfit for rock-climbing. The legend was started that such climbing was suicidal – a legend which persisted in many circles well after publication of the guide.

However, by 1970, development in Derbyshire had progressed to a point where a good number of quality routes of E2 and E3 had been established, particularly at Stoney Middleton, which became a forcing ground for limestone climbing. Yorkshire still lagged behind at this time but took a major leap forward with the arrival of Peter Livesey. Recently converted from a background of high standard caving, he was ready to push grades to a level well above that yet achieved on limestone, and ultimately of that on crags in established mountain areas. *Our Father* at Stoney Middleton, a major route of E4 grade climbed by Proctor and Birtles in 1967 and way ahead of its time, set the bench mark for the next phase of Pete's Yorkshire development.

When Pete and I managed to free *Face Route* at Gordale Scar it broke the established Yorkshire mould and caused a considerable local outcry, but it was actually on a par with existing Derbyshire routes. Looking back, it's easy to understand the reluctance of the establishment to accept that usurpers had the intent and ability to bring Peak District standards to a very conservative and insular Yorkshire. However, we were initially unaware of the controversy surrounding the ascent of both this route and the harder ones shortly to follow, which appeared to be centred within the mainstream and senior Yorkshire Mountaineering Club. If Pete and I owed any allegiance to organised climbing, it was to very peripheral clubs made up of small groups of like-minded friends. In any case, as Pete later said, we were doing our own thing and for ourselves, with little concern for what others thought. It was very personal, an attempt to see what we could do, competitive only within our small closed circle. I don't believe that at that time Pete had any real idea or desire for wide public acclaim. It seemed to me to be more a case of exploring his ability to see how he shaped up against a yardstick set by more established climbers, and measured in terms of the hard, documented routes of the day. Obviously he was satisfied with what he found. He accepted that his future routes would have implications for the wider climbing community and also the clear possibility that he was capable of performing with the best. He even progressed well beyond what was then accepted as the upper limit of difficulty. It was unfortunate, and at that time unusual, that Yorkshire felt unable to support its own.

Fame outside Yorkshire didn't come overnight, nor was it achieved, as sometimes claimed, by a blatant disregard for the traditional ethics of climbing. I well remember us inspecting the virtually untouched Troller's Gill in the early 1970s. He declared the obvious lines to be impractical without resorting to excessive peg protection given the modest height of potential lines and we came away empty-handed preferring the far inferior Loup Scar. Troller's had to wait another decade before it could be developed, and by this time Pete had moved on and away from Yorkshire limestone. With hindsight, even at that time, he was easily capable of free climbing several of those lines using conventional protection of the day. The time wasn't right, he was still learning.

That Pete's early Yorkshire routes were inspected prior to their ascent was never disputed. Indeed, given that at the time of the first ascent, *Jenny Wren* was possibly the hardest rock-climb in the country and on occasionally dubious rock, I doubt anyone would have attempted an ascent in any other style. What was greatly exaggerated was the amount of practise that was employed. At the time his cheeky article in the climbing press perhaps further confused things. He put forward a list of the hard routes on Pennine and Peak limestone. In this he made reference to top rope practice as he understood it. Top rope to Pete meant the practise of crucial moves of a projected climb and emphatically not, as the term was perhaps commonly used, the ascent of the complete route. Even I couldn't have been persuaded to buy a rope long enough to top-rope *Jenny Wren* for example. How it could have been accomplished on such overhanging, devious lines, I can't imagine. Pete's approach was to abseil the line to establish the existence of holds, pretty fundamental to the feasibility of any route. A second descent might be required to remove dangerously loose rock and to test how vital crux holds could be used. This would be done on the abseil rope and could involve climbing a couple of metres above a locked off Figure of Eight. The possible consequences of even a short fall onto such a device could be rather severe and Pete was far too savvy to wander too far with such dubious security. The route would then be attempted ground-up, with no top-roping and no guarantee that it was possible on the lead. He was a bold adventurer but he wasn't a fool. I would follow a successful lead on the rope and without aid. The unspoken but recognised plan was that if he could lead it after inspection, and I could follow it unaided, then we could come to a very fair assessment of its future grade.

A few years after the early Yorkshire climbs we were in the Lakes, intent on a line on Goat Crag that would become *Bitter Oasis*. He checked the line and cleaned the first pitch, placing a very poor peg above the stance. That evening we were in a Keswick pub and engaged in conversation with Ray McHaffie, a Lakes legend who, as outsiders, we were meeting for the first time. After a comical hour, Ray said, *'Allan (Austin) says yer not a bad lad, but you cheat a little bit.'* Next morning we arrived at the crag to find Ray and supporters occupying grandstand seats around the foot of our desired route. Goat can be a pretty dirty crag but the climb went without a hitch other than the mental numbness I experienced following the top pitch, which he hadn't bothered to clean, expecting it to be straightforward. We arrived back at the foot of the crag as Ray and entourage were leaving. *'Well, there were nowt wrong with that,'* was his departing remark. I hope the verdict went back to Yorkshire. I suspect it did.

Fondness for the unrelenting steepness and infinite variety of limestone continued as the net was cast further afield. Almost inevitably, given Pete's vision and restless nature, thoughts began to turn to more distant horizons, not so much with a view to free climbing existing aid routes, but to travel, explore, and most vitally, experience the apparently endless and far greater walls of Europe. This then was how, in the summer of 1972, we found our way to the Wilder Kaiser of Austria, in search of routes that I saw as traditional Alpine climbs but which Pete saw, realistically, as simply much higher versions of what we were already about. We were pretty sure to encounter the then prevalent Continental approach to rock-climbing, but intended to have no truck with peg pulling and resting. It was going to be interesting to see how standards compared. To this end we each purchased lightweight rock boots as a nod towards tradition, later to be hastily abandoned in favour of our infinitely superior EBs. Thoughts of sacrilege and niggling conscience would soon be forgotten; some of the routes when done completely free proved to be hard.

It was our first non-stop journey through, for us at least, a largely unknown Germany, ending finally in a bar in Kitzbühel. Things didn't get off to a good start as a large, lederhosen-clad drunk, came across the room to spit a mouthful of partially chewed nuts directly into Pete's face. We figured it was time to leave town and made a hasty retreat to St Johann, where, to our relief, we were welcomed and shown to a handy campsite, home for the next two weeks.

In superb, summer weather we proceeded to tick off some of the classic climbs of the region. The Wilder Kaiser proved to be an idyllic mountain area, set above beautiful Alpine meadows and located conveniently near to picturesque Tyrolean villages and bars. At first sight the range appeared remote and inaccessible but closer acquaintance revealed good roads leading to attractive taverns from which well-organised paths led into the mountains. Our preferred approach was from the north side of the range and into the Steinerne Rinne, apparently roughly translated as 'the stone trough' a massive, vertically sided rift, which completely severed the range. The approach walk-in followed an easy path from the inn of Griesener Alm, finally ascending into 'the gutter' by an almost vertical section of hewn steps. Towering walls of the famous Predigtstuhl and Fleischbank faced each other across the 200 metre wide ravine, rising vertically for 350 metres. These walls, and particularly those of the Eldorado of climbing in the Kaiser, the East Face of the Fleischbank (the macabre 'Butcher's Shop'), would come to contain impressive, modern, super routes put up by the likes of Stefan Glowacz, Thomas Huber and Wolfgang Muller. At the time of our visit, however, the route for the romantics among us was the *1912 Dülfer Route*. At the time of its first ascent, it was regarded as the ultimate in difficulty and that with considerable artificial aid, it now yielded to a more modern approach in three hours. It remains, however, a classic route, 500 metres of climbing in a superb position, undiminished by time, and deserving of respect for its early pioneer.

Initially the difficulty of these classics was of a considerably lesser order than on the relatively small walls at home and long multi-pitch routes were easily completed in an afternoon, following the longish approach walks undertaken every day without break, largely at Pete's insistence on frugality. A traditional night of Tyrolean hospitality in the atmospheric Alpine huts was denied me and the grind became something of a daily ritual. Given that we regularly climbed at E3/4 in Yorkshire, the Kaiser routes of a lowly HVS and E1 felt pleasantly easy. Conventional protection was plentiful and double 70-metre ropes allowed massive run-outs as pitches were run together. The climbs were real quality on good rock, making up in atmosphere what they lacked in technical difficulty.

Inevitably, ticking our way through the old English guide, the charge slowed as we finally encountered a climb that gave cause for a more serious approach. The *South East Diedre* of the Fleischbank, or *Sudostverschneudung* as it was more impressively named in the German guide, was a superb outing, following a powerful line in impressive situations. First climbed by Weiss and Moser in 1944, in its free state it felt probably E2 or 3, quite respectable on a short Yorkshire climb in those days, and certainly cause for thought on a 350-metre sustained face. Down early after the usual two-hour race to the summit, I retired for a pleasant afternoon snooze under a boulder. Pete went off to solo the *Dülfer Route*. An hour or so later he was back with tales of having fainted due to heat exhaustion and fallen off the famous traverse, to be saved by a fortuitously clipped peg. Good old Hans Dülfer.

Back down to the valley for the 10th time we were to be met with another epic. Driving through St Johann, we were amazed to see an airborne fourteen-stone fraulein disappear over the bonnet of my car.

After we'd found her bike and checked the damage to my new vehicle, we stood awkwardly at the road junction awaiting the arrival of the ambulance and police. The fraulein looked okay to me, just a little scratched, and it was clearly her fault for not stopping at the junction in her headlong flight down the hill. Perhaps her brakes had failed, or perhaps she'd gained so much momentum that it would have taken a parachute brake to slow her. Either way, Pete's face fell a foot when I was instructed to report to the magistrate's court the following morning. It had been a pretty dramatic way to get a day off climbing, but I anticipated enjoying it to the full.

Next morning I entered a dimly lit, underground cellar and into what appeared to be a medieval courthouse. Things did not look good. Three judges, complete with black robes, sat on a raised dais above me. They spoke no English, or were not prepared to, and I only had guidebook German, and even that was limited. An incredibly attractive female, also in black, was apparently my defence lawyer, and she spoke perfect English. The trial, for apparently that was what was happening, started with the resulting three way proceedings. After each pronouncement by the chief judge, she would turn her back on the bench, and with a huge smile, inform me of what had been said. All seemed to be going well, until, after a long, stern lecture from the judge, she turned and unable to contain herself further, announced between giggles unseen to him, that, 'When I was in Austria I must not run over local frauleins'. The absurdity of the situation, and her lack of control, was more than I could take and I too had to choke back a laughing fit.

The judge didn't take kindly to my lack of respect and promptly put on a black hat before passing sentence. Now this was no longer funny. Had they got me in the wrong court and mixed me up with a local mass murderer? Thirty pounds was the punishment, something of a relief, but quite a lot of money in those days. It was going to be an expensive day off, particularly when I hit the nearest bar. Out into the blinding afternoon sun, to be met by a waiting Livesey with two packed sacks, *'Come on, there's still time for a route.'* What did it take?

Next day it was the *Schmuck Kamin*, eventually climbed in 1949 by Markus Schmuck of Broad Peak fame; it was the route on which Buhl took his 50-metre flyer 'into life'. A stunning line on the Butcher's east wall, when seen from the Steinerne Rinne it appears as a huge chimney scything in a vertical straight line through much of the face. Chimneys were not normally our scene, but this was supposed to be the hardest route in the Kaiser and hence an obvious target. In fact, the chimney proved to be a fissure often too wide to bridge, and with hard off-width cracks that offered scant protection. Without doubt the hardest climb we did during our stay, we could only liken it to an endless series of Curbar-like routes stacked one on the other. Pete used the legendary Livesey bridge between the bounding walls. I followed, leaping from crack to crack, quite unable to span the gap. Shouts for a tight rope were met with the response that the belay was poor and that if I didn't hurry up he was likely to fall out of the crack he was wedged in. Sustained and difficult to protect, it's without doubt a magnificent route and a brilliant testimony to the men of yesteryear, still deserving of E3 today.

The main point of our visit to the Kaiser had been to prepare for the Laliderer Wall of the Karwendel, and it was to this major range immediately north of Innsbruck that our thoughts now turned. First though, was the problem of the campsite fee. We'd already made a hefty first payment and the final instalment had been jeopardised by my court fine. A scheme devised over a final afternoon beer was put into action. Pack all the gear quietly into the car, retreat to the tent and contrive to take it down whilst still in it, leaving only the flysheet, supported by four pegs, to camouflage our intended, wicked action. As dusk fell we emerged from cover, ripped down the fly, stuffed it in the car and made our escape under the nose of the guardian. Hints of unfair play were eased by the excuse that they had already had my £30 for something that wasn't our fault. Had I been able to foresee the future, I would have had no second thoughts. I eventually arrived home to find my insurance company had paid out a fortune on the strength of my conviction and promptly doubled the premium. I had to sell the car and buy a van.

The Karwendel ranges are enclosed by a vast Alpine Park, covering an area of 700 square kilometres. It's a beautiful but strangely complex place of picture postcard Alpine forests and meadows with well-organised tracks leading up into stark limestone terrain and remote summits. At the time of our visit approaches to the climbs involved long valley hikes or clandestine car trips along closed toll roads; probably still does. Following our brief English guidebook we sneaked in as far as a final barrier, which couldn't be persuaded to open, and camped in the nearby woods, concealing the car with branches.

The 40-kilometre Main Ridge, containing the summits of the Laliderer Spitze, Lamsenspitze and, highest of the Karwendal mountains at 2,749 metres, the Birkkarspitze, proved to be an altogether more serious affair than the Wilder Kaiser. Difficult access due to closure of the forest roads, long approach walks, huge 800 metre faces, loose rock, severe stonefall and unpredictable weather, in short, we had exchanged our Eldorado for serious mountaineering, and there was a real question on the advisability of our lightweight tactics and gear. Pete reduced the issue simply to one of scale. If we could complete difficult 350 metre Kaiser climbs in a couple of hours, it must be possible to do the same on technically easier Karwendel rock in about twice as long. Simple!

We decided to put his theory to the test and selected the Lamsenhuttenturm as being a suitable test bed – an impressive pinnacle more accessible than the Laliderer Wall and much shorter. In 1947, the great Hermann Buhl made the first ascent of the *Gelbe Kante*, the *Yellow Edge*, resorting to the use of wooden wedges in the upper difficult pitches. This was the one for us, a two-hour approach, brief by Karwendel standards, only a four-hour guidebook time for the route, an impressive line and a name to collect. What could go wrong? The hut guardian's advice that Karwendel grades were much harder than those in the Kaiser was only an added incentive. Loose, brittle rock, that's what could go wrong. We casually ignored the widely accepted fact that the rock in these ranges was often highly suspect. It couldn't be as loose as parts of Gordale, could it? Stands to reason.

The initial pitches went easily enough but simply moving the rope brought down showers of small stones. Belays were indifferent, but adequate for the grade. Above us towered a huge prow, yellow and overhanging. Given the state of the rock, the route obviously didn't go up there; we'd reckoned without Hermann. The next pitches gradually steepened and led inexorably towards that hanging prow. Things became serious as Pete led up an inverted staircase of loose rock, rotten wedges and old pitons falling out at the slightest touch. A poor, overhanging belay secured only by two loose pegs, marked the start of a nightmare pitch. Pete led on into space, he'd gone very quiet and was moving slowly and methodically as he disappeared over the next roof, progress marked only by sporadic jerks of the rope and falling lumps of limestone. In response to my anxious calls, the repeated words, 'Good old Hermann,' could be heard, doing nothing to ease my growing sense of unease. Eventually he called down that the next pitch looked even worse and that his belay was useless. When I shouted back asking for clarification of useless, all I got was the faint reply, '*Don't fall off.*' I removed my belay pegs with a gentle pull and started up the overhangs with a numb, detached feeling, knowing that a fall would be the end of us both, but with enough awareness left to register that this had been the lead of a master climber. The stance finally appeared, huge, flat and solid, with a grinning Livesey firmly attached to the summit crucifix; it was enormous, solid steel, and totally immovable.

Down at the hut the guardian bought us beers and told us this had been the first ascent for two years, owing to a massive rockfall, which had removed the upper pitches containing the wide crack-line that Buhl had followed. The resulting massive scar that we had unwittingly climbed had left us both shaken but Pete answered with a look of disbelief and the comment that it was technically easy, just a little loose. Secretly relieved to be down safely, we headed for the valley, thoughts of the Laliderer Wall forgotten.

Back home, *Deliverance*, aptly named I thought, was climbed in March 1973, weighing in at E4 with one point of aid. We were convinced there were no holds on that beautiful little wall, and Dougie Hall's impressive elimination of the ancient bolt nine years later proved that Pete had still some way to go. But go he did, pushing his own standards ever higher with routes like *Limehill*, *Claws* and *Mossdale Trip*. Apart from seeking hard, cutting edge routes at home, Pete was becoming focused on using his now proven talent in order to make free ascents, or substantial reductions of aid, on existing, long multi-pitch climbs further afield; a pursuit which may well have unconsciously started with his early repeat of the Troll Wall with John Stanger way back in 1967. After Austria we wandered further afield, both of us in search of bigger walls and pastures new, separately to Yosemite and the Western Alps for several trips, and then, in the spring of 1976, together to the Verdon.

PART TWO

THE ORIGINAL ROCK ATHLETE

Arms Like a Fly

by Pete Livesey

Hell! he's got big arms, and that blue-eyed, god-like expression doesn't help either. The object of my scrutiny was John Syrett, who'd just failed to get up Kilnsey's Central Wall on what could have been the first free ascent. Could have been, yes, but would it ever be now that the reincarnation of JME (John Menlove Edwards) standing over at the bar had turned back on it? The pace was hotting up in Yorkshire now, we'd had it virtually to ourselves for six months, now here were two teams scrapping for Kilnsey's prize. We'd snatched *Diedre* the week before, lifted it from the same team that were ahead of us in the *Central Wall* stakes.

The Saturday after and heavy rain shrouded John and I as we slipped over the edge on a long, airy inspection abseil. The route looked steep but possible from out there in space. Syrett's two aid pegs grinned tantalisingly, though I couldn't see any reason for the second one, but it's alright talking from a floating bath chair. A climber's van pulled up on the road below and two disinterested looking climbers sidled straight towards us. We sorted and resorted our gear, arranged it in rows and piles; anything but look at the rope hanging there 30 feet out from the base of the crag. The lead sidler approached, appearing to ignore the rope and asked important questions about the weather, which was still deluging outside, and about 10-foot crags down the road. He sidled away backwards to the next dry route where he climbed and re-climbed the section in full view of our rope. I thought about his big arms as we scrambled to the top to retrieve our rope – bigger than Syrett's; hell they must be good. I kept looking at my withered little arms and decided it wasn't fair. That was it for the day, I was demoralised, the climb was steep and they'd all got bigger arms than me. Even Sheard's arms seemed to be bulging Popeye-like under his Ben Sherman shirt. John always climbs in that kind of gear, he's never been the same since he saw Rouse at Stoney in his velvet loons. No, you just couldn't attempt a new route with the cards stacked like that.

We shot off to Loup Scar where we just managed to put up *Lapper*, an all-weather fun route that should become a classic, it had been waiting a while for suitably wet conditions. Pulling over the final three-foot roof boosted confidence in my demoralised muscles. I was subconsciously preparing for the day after. I reckoned if we weren't at Kilnsey on Sunday, Syrett and RBJ (Baxter-Jones) would have it during the week.

Sunday morning rolled over and it was wet again. This bird kept sticking her foot in my ear, so what can you do but get out. I could have hidden for a day in bed. Sheard arrived two hours late, that's good for John so the sod must be keen. John's car pointed inexorably towards Kilnsey, wipers at double speed vainly scraping at the weather. I was getting edgy now, only half confident that the route would be wet. Kilnsey loomed up, a black dripping hulk with a laughing patch of powder dry rock right where *Central Wall* should have been wet. A finger of wet crossed the route at one point but fate said it had to be done. John said nothing, just handed me his store of slings and krabs. Neither of us said much – I was now engrossed in fright. The start is a vicious little pull over a roof to gain a ramp rising leftwards. Ten feet of climbing and you're committed, but so far the holds were good and I was finding lots of little threads below the guardian overlap I was following. I felt very unhappy up there, I'd used a lot of energy getting over the initial bulge and things were going to get a lot steeper in the next 100 feet. The wall steepened as it merged into the overlap, a high side-pull enabling Syrett's first aid peg to be reached. I was just about to swing on it when I noticed a little hold above it, would it do? I climbed down a few feet for a look. The problem was to get my left hand on the hold and make a huge swing right for a flake, but the move was perfectly protected. I kept thinking, if I fall onto the peg, will it be aid? I was still trying to resolve the problem as I lunged off rightwards and made the flake. It was a case of climbing fast now for 20 feet to a loose block with a resting ledge. I just made the ledge as the familiar finger fade symptoms crept on. Nearly halfway now with a long steep groove ahead running out in a blank wall. The groove looked obvious but I hadn't a clue about the blank wall, still, limestone being limestone ...

You've got to go soon when you're plastered on a blank wall like that, so off I went. The groove went very quickly, a good nut too, but I took a long time working out an exit to the foot of the wall. Eventually I reached a little overhung ledge on the right, heartbeat ledge, and smiling down slit-mouthed from above were a couple of handhold-like breaks. Lunge and lunge again? Both were handholds, and I was there, at a peg on *Trauma Traverse*. For the first time I felt happy, then nearly fell off traversing left over grease squeezed out of cracks by the sheer weight of the crag.

The tree belay grows horizontally out of a crack, forming an airy seat (so I had a peg as well) from which I could gloat down the great overhung wall at John. The slack was up and in came John, powering up on fingers and the occasional toe. He started talking again at about three quarters height, that must be where it eases off, I was too gripped to notice any easing off. John arrived and hung his arms around his ankles for a while. Next was an overhang with a corner above, disappearing as it eased to vertical. This was unseen ground but there looked to be plenty of holds lurking behind the grass.

I climbed the tree until it bent too much to be of any further use, got a finger jam and a nut in the same hole and swung off. The steepness of the situation became immediately obvious, and the holds above jammed full of sods. I gave in, sat in the sling and gardened the groove above. The holds just below the overhang were now apparent, if still muddy, so off we go. I could quite happily fall off now, you know how it feels, nothing can go wrong – the main pitch was done. Above the overhang the climbing eased to VS on large holds and in 40 feet it was all over. John joined me in the rain and cold on top but it didn't matter now, we'd done with Kilnsey for the time being. We could just drift euphorically away without looking back; we wouldn't have believed it anyway. It's almost a pleasure going back to work after a route like that. Can't wait, give the kids a stack of maths and write up the route for the glossies, hell! my arms look big now...

First published in Rocksport *December 1972.*

A First Encounter with Pete Livesey

by John Cleare

A new star had appeared in the climbing firmament and Dennis Gray, the gossip columnist Fifi on *Mountain Life* magazine, assured us that he would make an interesting subject for a profile feature. Editor, Chris Brasher, was especially intrigued, for by all accounts this character was not only a brilliant rock-climber but also a first class field athlete, intrepid caver and champion kayaker. We commissioned Jim Perrin to write the piece and I whizzed up to Bradford to shoot the pictures. It was an eye-opening insight into a different world, the Yorkshire climbing scene.

Pete Livesey, for he was the star, and his 'oppo', John Sheard, were welcoming and most hospitable. It was a cold, damp morning in early May and the Saturday morning ethos at Ilkley Quarry was quite intense, yet the pair seemed so relaxed, diffident almost, and were quite happy to be pointed at gripping situations, and to be pushed around and directed to satisfy my requirements. Nothing was too much trouble. Pete's style was athletic and the way he powered straight up *Wellington Crack* was, I thought, most impressive. In the afternoon we moved on up to the limestone where Pete was keen to show me *Jenny Wren*, his pièce de résistance, on the awesome walls of Gordale Scar. As a Cheddar veteran with weak fingers and a poor power/weight ratio, I had a shrewd idea of what was involved, and only thankful that it was unnecessary for me personally to leave the ground. Climbing swiftly, almost rhythmically, Pete moved out and up the leaning limestone with apparent ease, precisely placing his protection and pursued by light-hearted banter. It was surely no place to hang around but I was watching an extremely fit man with steel fingers, an efficient, forceful and fearless climbing machine.

It was already early evening but there was just time to slot in a few frames of John coiling a rope for an advertising requirement, before the rain started in earnest and we repaired to the Buck Inn at Malham for several pints and a couple of hours of laughter. Thus it was very late when we reached Bradford – too late, in fact, to find a 'regular' meal. But to my hosts this must have been a familiar scenario, for we proceeded down a seedy looking back street and down a flight of stone steps to a basement door. Doubtless there was a sign of some sort that I'd not noticed? We opened the door and confronted a large Alsatian chained to an equally large, iron-visaged policeman. No one batted an eyelid. A dozen or so tables filled the dimly lit room and the figures who sat at them, eating with their fingers off tin plates, appeared mostly to be bearded and be-turbaned.

'*You okay for curry?*' asked Pete.

At the counter we paid over what I recall as a half-crown each (that's 12p in new money) and a large chapatti followed by a dollop of steaming curry was ladled onto each of our tin plates. We found space at one of the tables and eating with our fingers, enjoyed a delicious if somewhat bizarre supper. Neither the dog nor the policeman moved. And that was my first encounter with Pete Livesey.

Livesey repeating *Wellington Crack* E4 5c, Ilkley Quarry in 1974.
Photograph by John Cleare.

Pete on *Mortlock's Arête* E4 6a during the race for the first free ascent in 1976.
Photograph by Geoff Birtles.

Pete bouldering out the start of *Central Wall* E4 6a, Kilnsey Crag.
Photographer unknown.

Pete and Jill Lawrence in Llanberis Pass.
Photograph by John Sheard.

Pete on a rare visit to sample the snow and ice of the Alps in 1974.
Above: At the summit of the *Frendo Spur*.

Below:
Left: Looking down at Pete on the classic ice crest of the *Frendo Spur*.
Right: At the bivouac on the *Frendo Spur* demonstrating his penchant for alpine fashion.
All photographs by John Barker.

Livesey in action on *Dream* E3 6a Great Zawn Cornwall.
This photograph was taken by John Cleare during filming for *ABC TV* New
York and the making of *American Sportsman in* 1976.

Pete on *Déjà vu* E3 5c Great Zawn, Cornwall.
Photograph by Brian Cropper.

Left: Soloing *Sickle* Clogwyn y Grochan.
Photograph by John Sheard.

Below:
Left: Livesey leading (just) *Ulysses* at Stanage (mid 1970s) belayed by Jill Lawrence.
Photograph by Dave Croaker.

Right: Pete making the first free ascent of *Zukator* E4 6b Tremadog 1974.
Photograph by John Sheard.

With Chris Bonington at the Harrogate Trade Show.
Photograph by Chris Tullis.

International climbing meet at Plas y Brenin 1976

Top row from L to R: Don Roscoe; Pat Littlejohn; Claude Remy; unknown; Tom Proctor; unknown; Pete Boardman; unknown; unknown; Phil Burke; Bill March (checked jacket); Calvin Torrans; unknown; Pete Gomersall (stripey shirt); unknown. *Bottom row L to R*: unknown; Al Evans; Pete Livesey; unknown; Geoff Birtles; unknown; unknown; unknown.

Pete making the first ascent of *Lunatic* E3 5c at Chapel Head Scar, in 1974.
Photograph by John Sheard.

I Feel Rock – Wellington Crack

by Pete Livesey

There's not much to recommend *Wellington Crack* to the seeker of the aesthetic in climbing. The ugliness of the situation is enveloping, the crack itself more of an evil unnatural slit, no comparison with the perfect Yosemite crack carefully dividing and apportioning sweeps of clean rock. No, if any beauty is to be found in *Wellington Crack*, it can only be through feedback from the body and its movement.

From bottom to top the crack demands unending attention to movement that is at the same time delicate yet strenuous, dynamic yet slow and balanced. Every foot requires something different of the climber. Every movement of every part has to be considered. Every movement is deliberate and worthwhile. A knee or an arm too far out and the layback doesn't work, or balance is lost. Too far in, and you begin to swing outwards slowly but irrevocably; in three or four seconds finger friction will be lost, and you'll be away. You'll realise the reason at the top, take pride in five minutes of perfectly controlled movement, and the graffiti and litter and tourists' dogs are unimportant.

Cow and Calf Rocks, Ilkley, Yorkshire, 50ft, XS (E4) Livesey/Sheard 1973.

First published in Crags 7 1976.

Innovation and Provocation in the Lakes and Yorkshire

by Martin Berzins

ete Livesey provided me with an introduction to climbing on big cliffs that was a small but significant step in my misspent youth and adulthood. The date was May 1972 and the Leeds Canoe Club was having its annual canoe surfing meet at Abersoch on the Lleyn Peninsula, alas without any surf. I think that there was some plan that Jeff Slater (of the canoe expeditions' fame) and I would climb. There were many connections between Yorkshire canoeists and somehow Pete showed up with a crew of climbers. The idea was that we should all do *Dream of White Horses* in Wen Zawn on the Gogarth cliffs of Anglesey. As the novice tag-along I hid at the back awed by lightheartedness, the serious surroundings and all the real climbers. At one point I asked Pete if I would be okay, given that I had only done some Malham VSs. '*Oh yes, you will be fine – these routes are much easier,*' he said. The grassy scramble above a void and the abseil down towards the sea that followed, were both gripping and atmospheric for someone so inexperienced. Once down it was cold in the shade and Jeff and I were at the back of a long line of climbers. The climbing was just a little bit scary but it was, indeed, fine even though we only did the top two pitches of Wen, and it was easier than the notorious Malham VSs which were my usual fare.

Indeed it was at Malham, one weekend in September 1972, that Mick Hillas and I (both long-haired youths) repeated Allan Austin's test piece *Sundance Wall*, watched by Pete. Mick then cleaned and led what we were sure was a new route, *Junkyard Angel* on the right wing. We asked Pete if anyone had done the line, '*Oh yes,*' he said, '*the Heys brothers did it I think.*' At that time the mysterious Heys brothers were supposed to have climbed every blank bit of rock in Yorkshire. Incredulous, we couldn't square this with the loose rock that came off the crux, only to understand much later that this was, perhaps, a typical Pete wind-up. Anyway we chose to ignore the comment, recorded the climb and never heard any more about the Heys brothers. We couldn't really walk away from it as, in the 'free-for-all atmosphere' of the times, Pete or someone else would have quickly climbed and claimed it. The next day we saw Pete on *Sundance Wall*, looking lost, so we gave him directions and a little later we watched him fail on John Syrett's bold *Midnight Cowboy*. It was reassuring to see that Pete climbed like the rest of us on existing routes. The interesting point here, was that it would take me a while and a further conversation with Pete to understand that there was not necessarily any discrepancy between Pete's audacious new routes and more normal days like this.

A year later we saw Pete do two first ascents. The first was *Arnold Freerouter* on the left wing of Gordale Scar. The climb wasn't a great one and probably does not get done these days. My logbook only says that John Sheard had some problems, but if I recall, the ascent was done really quickly. Much more impressive was the first ascent (or what we saw of it) of the very impressive *Limehill* on the exposed continuation of The Terrace at Malham. We saw him at the start in the initial corner and then walked around hoping to see the ascent from a better viewpoint. To our astonishment he had finished the hard climbing and was almost at the top on easy ground. Later still we asked him about the ascent, '*If I know I can do it I don't worry too much about protection,*' he said.

Thinking back, this was a good example of the kind of bold approach on mostly natural gear that transformed Yorkshire and

Derbyshire limestone. While there was a strong free climbing tradition on cliffs like Malham, the difficulty, boldness and sheer élan of ascents like *Jenny Wren* and *Mossdale Trip* at Gordale set the stage for many very bold traditional ascents on Peak and Pennine limestone, often on cliffs on which there is now a mixture of sport (all-bolted) climbs and bolder more traditional climbs. As Paul Clarke, an avid Yorkshire new router, noted in 2013, such traditional climbs on limestone are not that popular now. This is not surprising as the everyday athleticism of climbing provides no training for the kind of mind games needed to obtain the almost intoxicating rush from the combination of long run-outs, doubtful rock and thought-provoking difficulty. As Niccolo Machiavelli puts it, in a somewhat different context, 'Never was anything great achieved without danger'. As if to show that the activity is not quite dead on Yorkshire limestone, Nik Jennings did climb a notable E8 on Kilnsey in May 2013.

This boldness of Pete's did not appear to be a sudden thing. As a penance for something or other I was asked to check Pete's climbs at the mighty Langcliffe Quarry near Settle for one of the limestone guides. This large but not particularly compelling cliff towers above what was then the municipal rubbish tip. The rock does not run to cracks for protection and, in its 1960s and 1970s heyday, bolts were not used on free climbs there. An early article in *Rocksport* magazine showed Pete in canoeing crash hat climbing there if I remember. It was hard not to be impressed by the boldness of routes like *Sickler* at E3 and to (sensibly) stay off leading them if they were not an overriding obsession. Suffice to say that the combination of ambiance and lack of protection did not make these routes popular, but their boldness was a pointer towards the future. There was boldness too on his ascents of routes like *Central Wall* at Kilnsey (climbed with John Sheard) with its intricate and forearm pumping climbing and well-spaced protection, particularly at the top. Repeat ascents were few and tentative. In my case, incompetence led to a very long fall on an early attempt, but fortunately I also gained the realisation that small wires can hold very long falls if placed properly. This gave me a healthy respect for what Pete had told me after his ascent of *Limehill*; '*If I know I can do it I don't worry too much about protection.*'

Pete's ascents stirred both the guardians of Yorkshire and Lake District climbing, the Yorkshire Mountaineering Club (YMC) and the Fell and Rock Climbing Club, (FRCC). The reporting of these routes in magazines like Ken Wilson's *Mountain* also passed the news more quickly than the sometimes tightly controlled guidebooks from the YMC and FRCC. Both clubs were populated by a 1960s generation that was starting to age and, in some instances, was resistant to change and only partially aware of the change in standards that came about through training. At the time decisions were made to leave routes out of these guides if the routes were too poor and/or climbed in a way that the guide writers did not approve of (or also perhaps of a difficulty of which they could not conceive).

The Yorkshire Mountaineering Club clung to the idea that nothing could be much harder than Hard Very Severe on Yorkshire limestone and failed, at first, to see how training was changing what could be done. Pete's routes were left out of the guides or half-heartedly included, sparking a very critical review of the 1974 guide by Pete in *Mountain* 40 magazine. These omissions were even stranger given that Pete brought out a supplement in 1973 that described recent developments on limestone. By 1980, however, Pete was one of the YMC guidebook writers and in some ways part of the climbing establishment. Pete's efforts to supply more accurate information continued with the *Lime Crime* guidebook that he wrote with Graham Desroy in 1982. The combination of this and Desroy's 1980 *New Grit Supplement* started the revitalisation of the Yorkshire guidebooks, which Desroy then led with typical flair and imagination through the 1980s.

To be fair to the YMC and FRCC, they did eventually start to acknowledge the changing standards and bring in new blood but not in a way that always made them comfortable. As one of the FRCC stalwarts blurted out after seeing me and my brother climbing on a cliff with our long hair and youthful looks, 'There's two women climbing really hard routes down there. They are really ugly but they can't half climb.' Pete, however, probably had no need of those clubs as he had his own active group of climbers.

The confused and fast-changing nature of climbing at the time was shown by a debate in *Mountain* magazine in 1976. '*John Allen free climbs Great Wall but uses chalk*' was one headline. After I wrote a letter to *Mountain* praising chalk over aid, Ken Wilson brought together the good and the great to pontificate about how they would never use chalk or only in the smallest amounts. Pete's response was pretty clear, '*Chalk? Sure it leaves marks but so does making little yellow holes in the snow up Zero Gully.*' Needless to say chalk is ubiquitous today, as perhaps are little yellow holes in the snow of *Zero Gully*.

The first Yorkshire climbing walls gave Pete and other local climbers a critical advantage in climbing new routes. In the early to mid 1970s the crucible for this was perhaps the Leeds University climbing wall, which was also a stopping-off point for climbers from far and wide. In his review *The Grade of Things to Come* (which is re-produced in this book), he predicted that '*6b and 6c moves were being strung together on the Leeds Wall, when this form is reproduced on the outcrops standards will rise two grades*'. They did too and by the late 1970s some hard gritstone, limestone and even mountain routes were sometimes climbed in a way that resembled the tactics used today, headpointing, abseil inspections, multi-day ascents and pre-placed protection. Occasional aid was still used, but only infrequently. Many years after Pete's groundbreaking ascent of *Wellington Crack* in Ilkley Quarry, with a sling for resting, he saw Paul Clarke, a local

Yorkshire climber, fail to free climb *Wellington Crack* at the end of a long climbing evening. Pete shouted up to Paul, '*I hope that you are not going to claim that ascent.*'

'*No Pete, I am just trying to recreate your first ascent,*' replied Paul as Pete exited the Quarry.

Of course, this new professionalism did not go down too well in the Lake District where the Fell and Rock Climbing Club was still lined up with Allan Austin's admirable but sometimes not consistent view that '*I do not see crags as impressive backcloths where ruthless men can construct their climbs*'. (*Mountain* 29 September 1973). Abseil inspection and aid points placed in that way were not accepted. Of course, this did not always apply to their own and the ascent of *The Cumbrian* on Esk Buttress, one of the finest unclimbed lines in the Lake District, by Paul Braithwaite and Rod Valentine with two aid points came in for justified criticism by Pete and others. Pete's ascent with Al Manson appeared to have cleaned up that issue, as he stated in *Mountain* 39, until rumours began to circulate.

Sometime later my brother Bob and I were climbing on Shepherd's Crag in Borrowdale when Pete showed up looking for someone to climb with to do a new route. The line he chose was an eliminate in the Chamonix area of the cliff. Bob and I were more than willing accomplices. The ascent was uneventful and indeed the only memorable thing about the route was the monstrous fart that Pete let loose on the crux. Of course, we wanted to name the route after this but he settled on *Bob Martins*, a dog food brand, to which we could only growl and whine in response once we found out that we had been the victims of Pete's provocative sense of humour.

After this ascent Pete's competitive nature led him to solo up *MGC* (E2) behind our roped ascent. The somewhat harsh judgement in my log book reads, '*Livesey tried to burn us off by soloing it, but had a desperate time, basically he is crap and so are we*'. My log book also records a couple of classic quotes by Pete. Regarding his ascent of *The Cumbrian* he said, '*I didn't mean to use aid but someone saw me hanging on a sling.*' On new routes in general he said that, '*Yes, you can climb a full grade harder on new routes than on repeats.*' So this was the key. The fact that detailed and careful inspections, coupled with a passionate desire to succeed, made it possible to do new routes that were somewhat harder than one's everyday climbing. I took that comment to heart for about the next forty years and also climbed *The Cumbrian* free, without ever really knowing what happened on his ascent. I recollect not stopping to place any protection in the main groove for fear of having to rest and only finding it at the top break. Maybe Pete had taught me something about boldness too.

My brother and I, with others, also took it upon ourselves to repeat his routes and were amazed by the quality of the climbing and the consistency of the imagination employed in the choice of mostly classic lines. Routes like the magnificent *Footless Crow* (climbed with Robin Witham) meant that would-be early ascensionists had to improve their game or spend multiple days in order to succeed on its tricky and unobvious crux. The boldness of his solo back-roped ascents of *Dry Gasp* and *Nagasaki Grooves* was extraordinary, although entirely typical given some of his solo ascents of existing routes such as *Capital Punishment* on Cwm Idwal's Suicide Wall. Amazing new climb followed amazing new climb and provoked the rest of us to look at unclimbed rock just as carefully as Pete obviously did. The boldness and speed of ascents that typified Pete's routes were important, as the anarchic attitudes of the time meant that you had to climb new routes quickly or expect someone else to. This was a far cry from the multi-day, week or year 'projects' that sometimes linger today, mine included.

Amidst this extraordinary set of ascents, there were some curious incidents in which Pete very successfully stirred the pot with the

FRCC for reasons that don't entirely make sense today. Allan Austin was very protective over a very average route called *The Ragman's Trumpet* on the left side of Pavey Ark. Pete did a route at about the same time that climbed the same main pitch and then climbed up to a prominent groove, *Sally Free and Easy*. In the debate that followed, Allan Austin was convinced that the FRCC team had climbed the first pitch before Pete and in his counterblast Pete disagreed and described the upper groove (tongue in cheek perhaps) as *'eminently sound and holdless'*. Encouraged by this description in 1974 my brother and I went into the groove and found it to be of poor quality to the point where we had clearly been victims of another Pete wind-up. Recourse came when I said in print that *'only a mind lobotomized by some of the more tottering attractions of Langcliffe and Gordale would describe it as sound and holdless'*. Perhaps Pete was not alone in being provocative, but those were the times.

Perhaps one of the best of Pete's lines was *Lost Horizons* on Scafell, which he climbed with Jill Lawrence, again with some controversy about the style of the ascent, pegs being placed from abseil and the top one used for a handhold. Regardless of this indiscretion, it was the sheer audacity of this ascent and the quality of the resulting route that left people stunned. The peg for aid lasted for a while until it was eliminated by my brother Bob. The pinnacle of Pete's achievements in the Lake District was probably *Das Kapital*, climbed with Pete Gomersall in 1977 on Raven Crag, Thirlmere, with its high degree of difficulty (E6) on the crux and swooping falls if (when?) one failed, as this one did many times. This climb seemed to be an order of magnitude harder than anything else he did in the Lakes. Pete's routes raised standards in the Lakes where his ability to stir up debate made the whole climbing scene there much more dynamic and helped make the Fell and Rock climbing club change its mindset.

This ability to find outstanding lines was also translated into

Pete's later limestone routes. One of the better examples was *Claws* at Kilnsey. The first pitch of this is a piece of superb limestone wall climbing with just enough protection in the shape of small wires. The top pitch is in spectacular position but really not as good as the first as it features a struggle with a bush and then a controversial series of chipped holds. One of my complaints was that these holds were on the small side and rather hard to see. The overall climb is magnificent, and while the tactics used were rightly condemned, in the grand scheme of things they are less significant than they might be, especially when glue now holds together many routes. There were some more mysterious ascents such as *The Gorgon* at Malham, again climbed with Jill Lawrence. The first pitch of this is very loose indeed and the crux bulge above a peculiar tufa pillar has a particularly hard move that is now part of *Gorgon Direct*. This route must have been an adventure comparable with the Gordale routes and one that never gained the recognition it deserved for a very bold ascent.

It was a shock to hear that Pete had stopped climbing and moved to Malham. I somehow expected that he would continue to innovate and to stir things up for years to come. Often we would see him running up to Gordale Scar as part of the training for fell running. He would stop to chat but seemed to have a disinterest in what was happening. In my mind I still see him, frozen in time, running up that gorge, fit, athletic and graceful, still curious about the activity he had done so much to shape but looking dispassionately at what he had moved on from.

Castaway on a Gritstone Island

by Pete Livesey

Beyond the mainstream cliffs of Derbyshire gritstone swells the dirty grey-black sea of Yorkshire industry. Cross the sinuous industrial fjords of the West Riding and you arrive abruptly at the heathery moors of the Yorkshire Dales. You won't find the long lined gritstone tiers of the south here, but crags twinkling from a moorland setting, pinpoints of black light.

The harsh weather, small crags and dour guides have never offered much encouragement to the visitor. Coming here, one usually found the routes easier than one had imagined, although some gems of the dark days of Yorkshire climbing stood out. Austin's *Western Front* and *Wall of Horrors* were morbid lures to Almscliff, aspirants more than likely struggling to capture the barely lesser jewels of Dolphin's era: *Birdlime Traverse* or *Demon Wall, High Street* at Ilkley, Heptonstall's *Forked Lightning Crack* and Crookrise's *Shelf* were all fine but rarely climbed XSs of the 1960s.

We've heard all this before, though. Austin's nine sweaters, Whillans's fists; we know more about them than the routes. But now, now the barriers are down. The five years that have passed since the publication of the guide have seen the internal aspect of Yorkshire climbing revolutionised; irreverent intellectuals vie with irrelevant non-intellectuals for revelationary routes. There's a throbbing youth cult hammering away at the rock, with fingers, fists, feet, and even some heads. The rock is climbed for the routes, for the moving, for the thrills; no one cares who adds what to the age-old defacements at Ilkley. Aestheticism is derived from the totally consuming difficulty of the routes, rather than from the surroundings. Older aspirant youth-cultivators try to alter their image, in order to belong once again.

A fresh emergent rock group rehearses hard at Leeds University – all lead players in an innovatory band. Concrete-backed brick edges wince at the bite of fingernails belonging to solid arms. Bodies revolve about those arms, gaining height with scant regard for traditional posture. The members of the band look alike, all Perrin's skinny ape-armed type, embellished by pop group looks. Concentrated competition drives them to perfect ever more ridiculous moves. Hand-holds approach footholds as the distance to the next pair increases. Kinaesthologists would marvel at the vertical awareness of these performers utilizing every inch of their movement sphere from two small central holds. New techniques, knee pressing, arm locking and two-dimensional movement emerge quickly in the competitive but sociable atmosphere; these are friendlies, soon to be played for real when the shrieking winter gales abate from those gritstone outcrops. On the other hand, it may be that the outcrops provide training for Leeds University's Wall. Groupie Bernard Newman weight-trains, runs, and has even been seen climbing in the Alps, in preparation for his winter season on 'The Wall'.

Don Robinson is the man to blame; a 64-year old lecturer at Leeds University, a skilled caver and a climber of moderate ability, he conceived the wall as an indoor teaching space for his students. Built for only a few pounds, its superiority over earlier and later architect-designed monstrosities was soon apparent. Today, as every day, it draws climbers from all over the county to play on its ferociously gymnastic possibilities.

The results that can be achieved on such a training ground first became apparent to the climbing world at large when John Syrett, non-climber, emerged from a year on the wall to tear about the country climbing everything from XS and up. His progression from nothing to a sight lead of *Wall of Horrors*, inside 12 months, set the scene. The conditions of some of his ascents emphasised the inadequacies of the technical difficulties as tests for his ability. New routes and new names soon followed, but Syrett, sober, was nigh on impossible to follow. His first ascents, often solo, were technically new, and they see little of the traffic that routes like *Wall of Horrors* now bear.

Traditionally trained climbers did not sit back and applaud this artificial effrontery. Old men with short hair, raggy sweaters and gnarled hands were heard panting and grunting in dimly lit corners of climbing walls. Ken Wood replied to the University challenge with two routes of his own, *Chopper* (XS) at Earl Crag, and *True Grit* (XS) at Brimham. Both are unrepeated; *Chopper* is off-width, and *True Grit* is a vicious finger-crack looking dispassionately north from the northern shores of Gritstone Island. Syrett also came north and added *Joker's Wall* to the fiercely overhanging side of Brimham's Cubic Block; you're too high to jump off before you know it – then it gets mean.

Of all the crags offended by these forays into the impossible, none has received the continual battering nor nurtured and harnessed the energy so well as Almscliff. Almscliff the friendly wart, no, more like a Freudian nipple – a barometer of the state of the art. Syrett's *Big Greenie* (XS) was a high bold problem on the nipple's biggest blank, a good starter for a concentrated but prolonged attack by the University climbers.

Almscliff, armscliff, every day;
sunny Sundays or Thursday at three,
three feet a day will fill
a route in 10.

Al Manson, without doubt the first man to make the real breakthrough in climbing wall standards, brought his ability to Almscliff and linked two unrepeated problems to produce *Rectum Rift* (XS). The highly technical start and stretchy tenuous finish make this obscene route one of the hardest technical challenges on grit, a bold statement that someone has yet to refute. The weediest climber in Britain, Pete Kitson, soloed two boulder problems on Virgin Boulder. At HVS, the 35-foot lengths of the *Gypsy* and the *Virgin* are shattering. In August 1973, when the inhabitants were sunning in Greece or voyeurging to the Calanques, Lancastrian Pasquill sailed in and poked out the *Goblin's Eyes*. Climbing an eight-foot roof on eye-like pockets to a long, long finishing pull, he led what Syrett had failed to top-rope. Home teams could not answer. Livesey came with *All Quiet* (XS), a beautiful climber's route, starting up *Wall of Horrors* and swinging from jug to jug across the wall to *Western Front*, then across again to *Crack of Doom*; 70 feet of high quality climbing in a continuously overhanging situation.

One could almost see a tearful sorrow in the eyes of spectators at Almscliff and other show grounds, as they watched the passing of the Average Climber. They could see nothing familiar, nothing to identify with in the preparations of the Lean Men: the Spiny Normans with their chalky hands, deep breathing, vest and shorts and quick-draw shortened runner racks. But come back after the show, you ordinary men, see when all's quiet what they have done; look at the needle-straight cracks of Ilkley's *Wellington Crack* or Heptonstall's *Hard Line*; contemplate the audacity of *Goblin's Eyes* or the technical beauty of Crookrise's *Small Brown*.

Attempts were made to strengthen the Western Ramparts. Heptonstall, first line of defence against the Invader, was fortified with Syrett's desperate-looking *Thunderclap* (XS). Livesey came next with the similar *Hard Line* (XS). Both routes follow thin, relentless crack-lines and are unrepeated. Peel and Rawlinson answered back for the invaders with *Cream* (XS) and *Strange Brew* (XS), two more steep lines.

At Ilkley, the first new route for years appeared on a most unlikely blank wall in the quarry. *Propeller Wall* was given the joke grade of VS by Syrett. Repeated twice, it is said to be harder than the neighbouring *High Street* (XS). Syrett soloed it. Livesey followed with *Waterloo* (HVS), similar but better protected. Something bigger was brewing at Ilkley though. Someone had cleaned the rotting wedges from the painfully obvious *Wellington Crack*, a thin diagonal slash up an otherwise featureless 40ft wall, slightly overhanging with an undercut base. It was going to be done soon, but by whom? Livesey stepped in, inspected it from jumars, then failed. But still no one else came. Three months later, Livesey returned and got to within a foot of the top, where failing strength forced him to grab a nut to step down for a rest, but the route was completed. Never technically ridiculous, its relentlessness can only be compared with that of its American cousin, *Butterballs*.

Nineteen-year old Ron Fawcett was quietly making his mark on the crags about his native Skipton. A narrow lad with a wide appreciation for climbing hard routes, Fawcett can stretch up and surely insert his club-like fists a foot higher than you or I. See him on Ilkley evenings; on a windy climbing wall – a wind that for some cools the heat of competition. Follow Fawcett solo round the routes; you can't – should have taken notice of those athlete's shorts and vests. At 18 he'd already done more, and harder, routes than Brown and Whillans put together. No one can repeat his free ascent of *Small Brown* at Crookrise, technical and strenuous in the extreme.

The rise in standard is by no means ebbing as climbing wall training gains momentum. A new wall opens on Gritstone Island, at Rothwell, it is bigger and better, another Robinson-built effort that is already incredibly popular. Climbers perform un-roped, a must for effective training; no meddling regulations here. What will it bring? Certainly routes like the Cows right-hand arête and *Milky Way*. Too hard for now, but soon to become a reality. But then, who knows when to stop?

First published in Mountain *42 1975*

Footnote by Mark Radtke.
Milky Way E6 6b, finally fell to Fawcett in 1978, but it was 12 years before Livesey's prediction about the right arête of The Cow came to fruition and was finally climbed by John Dunne in 1987 to produce *The New Statesman* E8 7a.

'The weediest climber in Britain, Pete Kitson, soloed two boulder problems on Virgin Boulder. At HVS, the 35-foot lengths of the *Gypsy* and the *Virgin* are shattering.' In 2014 the grade of the *Gypsy* and *Virgin* stand at E3 6a (Font 7a) and E3 6b (Font 7a+) respectively.

Great Days with Pete

by Peter Lindsey Gomersall

In the midnight hours

I was tired and perhaps a little deflated after an eight-week trip to the Alps. It had been my first climbing trip abroad, September 1975. I had visited the Dolomites and the high Alps around Chamonix. It had been enjoyable, eventful and relatively successful but, as was typical for me with long trips, a little tiresome towards the end. Maybe this is not the case with all climbers, but it definitely seemed to happen with me. On my return I started packing to leave home for a longer stint than the usual eight weeks. Not for a climbing trip this time, but for life as a student. Bingley had not been my first choice college, but at least I was going somewhere and what the hell, you don't always get what you want.

At this point in time I can't remember if I even knew that Pete Livesey was at Bingley, but this was about to change. I was enrolled on a new, modular, four-year degree course to become a physical education teacher. Unfortunately this turned out to be a little erroneous and I quickly changed to a straight degree with no teaching component. The 'modular degree' that year included an introduction to human movement studies, an outdoor pursuits class and a couple of geography classes. The two 'physical modules' involved a Monday morning contemporary dance section which us boys called 'prance' and then real PE later in the week.

Over the preceding few years I had become a pretty good climber, not surprising I suppose considering that my peers hailed from Skipton, and it seemed like everyone from the town who climbed was also good at it. I'd already started to do first ascents and this continued at Bingley College. My first involvement with Pete was in the outdoor pursuits class at the college. I'm sure I'd bumped into him out and about on the crags, but I'd not really met him in the meaningful sense of the word. My awakening came when out of the blue Pete asked me about a route I had only just put up at Malham. It was a case of, 'Wow, this person actually knows who I am!' I suppose it completely changed my perspective of him and also forged the start of a long friendship. By Monday morning, however, things were already a little clearer about this relationship as he tells me my *Seventh Grade* was a nice little route and, oh yes, he'd managed to dispense with some of the aid I had used. A clear pointer to his competitive streak, and my lowly position in his climbing world. From small beginnings I was pulled into this world and climbing life.

Pete was living in a top floor bedsit in Saltaire with his girlfriend, Florrie (Jill Lawrence), an aspiring climber herself. Over the coming year I became more and more involved with them. Highlights of this time concerned a trip to Cornwall for Easter with what seemed like the whole of Yorkshire's climbing glitterati camping on the field outside The Count House. During this trip virtually every major route in the area was climbed. Somehow the trip ended with me and Ron (Fawcett) having a lift back with Pete and Jill; everyone else had gone home having had shorter breaks. The trip ended with a stop-off at Pentire Head on the way back, with Ron and me doing *Darkinbad* while those two did *Eroica*. Pete had freed *Darkinbad* on the way down a few days earlier.

Later that year there was a great Buxton conference where Peter was a guest speaker. All I remember were very late nights with about six people on the floor of his guest bedroom. After staggering back to the room I was pressed to the floor by his lodger (who at the time had a full leg in plaster). It brought new meaning to the rest of his guests with the constant bonk, bonk, bonk of the pot on the floor. During this time we began to make more and more visits to the Junction pub in Brighouse on a Friday night. It became a bit of a scene where members of the Phoenix Club hung out. I believe it became popular, not because of the pub, but the fact that Christine Crawshaw's house was right next to it. Everyone could stagger over there after last orders and could continue the partying – more drinking, food, good company and a lot of old films on the 'telly'. It was during this time that Pete coined the phrase 'zero hour', which he described as that period in time that didn't cost anything. Zero hour would be used to travel to places and not take up important parts of the day. An example of this was after an evening in Chester for a party with Al Rouse, Rab Carrington and the Burgess twins when we hit the road in the middle of the night back to Stoney so we could climb the next day without wasting any time. They were hedonistic days, but my God did we pack stuff in.

Crème du Menthe

One of the problems with new things is that they don't always turn out to be great, or even come close to what they were supposed to be. This was the case with the new modular degree at Bingley. The college became strangled by lack of funding. The net result was that the, 'you can combine any module with any other', approach that had been sold to me was now out of the window. My second year at the college, which was basically sports science type studies, resulted in me having to fill an empty slot with the only thing available – an art class. The resulting lack of enthusiasm on my part ended up with my taking a year out and studying in the real world, working at a bath factory. It turned out it was not too bad either as Ron Fawcett joined me on the assembly line just to keep me company.

Sometime prior to Easter that year I went to Wales with Ron and Gibby (Chris Gibb) but it turned out to be a really wet weekend. All we did was boulder at Hyll-Drem, and for my troubles I ended up with a broken wrist, having slipped off. The good news was that I couldn't make baths for a while and I was able to tag along with Pete and Florrie on a trip to the south of France. The original plan had been for them to meet up with Bonny Masson (my partner) and Chris Gore, a new up-and-coming upstart from London. With my enforced leave from work I jumped aboard. All I could think about was the ordeal of five people in a Citroën Ami. As was customary back then, it was a non-stop drive to the south of France, with us like sardines squashed in a tin heading for a place called the Verdon. It was dawn as we drove the last stint between Castellane and La Palud. I recall that it was a dreary misty morning, but we were awakened by the ever increasing impressiveness of the canyon as the full impact became apparent for the first time. The mists parted and we looked down into the full grandeur of the east end of the Verdon.

This was an early trip by British climbers to this 'new place', which in the span of just a year or so, would evolve into a Mecca for the modern rock-climber. Pete had already visited the mighty Vercors at that time, but it was obvious from his comments that the Verdon was an entirely different animal, and in a wholly different league. That night it snowed and we spent the next day trudging around investigating the gorge. Later that evening at the bar in La Palud, we found our luck was definitely out and rain and snow was expected for the next few days. The only bright spark was obtained from some locals who told us of a climbing area in the foothills above Nice called Saint Jeannet, where we were assured it would be warm and dry. Even though the Verdon was wet the huge amount of rock left a lasting impression and we'd have to come back. The next few days were spent sampling the delights of Saint Jeannet, sleeping in the vine terraces just above the village, eating in the wonderful family restaurants and being serenaded to sleep by the clicking of cicadas in the warm night air. Looking back it was such a wonderful experience and still so unspoiled. I wonder if we could still sleep out on the terraces today? Somehow I doubt it. How could it be that we were such a short distance from the dreary mountain weather that the Verdon was subject to? It's all so obvious today, but back then every day was a new adventure.

I had itchy fingers and I couldn't climb, not with a cast on my arm. I managed a few top-ropes to satiate my thirst. Pete and Chris did a free ascent of a big route on the main face at Saint Jeannet, and it seemed like a good time to return to the Gorge. Sadly as our hopes rose, our hearts sank and the weather closed back in. Snow was still deep on the ground, there would be no climbing in the Verdon this trip. We were forced to pack the tents and head back to Nice.

It was just rock and more rock as we headed west and moved to Saint Victoire, where we spent the remaining days of our trip. Its nearly forty years ago, but isn't it strange the little things you remember from times past? The pain in your toes, that funny little sling glued into a hole for protection, and the gorgeous lapin ragoût we had in the auberge at the foot of the cliff. So we began the long drive home and even that became a strange experience. For the next 400 miles we had to stop at every autoroute service station until we hit Paris. The sole intention had been to see who could steal the most from the gift shops. Another of Pete's games, and the beginning of his love affair with Crème du Menthe.

The first ascent of Strawberries

So my year out from college was coming to an end and I had been left some money by my grandmother, who had just passed away. I spent it on two flights to San Francisco for Bonny and me. We'd planned a visit to Yosemite and a cross-America road trip with Pete and a bunch of other villains. We were really psyched for this trip. It was about two weeks before we were due to leave for the States and Pete called me. *'We've got to go to Wales to try those routes before we fly.'*

The next day, or should I say night, we were en route to Wales, as usual in the zero hour. In the morning we breakfasted at Ynws and discussed the day. We talked about 'the crack' on the Vector headwall. Later, after coffee at the Tremadog café we walked along the road below the cliffs chatting about the line and where to go. We decided there was plenty of unclimbed rock below and to the left of the headwall. Pete climbed a line roughly between what is now *Weaver* and *Nimbus* and belayed on the top Vector traverse. I followed and then headed right across the grey slab. I fought my way around the corner on the narrowing slab squashed between a roof and an overlap, pulling at bunches of ivy and peeling them off the rock as I went. Once around the corner, I steadied my breathing and began to head up the crack above. After about 10 feet, I was shut down by difficulty and rope drag and had to scuttle off left to belay on the spikes below the top of *Cream*. Pete came across and tried the crack, getting about fifteen feet before grinding to a halt. He stripped the gear while down climbing. Discussing the problem we decided we needed to clean it properly and would have to come back later. Pete shuffled off right and scampered up the gully to the top of the *Shadrach* wall.

We decided we had plenty of time to do a line we had seen directly up the wall below us, and so we abseiled down, pulling the ropes. I headed back up, sticking a couple of nuts in at the top of a flake before stepping out right onto a nice little steep wall. Further up as I was stepping on a little foothold and pushing against a thumb sprag, the tiny hold snapped and I was flying though air. An audible crack signatured my impact with the ledge. Pete slowly lowered me to the ground. My head was spinning, but I thought I was all right. Once I came to my senses, it didn't seem so bad and I tried to stand, there was an unsavory grating sound from my leg. *'That doesn't sound too good,'* said Pete.

'It's broken,' I replied. At that point he started to remove his gear. Next, he was off, soloing up the wall and I shouted out, *'What about me?'* He nonchalantly replied with a wry smile, *'If Doug Scott can crawl down the Ogre with a broken leg, you can get to the café!'* Of course, I knew he wasn't joking, so I started to drag myself down the boulder field. I had just got down to the road when another climber found me and gave me a piggy-back to the car park. Half an hour later Pete appeared with all the gear from the top of the cliff: *'I guess we are off to the hospital?'* he said with a smile. I replied sharply, *'Yes, but not Bangor. They're more likely to take your leg off there than try and repair it.'* Bonny who'd worked there previously had warned me about this. *'Never go there for anything,'* she'd often counseled. Pete packed the car and I dragged myself in and we headed off home. *'Here you are, ten should help the pain until we can get to Airedale.'* Pete handed me an aspirin bottle.

'That looks nasty, 'Pot's Fracture'. You'll need to go to surgery,' the surgeon said. The next thing I remembered was Pete helping me out of the car at my house and handing me a pair of crutches; it was the zero hour again.

He got back in the car. *'Where are you going?'* I shouted.

'Home, I've rung the bell, but there's no way I'm seeing Bonny tonight with you in that condition.' He wound up the window and was off. The front door opened and Bonny stared out at me looking at the long plaster cast on my leg.

The glare in her eyes said it all. She didn't speak to me for weeks. That was the conclusion to our brief attempt at what was to become *Strawberries* and what should have been my first trip to the States. The insurance money that we got back for the cancelled flights went towards a new car; they even took the Morris Minor in exchange. Pete climbed a new route a month or so after his trip to the States and called it Leg Break.

Dresden to Das Kapital

Pete had received an invitation to visit the sandstone towers of Elbsandstein near Dresden in East Germany. The trip was planned for the Spring Bank Holiday and we had to get visas. It was Saturday morning and hot. Pete, Christine Crawshaw and I headed down the M1 and onto the North Circular, and then off down south to Highbury, cutting east to the Dartford tunnel. We were flying and soon headed onto the M2 towards Dover. Maybe that was the problem as suddenly a large plume of steam started to appear from the front of Pete's Ford Escort. We chugged into the services at Faversham. After a brief discussion, the radiator had cooled and we could pour in the guppy, gunky 'seal anything' promised on the tin. Soon we were off again. Trouble was we all knew that the car was never going to get us to Dresden so we turned tail and were soon flying back up the M1. Was it a problem? No, not for us, we always had plenty of other things to climb.

Sunday came and this time we were flying up the A65 through Yorkshire. Maybe we should have put more faith in the gunky stuff and kept with the original plan? Hellifield went flashing by; Settle, Ingleton, and soon we were passing Kendal. Within what seemed like minutes we crested Dunmail Raise in the Lakes and parked up at the north end of Thirlmere. We were heading up to Raven Crag. '*Looks like they're already here,*' Pete said as he pulled the sack out of the boot. Bonny and Florrie were at the crag; I suspect they weren't thinking we'd be there to keep them company though. It wasn't our first visit; we'd already made the second ascent of *Gates of Delirium*, which had been followed by our first ascent of a tough line that we'd called *Peels of Laughter*. *Peels* hadn't been planned; having led the second pitch of

Gates, Pete had traversed off left to look at a line covered with chalk, which we'd noticed when we walked-in. We thought we should take a look. When I scrambled over, he wasn't belaying but setting up an anchor for an abseil. This sturdy anchor was a hawthorn bush, which was all of thirty millimetres in diameter. I looked at him quizzically and he flashed back a wry smile and a quick: *'Hawthorns are strong!'* We managed to struggle up the line after a real fight at the roof. It was only later when we were in the Pack Horse pub that we realized that it was unclimbed and we had done the first ascent. Our involvement continued at Raven with a swift free ascent of a previously aided route that was now named *Blitzkrieg*.

Today, however, we were there for sterner stuff. We had our sights on a much steeper line up the most overhanging part of the cliff. The line went up an overhanging crack and groove system, then out left to what would be a tricky exit, before following another groove towards the top of the pitch. Pete told me he'd been up and 'prepared it' the previous Tuesday. It didn't take long to lead the pitch, but I could tell it was hard from the sound of his breathing, even though I couldn't see him. It took me all my effort to second the pitch. The tricky exit left and the little finishing groove proved really taxing. Sitting on the ledge at the top of the pitch below the headwall and panting profusely he piped up: *'Your turn now.'* I had become well-accustomed to this sort of summons. If it wasn't clean and he hadn't prepared it to his satisfaction it was always my pitch. After a short breather, there was no alternative but to launch out above the void and onto the headwall. Creeping out right, the wall steepened and I had to move out further, it then looked like I needed to break left. For me, it wasn't going to go that day. With the gear in place Pete also tried the pitch, but also scuttled back to our eyrie. We would have to return another day.

For some reason we had to drive to the crag separately the following Tuesday. When I arrived at the parking place he'd already headed up to the crag. As I cleared the tree line I could see him readying to abseil over the top of the cliff. Forty minutes later I was on top of the cliff and scrambling over to his anchors. I could hear the tap, tap, tap of a hammer and chisel. At the same time I was consumed by huge swarms of midges encircling the top of the cliff. I tried to find a spot in the air flow that would keep the devils at bay and covered my head with my hoodie. It was all to no avail, the infamous biters were everywhere. Eventually he pulled back up his ropes and arrived at the cliff top. '*It's your turn to finish the job,*' he said handing me the hammer. When I got down the wall I saw the little scratch he'd made in the rock. It must be iron hard I thought. It took forever to make a usable hold while I continued to be eaten alive. When I got back to the top my eyes were nearly completely closed from the midge bites. He insisted we went down and do the top pitch; I just said he must be bloody joking. We resolved to leave it anyway, as now even his blood had become tasty to the nasty midges.

Two days later we were back at the cliff and climbed the whole route. *Das Kapital* was just another example of Pete's desire to find the best and hardest routes; a means for self-expression and a need to be the best. It didn't matter to him that we had to chip a hold; it was the overall value of the route that was important. His routes were always pure and aesthetic. Even the preparation justified the end result in Pete's eyes. Cleaning, practicing, and chipping were all part of his game. As long as the end result was 'a great route' then he was happy.

Cars

I have mentioned the Citroën Ami going to the Verdon, and the Ford Escort that so horribly died going to East Germany. These were not the only cars that Pete became infatuated with. Looking back I do believe it was a case of boys must have toys and also that they act as supplicant when we can't have or have lost what we want or need.

However regardless of the Psych stuff Pete did love a nice car. Once he'd had a decent job for of a couple of years or so he could afford the Alfa Romeo Giulietta, a steady entry into the sports car field. Then there was the Lotus Elite from some dodgy dealer in Sheffield, a tasty machine that was in and out of the workshop every second week. We had one hilarious trip to Gogarth, racing Gibby and Ron in an extremely powerful Austin Allegro. Pete kept blasting past nipping in and out of traffic and hiding down the side streets of towns across Anglesey to then blast past the unsuspecting duo. After twenty odd miles of play, our respective teams called it quits and then proceeded on to make the second and third ascents of *Positron* to end the morning's frivolities. I can certainly understand Pete's emotions here; I too succumbed to buying expensive cars out of a gut wrenching need to placate oneself after going through a heart-wrenching breakup. He did learn though; he found that you can have a decent car and have a bit of fun too; just buy a Toyota Celica!

Accomplice

Life always has its ups and downs and even Pete was given his fair share of the shitty end of the stick. Jill Lawrence finished her degree at Bingley and got a job at Bewerley Park Outdoor Pursuits Centre near Pateley Bridge. She was also emerging from Pete's shadow as a gifted climber in her own right with some significant female ascents, like the first British female ascent of Pete's own route, *Right Wall*. Back in the day this was ground-breaking. I believe that this was an enlightening time for her as she was also realising her own personal sexual revolution. The resulting effect of the latter was devastating for Pete and inevitably they split. Things were not going well in the educational world either. Bingley had been killed off by people with clout in Bradford who decided to close the college and move everything to Ilkley. Fortunately for Pete, outdoor pursuits was seen as one of the areas worth salvaging and everything related to his area got migrated to the new and improved Ilkley Campus. It wasn't long though before Pete was at the top of the Principal's list. Not for being a bad boy, but on the list of research publications achieved. This was entirely due to Pete's monthly column in *Climber* magazine. Twelve publications a year in research was huge in academia.

Things were on the up again for Pete. It was during this period that he met and fell in love with Soma, a female PE teacher. Pete and Soma's relationship would be cemented in stone through a wild adventure, typical of Pete's making, but that's a story that I think only Pete himself could tell. We continued to climb together but I could see something was changing. We had a trip up to Tophet Wall in Wasdale. He effortlessly floated up *Supernatural*, but then failed to even second a steep crack climbed on the left side of the cliff, the name of which I can't for the life of me remember. On the way home he just came straight out with it and let me know he was finished with climbing. Those were the last routes we ever did together.

I continued to be close friends with Pete and Soma. My passion for climbing was never dimmed and I'd regularly drop in to see them at their house in Malham. It was great to see them both, now blessed with a beautiful daughter who they'd named Tai. On the wall of the living room hung photos of fell races won, Pete standing proud on the podium. The mantelpiece was decorated with trophies and medals from mountain marathons. He'd found a new game and typical of Pete he was champion once again.

What I have presented here are a few memories of great times I spent with Pete. It was always a learning experience for sure. Some of the things we did back then may seem less than pure, seen through the eyes of those born in the age of today's more politically correct values and attitudes, but that's how it was back then, we were pushing into new ground and Pete certainly liked to do things his way. I knew Pete for more than twenty years, but less than ten were involved with climbing. He was such an interesting character with many different facets. He challenged himself and those around him, he charmed and inspired people and loved to buck the system. I am honoured to have been his friend and accomplice in the great adventure. I truly miss him.

I Feel Rock - *Darkinbad the Brightdayler*

by Pete Livesey

A foreboding, harsh grey cliff glowering at an equally angry-looking sea. A 150-foot sheet of smooth wall is dominated by a leaning headwall seamed with ridiculous-looking grooves. The start of *Darkinbad* does little to ease your mind; a lurch from a boulder on to a wall of no return. Then suddenly things change, and the whole wall is a mass of tiny twisted cracks and holds, each one containing hundreds of friendly acrobatic shrimps – it's alive. Everything is enjoyable, you're among friends – millions of climbers whiling away their time on a vast handhold sanctuary.

Just wander up that vast wall, always heading for a shallow alcove below the nastiest of the hanging grooves above. You set out up the groove, steady laybacking to a roof where you gradually realise that you're trying to layback with your feet above your hands and there's no horizon left.

The shrimps above are disturbed by a blind hand creeping over the roof, feeling around, finding a flat hold with a useful crack down the back; a body and legs follow and all end up teetering on the flat hold with the useful crack.

The rest is a foregone conclusion, and you can lie in the sun in perfect Japanese filmmaker's grass until your second gets annoyed and begins to drag you over the edge, like a fish catching an angler.

Pentire Head, Cornwall 230 feet, XS (E4) FA P Littlejohn/ I Duckworth 1971 7 Pts FFA P Livesey /J Lawrence 1976.

First published in Crags *7 1976.*

Brain Damage

by Johnny Walker

It was the usual thing. I can't remember how I was drafted in as one of Pete's many portable belays, but there we were, charging up to the East Wall of Pavey Ark, in the Lake District, at a great rate of knots. The aim of the mission was to grab the second ascent of *Brain Damage*. The name seemed appropriate because, as it turned out, I must have been suffering from it.

When we got to the foot of the route, someone had beaten us to it. The legendary Allan Austin was already up there approaching the crux and shouting down to his partner that the nut that he needed was a hexcentric, and he'd left it back in the shop. I think Austin completed the climb, but whether he did it entirely free I can't remember. Pete was next, of course. He hovered briefly around the crux, but had little trouble with it and, as usual, was at the top in no time.

I was next and needless to say, I found it hard. The rope was pinging 'C' sharp as I was hauled over the crux, but the real fun was just about to begin. At the top of the route there are two or three narrow grassy terraces separated by short rock walls. On the first of these was a skittish looking sheep that had become crag fast. As I climbed up onto the ledge it became startled and off it shot. '*We can rescue it,*' said Pete.

'*How?*' I asked.

'*Well, if you untie one of the ropes, you can grab the sheep, tie the rope round it and I'll haul it up.*'

'*Right,*' said I, and not overly convinced with Pete's tactics, went to make a grab for the sheep. The sheep didn't want to be grabbed, however, and off it scuttled right to the end of the narrowing ledge.

After further instruction to, '*Follow it.*' Then, '*Dive on it.*'

'*Entwine your fingers in its fleece,*' said Pete. I was now contemplating a monster pendulum. A bit more encouragement from Pete finally persuaded me to make the grab. I wrestled the sheep to the ground and got the rope tied round it. Somehow, both my newly found, woolly friend and I managed to stay on the ledge and Pete dragged us back until we were below him. I shoved, whilst he pulled and eventually we got the creature up the short walls and back to the freedom of the fells.

Was it grateful? Not a bit of it. I untied the rope and the stupid creature buggered off back down to the ledge we'd just rescued it from. We laughed, coiled the ropes and left it to it.

It was another facet of Pete's character, one that I hadn't seen before. Under all that competitive drive there was also a considerable degree of compassion.

Gordale Scar

by Mark Radtke

As I advanced, the crags seemed to close in, but I discovered a narrow entrance turning to the right between them and then all further way is barred by a stream that at the height of about 50 feet, gushes from a hole in the rock, and spreading in large sheets over its broken front, dashes from steep to steep, and then rattles away in a torrent down the valley. The rock on the left rises perpendicular, with stubbed yew trees and shrubs starting from its sides, to the height of at least 300 feet; but these are not the thing; it is the rock to the right, under which you stand to see the fall, which forms the principal horror of the place. From its very base it begins to slope forwards over you in one black or solid mass without any crevice in its surface, and overshadows half the area below its dreadful canopy; when I stood at (I believe) four yards distant from its foot, the drops which perpetually distil from its brow, fell on my head; and in one part of its top more exposed to the weather, there are loose stones that hang in the air, and threaten visibly some idle spectator with instant destruction; it is safer to shelter yourself close to its bottom, and trust to the mercy of that enormous mass, which nothing but an earthquake can stir. The gloomy, uncomfortable day well-suited the savage aspect of the place, and made it still more formidable; I stayed there, not without shuddering, a quarter of an hour, and thought my trouble richly paid, for the impression will last for life.

Erskine Stuart 1892 Literary Shrines of Yorkshire.

A wide gravel path now leads through the camp site and guides countless visitors to the entrance of Gordale Scar, but despite the crowds, this Gothic cathedral of a crag retains all the drama that Erskine Stuart experienced back in the 1890s. It's the perfect stage on which to re-enact some Livesey classics.

Face Route **50 metres E3 5c, 6a Pete Livesey, John Sheard 1971.**

Face Route needs to be climbed when you're just cutting it well on E3s. Do it when you're comfortable on E5s and the moment will be lost. It's a game of two halves. The first half requires a bit of courage and will appeal to the adventurer. The second half is a boulder problem and requires the technician's mind. A bold start up the wall to the right of the obvious corner sets you up. Take it on and you'll end up on top. Bomber nuts soon arrive and in no time you're contemplating the roof. Spy out the driest holds and go for it, paste your feet high and layback like hell to jugs. Breathe easy, clip the tat and pull into the vertical, don't panic and press on scanning the right wall for footholds. Let the pump dissipate under the next bulge. The gear seems ancient and ancient it is, but enjoy the space beneath your feet as your fingers curl around intoxicating jugs. A bit of cautious technicality lands you on *Bikini Atoll.* Today some people choose to do Face Route in one long pitch, but do it like this and you're missing the point of Gordale. As you sit marooned on that oasis of a belay, gaze at the architecture all around and glean what you can about what lies therein. You'll need it, because after this you'll be back for more. Let your bouldering mate do pitch 2. It's a piece of piss if you're a boulderer. It's a cat and mouse game if you're not.

Jenny Wren 60 metres E5 5b, 5c, 6a Pete Livesey, John Sheard 1971.

The first pitch of *Jenny Wren* sets the scene perfectly. A creaky groove seduces you upwards. The climbing is never desperate but suspect rock and sparse protection make total concentration mandatory. The groove leads to a cave belay on a narrow rubble-strewn ledge. Any hope of escape upwards is thwarted by overhangs adorned with loose and unstable flakes of rock. The place has a sense of decomposition and decay. From here the way ahead is out leftwards round a blind arête and into the unknown; it looks blank and uninviting. A token runner in a small crack at the end of the ledge provides just enough protection to encourage tentative probing of the shattered wall. Eighty feet of space below your feet with no obvious runners and unhelpful holds cause hesitant to-ing and fro-ing. Eventually you'll get the hold combination which allows a stretch left round the blind arête. Fingers will lock onto good flakes and you're making steady progress leftwards over increasingly solid rock. Arrive at the belay, an oasis set in a sea of white limestone, and soak up the atmosphere. The third pitch is the crux of the climb. It continues up and leftwards linking technical pieces of bold climbing with cracks and features that offer a hope of protection and the possibility of rest. *Jenny Wren* is a subtle route, the way ahead is never obvious, runners have to be placed with craft; it's classic Livesey. The rock may be dubious and the line tenuous, but the quality of the climb comes not from purity of line, or excellence of moves, but from where it takes you mentally.

Deliverance 45 metres E5 5c, 6b, 5c Pete Livesey, John Sheard 1973 (1pt).

In the upper reaches of the gorge a huge ship's prow of smooth and featured rock juts temptingly above the cascade. If you want *Deliverance* then this is where you have to venture. The first pitch smacks you straight in the face with instant exposure as you swing out right around the arête, but the fear is kept at bay with good nuts in solid cracks; further on, a bolt calms nerves. In Livesey's day this was a rusting relic and testimony to why he was there. It was replaced in recent times and makes the moves to the belay ledge a veritable dance. The one point of aid used by Livesey on pitch 2 says it all. It took the talent of Dougie Hall to finally eliminate the errant aid point in 1982 and even today's wall-honed rock athlete is likely to be sorely tested. A crack in a smooth wall above the ledge gets you moving and provides gear so that you can stretch out and clip the bolt before taking the inevitable fall. Hanging off the bolt you can try and make sense of non-holds. If you manage to make some sense of the smoothness you might just claw your way to the break above, but beware, it's easy to be spat back down into the abyss from the deceptive roundness. If you're lucky enough to make the next belay then you can breathe easy; pitch 3 is in the bag.

Mossdale Trip **E6 6b, 6b Pete Livesey, Jill Lawrence 1977.**

To the right of *Face Route* a magnificent ocean of white rock, devoid of features and cracks rises out of the rubble-strewn floor and soars skywards. When seen in the afternoon sunlight this vast expanse of shattered limestone provides a temptation for those in search of adventure. No bolts intrude to interrupt your concentration. Holds are studied in intimate detail, tested carefully and gently weighted. Progress is slow, no savage pulls, no random slaps or snatches. No room for error, just cautious, calculated movement, mind and body in total symbiosis. An occasional rusted peg appears momentarily and then slips away into the void below – temporary psychological comfort, as the mind concentrates, the body obeys and all doubt is suppressed. This is no place for doubt. This is the *Mossdale Trip*.

Cumbrian Classics

by Ian Cooksey

Without doubt some of the finest climbing in the British Isles can be found in the Lake District. During the 1970s it was a hot bed of activity at a time when hard, free climbing was coming of age. Many of the remaining aid points were eliminated and numerous plum lines that had been deemed to be too hard by previous generations were climbed. At the heart of this free climbing revolution was Pete Livesey, a Yorkshire man who brought with him a new approach to climbing that would help to transform the sport.

A prolific new router, he left his mark on the Lakes with a clutch of climbs that, at the time, were at the cutting edge of what seemed possible. His route names stirred the imagination, *Lost Horizons*, *Fine Time*, *Footless Crow*, *Bitter Oasis*, *Eastern Hammer* and *Peels of Laughter* to name a few.

By the end of the seventies I had managed to climb some of Livesey's routes, including *Bitter Oasis*, with Pat McVey. We were both still at school and had hitched to Borrowdale to have a go. We had climbed *Cruel Sister* the day before and, with youthful swagger on our side, we were feeling quite confident. However, we found it technical and intimidating. Pat led the first pitch and I got the top one. I remember it took us all afternoon and at the time a mixture of pure terror and incredulity that we'd actually pulled it off made it one of the most amazing climbing experiences I'd ever had.

Peels of Laughter was climbed in 1977 by Livesey and Gomersall and rumour had it, at the time, that the great man had failed on the roof and had to hand over the sharp end to his partner. The first ascent is described in the guide-book as alternate leads. The route had a fierce reputation and had seen very few repeats on a crag that could never be described in the modern parlance as 'user friendly'.

In the spring of 1984 I was climbing regularly with Bill Birkett who was also very keen to make his mark on the new route scene. We spent quite some time establishing what was to become *Centrefold* on Raven Crag at Langdale and after that switched our attention to Raven Crag at Thirlmere.

Even on a beautiful summer's day I remember feeling intimidated by the menacing atmosphere that the crag seems to exude. Even getting to the foot of the route seemed to be an epic. Despite this feeling of impending doom I was reasonably relaxed, after all surely Bill would have the first go whilst I lay back in the sunshine and belayed. This was not to be the case. After sorting the gear out Bill produced a coin and heads meant I got to lead. This was not going according to plan. Taking my newly acquired Sony Walkman (remember those?) off me he settled back listening to music as I set off up the initial vague groove. Before long I had reached a large break but couldn't seem to find any decent gear. Placing an RP and some other dubious nuts I stepped left and found myself committed to climbing a steep wall on small holds. I remember feeling that the moves seemed irreversible and by the time I had pulled right into a shallow scoop I was pumped and gripped. Staring me in the face was a good nut placement, but taking a hand off to place it was not going to be easy. At this point I also had an audience; Mick Lovatt and another climber, who were watching with interest. Mick had done the third ascent of the route the week before and so proved quite useful as I was now in extremis! He knew the nut size. This saved valuable seconds, allowing me to place it and climb up under the roof where I could gain some respite.

The roof is described in the latest guide as *brutal* and cowering under it that day it looked impossible. After a few tentative attempts I managed to work out a feasible sequence and spotted a jammed wire, which was something to aim for. Back under the roof I settled myself until I felt ready to go for it. It was now or never, so with as much confidence as I could muster, I traversed left and climbed the weakness finding a good hold on the lip of the roof. I clipped the in-situ wire, which I tried not to scrutinise in too much detail and came to a grinding halt. Above me there was a vague rib but little else. Eyeballing the half jammed in rock 3 I attempted to pinch the rib above in order to turn the lip of the roof. This proved to be the crux of the route and with much encouragement from below I gave it my all. Using the rib proved awkward and technical, I recall almost laybacking it at one point, feeling totally committed, I pulled round and it was one of those moments when time seemed to stand still for a split second. After a few more moves I was standing more comfortably in a wide groove but with no obvious gear placements. With more advice and encouragement from below I made some awkward moves up and found some decent gear at last. I savoured the final part of the route relishing the exposure and the moves.

Relaxing on the ledge at the top I took some time to take in the view across Thirlmere, and to this day I can still recall the vivid colours, the sweeping valley and the hills beyond. It was an intense climbing experience that can only be gained from a fantastic route. *Peels of Laughter* is certainly that and one of Livesey's finest Lakeland test pieces.

Footless Crow is based on the old aided route *Great Buttress* climbed by Paul Ross and A Liddell in 1965 and required eight points of aid. Mike Thompson, writing in the Borrowdale guide in 1966, commented that, 'The man who transforms The Great Buttress from a peg route to a free route is sure of his niche in climbing history'. Pete Livesey did just that in April 1974. It remained unrepeated for some time and took the talents of Ron Fawcett to succeed where others had failed.

In the mid eighties it was our turn. Mark Radtke and I turned up at the crag and decided to give it a go. We had both seen the Channel Four series *Lakeland Rock* and watched with interest as Livesey re-climbed the route with Chris Bonington. It had not looked easy with both climbers having to use the odd point of aid. However, it did show that it was possible and that had spurred us on.

In terms of a line *Footless Crow* is not very distinctive but it does weave its way through some very impressive territory. I climbed the first pitch, which starts up *Athanor* and I remember belaying on a poor stance beneath the roof secured by a bolt and some old pegs. Rad then set about the main pitch. He spent some time arranging protection, including clipping old pegs and placing wires until he seemed to be satisfied with what he had. It's often hard to tell how hard something is when you're watching from the stance and Rad didn't seem to have much trouble with the crux and only applied the reverse thrusters a couple of times. Soon it was my turn to follow. Looking up steep beetling overhangs made progress look unlikely. Using the obvious undercuts to make progress was strenuous, and by the time I got to the top one the clock was ticking. An obvious crack to the left beckoned. Stretching left I managed to place my left foot on a small hold and bridge with my right on not much. Using a small undercut I managed to throw myself into the crack, retrieving the half friend an Australian friend had lent us in the process. The rest of the pitch went more easily following huge jugs over a bulge and a mossy slab to finish. I congratulated Rad on a fine lead and we both agreed that unlocking that desperate crux sequence was the key to climbing one of the most exhilarating hard pitches in the Lakes and a true Livesey classic.

Many regard the citadel of fine grey rock high above Mickleden as the jewel in Langdale's climbing crown. The central prow of Gimmer

Crag is steep and intimidating and it was Arthur Dolphin who first managed to find a way with his superb climb *Kipling Groove* in 1948. This route does weave round the central steepness and it was not until 1974 that a direct, and uncompromising, line was climbed by Livesey and Manson.

There was some controversy at the time about the tactics used on *Eastern Hammer* as it started up the old aid route climbed by Paul Ross and party in 1960. Livesey led the route using the old aid pegs for protection and then abseiled down and took them out! However, this proved to be the right thing to do as natural protection is plentiful and removing the ironmongery improved the quality of the pitch.

It was a beautiful spring day and the sun had warmed the rock as we geared up on *Ash Tree Ledge*. Looking up the prow I remember feeling quite nervous, it looked very steep. Once I started the pitch though, everything seemed to go quite smoothly and I soon found myself clipping the only peg left on the route, which is fairly low down. At this point there are also plenty of good wires that can be slotted in. The rock is superb and the moves flow as good finger locks are found and runners keep appearing. By now I was in what can only be described as a spectacular position. High above the Langdale valley on Gimmer's fine central prow was an awesome place to be. But there was no time to enjoy this view as the steepness started to take its toll. It had all been going so well, but now hanging in there below the final steep bulge I was starting to feel the strain. Looking down my partner Dale seemed to be more interested in the view than what was happening above. A bit of shouting encouraged him to watch the rope and I managed to reach a large flat hold and more perfect runners. It's amazing how good gear suddenly makes you feel less pumped. I remember being in two minds as to whether to go left or right and, in the end, I went direct, pulling on a small but positive hold to gain a standing position on the hold. Stamina counts at this point and luckily

I had enough in reserve for the final attack. Strenuous layback moves followed and at last the finishing crack of *Kipling Groove* was reached. Belaying Dale in the sun I marvelled at the glorious view and savoured every moment of what had been a magnificent climb.

I'll leave the last word to Lakeland stalwart Rob Matheson who said of this Livesey masterpiece in *Mountain* 54, '*Although only a one pitch climb, it is extremely tiring on the fingers and demands a confident approach. But the positions, out there on the front of Gimmer's finest bastion, are superb and the climb easily qualifies as one of the finest pitches in Langdale*'.

A Conversation with Rob Matheson

by Mark Radtke.

I t is clear from reading Ian Cooksey's essay *Cumbrian Classics* that climbing such Livesey routes can create a personal and deeply enriching experience and I guess that these are some of the ingredients that make certain climbs 'classic'. If you are able to take yourself back to the era when these climbs were conceived then they should evoke memories of Livesey as a class athlete at the top of his game, both mentally, dealing with the rigours of bold climbing, and physically pushing extreme technicality through stamina sapping ground. I was intrigued therefore during a conversation with respected Lakes climber, Rob Matheson, to hear him describe Livesey as 'The consummate climbing professional'. Matheson was a friend of Livesey and also a cutting edge pioneer of new routes around the same time as Pete. Rob's description of Livesey was an unusual turn of phrase and beneath the words I detected a slight hint of criticism. After the conversation I'd had with Rob I felt that I needed to report some of Matheson's reflections on Pete, but I've added what I hope is a bit of objective commentary of my own. In most sports where elite performers push the boundaries, there often exists a degree of rivalry. The climbing scene of the 1970s was no different and there certainly was a degree of friendly rivalry between Livesey and the local Lakeland pioneers. During our conversation it was evident that Matheson completely endorsed the quality of the new routes that Pete established in the Lakes, but he suggested to me that on the odd occasion, Pete's overriding drive to get the route in the bag sometimes brought the style of his ascents under scrutiny by the locals. Pete's first ascents of *Dry Grasp* and *Nagasaki Grooves* in Borrowdale were certainly unconventional back in the day. 'Soloed with a back rope', blurred accepted styles and left the locals questioning the validity of these first ascents. Pete was an accomplished soloist and I don't think anyone would question the fact that he climbed these routes free, but what Matheson alluded to, was how Livesey's back rope system might have reduced the element of risk associated with a more conventional lead, and in his eyes this is what devalued Pete's ascent on these occasions. Personally, I think these ascents need to be taken in their historical context. As a comparative illustration, it's useful to consider the tactic of 'yo-yoing', a style of ascent that was still prevalent in the 1970s, and to some was still accepted as legitimate. Routes established in this style were climbed ground up, but repeated yo-yo's sometimes meant that the crux of a climb might end up being essentially top roped. This was a decade of changing styles and attitudes, where differences of opinion and local rivalries inevitably fuelled the ethical debate.

I'm sure that the Livesey intellect and disarming sense of humour would have been able to present a perfectly reasonable counter argument on the case of his back roped solos. Rob commented that fellow Lakes climber Johnny Adams, who'd first climbed *Nagasaki Grooves* with several aid points, was appalled to discover what appeared to be 'chipping' on the route after Livesey's free ascent. Personally when I climbed *Nagasaki Grooves* I found it desperate, harder I think than I found *The Cumbrian* and *Footless Crow*, which I did around the same time. I certainly wasn't aware of any blatant chips. As well as finding the crux of *Nagasaki* technically extreme, it also sticks in my memory as being one of the most satisfying pitches I've ever led in the Lakes. History shows us that Pete did manufacture holds on a handful of his own routes, but only where he thought the resulting climb would be better for it. In his own mind it was a quality issue not a cheating issue, just read Livesey's article, *The Grade of Things To Come*, to gain a little insight into how his mind worked on this issue. The fact that Livesey was so outspoken about his own 'free style', and quick to criticise what he considered inferior styles of others' was, I think, at the root of what sometimes caused 'a raising of the eyebrows'. It was seen as a case of the 'pot calling the kettle black'. To a degree I can empathise with Matheson's words, '*At times he was simply just too professional*', but as Ian Cooksey has eloquently told us, Livesey's routes are bloody brilliant.

Based on a conversation with Rob Matheson in October 2013.

Right Wall

by Jill Lawrence

Although he was to go on to produce harder routes in later years, in many ways 1974 provided the zenith of Pete's climbing in the UK. It heralded a major breakthrough in standards and acceptance of what was possible on British crags. With confidence in his own stamina and finger strength, developed over the preceding five years on the vertical walls of Yorkshire and Derbyshire Limestone, he was now physically and mentally prepared for the obvious challenge of similar walls in the Lakes and North Wales. The audacious *Footless Crow* set the scene in the Lakes, and a certain inevitability led to the search for a similar leap forward in North Wales. The face to the right of *Cenotaph Corner* provided an obvious, vertical blank wall that had been thought unattainable by free means. The renowned Scottish climber Hamish MacInnes had even attempted an aided ascent of the wall placing bolts in the process, but his attempt came to naught. Given the limited sophistication of protection gear at that time, the prevailing attitude was very understandable. Pete, aware of his now proven technical ability, and with a confidence which was not dependent on closely spaced protection, nor likely to pale under extreme stress, made a preliminary abseil inspection of the wall and sorted out a possible line.

I'd become a student at Bingley College in 1973 and soon afterwards made my first climb on the local gritstone crag of Almscliffe. I'd gone there with John Stanger, a fellow student, on the back of his motorbike;

the thing was held together with bits of string so the ride was infinitely scarier than the climbing turned out to be. The route we did was called *Bird's Nest Crack*, a lowly severe, but I was hooked. Soon afterwards I met Pete when making my first attempts at climbing in Ilkley Quarry, where he gave me a top rope on a couple of VSs. I discovered that, by coincidence, he had recently joined the College as a lecturer and over the next months we spent more time climbing together. Under Pete's guidance I improved quickly having found I had the strength and natural ability well suited to rock climbing. Almost inevitably, given the standard that Pete was regularly climbing, a gap developed between what I could lead and what I could second. I did lots of routes with Pete in 1974 resulting in a number of hard first ascents, which was pretty unusual for someone so new to climbing. I was able to follow Pete on most routes but there were times when I needed to rest on the rope, or have some tension, so my confidence on the harder climbs wasn't very high. I still hadn't been climbing a year when Pete decided to go for *Right Wall* and I was pretty much in awe of his ability and ambition. That wall looked scary and completely blank to me and it never entered my head to even consider following his lead, but I obtained some satisfaction in knowing that he trusted me to handle the rope to safeguard his ascent of a futuristic and daunting new route. He'd previously cleaned the line and knew it was going to be hard and run out with poor protection; watching the ascent was enough for me. I thought if I could ever lead anything as scary and difficult as *Right Wall* my climbing ambitions would be fulfilled.

The first ascent of *Right Wall*, E5 6a, 45m; June 1974 – by Pete Livesey

If ever the history of British rock climbing were to be written on two pages, one might well compare them with the two great pages of Dinas Cromlech's open-book corner. Ranged here are six fine routes representing their respective eras – gauntlets thrown down for subsequent generations. *Spiral Stairs, Left Wall, Cenotaph Corner, Lord of the Flies, Right Wall* and *Cemetery Gates* are proclamations of climbing history, writ bold and plain for all to see.

The two walls are almost exactly 100-foot high, but they differ slightly in their degree of verticality. The left is just less than vertical, whereas the right is perhaps half a degree past, and it's amazing how much difference this makes to the feel of the climbing. With the exception of the *Corner*, all the routes call for a similar type of steep wall-climbing, following 'lines of greater holds', rather than crack, groove or corner lines.

The surface of the rock is smooth and relatively featureless, but it is pitted with a myriad of 'crozzly' pockets. Some areas have more pockets than others, and if anything can be said to give 'line' to the Cromlech routes, then it's the grouping of pockets, rendering some areas more climbable than others; the harder routes seem to gravitate from group to group.

One distinctive (and unnerving) feature of Cromlech wall climbing is that, although lines of weakness are obvious when one stands back from the wall, all semblance of line disappears once one starts up a route. I don't think I've ever been more frightened in my life when the whole of my pre-planned route for *Right Wall* became invalid as soon as I touched the rock; not a hold or a feature remained in sight; there was just the hold I was on, and possibly the next one.

The climb started up a lower wall of 10-foot or so, before embarking on the main face. A short crack was left for the first of the 'blind' climbing sections, where one goes from one hold to any other that can be reached.

Eventually, a right-sloping ramp of small handholds led to a resting ledge at one-third height where I arranged a couple of solid runners.

Had I fallen below this point I would have hit the ground. Above this first ledge a technical section led to a 'crozzled' spike in a large pocket. Thereafter, a difficult move left gained a deep pocket, straight above which, a rightward rising hand-ramp led to the second ledge; on my ascent, with only a tape draped over the weird spike between me and the ground. This ledge, which to the right becomes the stance for *Cemetery Gates*, provided another resting place.

After more technical moves a tiny pod-shaped depression was gained at which point I realised I had no idea where I was on my memorised route plan. With no apparent way on and 15-foot above protection, I retreated with difficulty to the ledge, untied, moved right and soloed off up the *Gates*. At the top, I borrowed a rope, abseiled down the top section, spied a possible solution and precariously retied back into the climbing ropes. A difficult move out of the pod got me to another right-sloping ramp leading to a non-resting ledge where I was able to arrange further protection before climbing quickly to the top.

And so it was that *Right Wall* was first climbed. Subsequently, pictures appeared in the magazines, showing the line with varying degrees of accuracy. Those who came after soon discovered the futility of trying to follow a line on such a wall by means of a photograph.

First published in Extreme Rock 1987.

Jill Lawrence takes up the story again.

It was to be another two years before the route received a second ascent, almost inevitably by the Yorkshire team of Ron Fawcett and Chris Gibb. Failures by other leading climbers, sometimes resulting in huge falls onto distant protection, did nothing to lessen the reputation of the route, or change my thoughts about that wall, that I'd originally formed watching Pete's first lead of it. Eventually, ascents became more frequent and it was only a matter of time before *Right Wall* would come to the attention of a newly emerging group of talented and ambitious female climbers.

Having completed my course at Bingley I worked at Bewerley Park Centre for Outdoor Education from 1977 to 1979. Time off didn't often coincide with Peter's and so I started climbing with other people. My leading ability dramatically improved and I began making my own choices about which routes I wanted to attempt. I felt in control of my own destiny with all the emotions that went with it, elation at successes, disappointment with failures, and the omnipresent feelings of fear. There was no longer a stronger partner to get me out of trouble, it was down to me and that was the bottom line.

In 1980 several French women came to Britain at the invitation of the BMC. There were a number of good climbers, but Catherine Destivelle stood out from the rest for her boldness and ability to push beyond her physical limitations. Catherine and I climbed together and the results were remarkable. She led some extremely difficult climbs, certainly the hardest leads so far achieved by a woman in Great Britain at that time, including Vulcan and Void at Tremadog. For me this was the first time I'd met a female who climbed as well as I did. In fact she was far bolder than I, and jumped on routes I was still 'building up to'. Catherine made me think about my own limitations. Physically our ability was comparable, but psychologically she was the stronger. I realised I needed to become more resilient mentally and decided that the best way to develop my confidence would be to climb as much as I possibly could. In 1982 the Women's International Climbing Meet was held in Britain. Rosie Andrews and Catherine Frier from America climbed some really hard stuff, which gave the British women a real kick up the backside. The attitudes and abilities of these women really inspired me. I wanted to see how far I could push myself so I decided to go for broke. I packed my job in, sold my car and went on an extended climbing road trip across The States. Needless to say I gained a lot of experience climbing on different rock types in places like Eldorado Canyon, Yosemite Valley and Joshua Tree. By the end of that trip my self-confidence on the rock was pretty solid.

I was back in Britain for the planned BMC Women's meet in May 1984. Rosie Andrews was climbing with me and we were both in good shape. I was now ready to tackle a number of routes I'd not previously considered doing: *Cream*, *Pippikin*, and *Zukator* at Tremadog increased my confidence further, but *Right Wall* was the route that was constantly at the back of my mind. It still looked as blank as ever to me and I was still incredibly intimidated by its reputation. The route still saw good climbers taking long falls on it. Before the meet I'd hoped no one else would try it, I knew if this happened pressure would be on for me to have a go. It was naive thinking of course. Rosie, Catherine Destivelle and Christine Lambert from France all had aspirations for the route. It seemed there was simply no way out, I'd have to give it a go.

During the week of my attempt it had rained and all the 'tell-tale' chalk which usually marked out the line were gone. As I stood at the bottom of the wall Rosie Andrews flipped a coin to see who'd get the first lead. I won the toss. So I'd lead first, abseil the line to strip the gear and then it would be Rosie's turn. I remember that I was pretty keyed up, the adrenaline was nearly pushing me into a fear crisis, but I took some deep breaths and set off. The route has three cruxes and I was soon staring the first one straight in the eye and starting to panic. 'Stopping, I hold on tight and stare at the last moves of the sequence, freezing there; my mind refusing to let my body function. Climb down, try again, freeze! Mind over matter? The protection is good just here. Flash, done it! How? It's a blankness. Total concentration? Maybe, but I'm above the first crux'.

The next moves presented a similar scenario. 'No, no, I can't do it.

119

I'm scared, what am I doing here; breathe deeply, count to ten. Calm, flash, done it'.

I climbed the route slowly, pacing myself, gathering my physical and mental resources at the good resting points after each crux. I've really no idea how long it took to climb the route, but the feeling from people around was really positive. There were women on *Left Wall*, *Resurrection* and the *Corner* and their smiling faces and shouts of encouragement spurred me on until I made the last few difficult pulls and I knew I was there, an ambition finally fulfilled.

Right Wall was a significant personal achievement for me in climbing. Technically there are no real stopper sequences, but you have to make hard moves well above gear and that requires a lot of mental control. I guess that's why E5s are E5 and frankly they scare me. Without the pressure and knowledge that other women had designs on *Right Wall* back in '84 I'm unsure whether I'd have even tried.

The Grade of Things to Come

by Pete Livesey

The rock is the race in our game, and the routes are the racers, not the climbers. The winner has achieved supreme difficulty of line. The openly competitive athlete's time is comparable to the ineptly concealed competition of the climber's line.

The record breakers are climbs instigating new levels of difficulty – other new lines of the same difficulty merely serve to reinforce the acceptability of the record. *Central Buttress*, *Slape*, *Diglyph* and *Hangover*, *Great Wall* and *Wall of Horrors* are all routes in the record breaker class. Other, newer routes may be seen later to be in this class. You don't just go out and climb a new line, you go and climb a hard new line, better still, a horrifying new line. Not now a case of chipping holds to make a climb possible – no, chip them off to make it nearly impossible, you'll see. It's an idea to make a principle of never putting out a route that's not the hardest on the crag, and when you really get fit the next route should always be harder than the last one.

But all this is chit-chat about the present, although they are pertinent points now that will perhaps be axioms of a future generation. What we are about is the future though, where our sport is going. I'm not talking now about the high pressure politics and the world, and the Olympic championships that Dennis is going to sort out, no, I mean the progress of the climber himself and the standards of the climbs.

Hundreds of people are now climbing what were top grade routes ten years ago – this top heavy condition is to be expected. Given basic aptitude, motivation and fitness, many climbers are able to get up top grade routes with a little practice. The climbers who rise above the mushroom's head will do so by training: hard, regular and frequent training. Strength of a very particular type will be required to string together a series of boulder-type moves, strength necessarily gained by applied specialised training. Finger strength and stamina combined with height, reach and a light frame will be essential.

This abnormal strength and stamina must be gained by weight training, climbing frequently on outcrops or boulders, or climbing wall training. Indoor climbing walls are of intrinsic value when training, whatever their degree of artificiality. Leeds University's wall is realistic, but not easy to train on. Future training techniques will demand more open, lower standard walls, common at sports halls; these are ideal for interval training if not for gaining technique.

6b and 6c moves are being strung together into routes on the Leeds wall – when this form is reproduced on the outcrops standards will rise two grades. Progression of outcrop grades to mountain crags will also occur at some later stage. Modern limestone grades are now rearing ugly heads on Lakeland crags. *Paladin*, *Pink Panther* and, more particularly, *Footless Crow* show that the equalisation of grades has already happened. We now await the next rise on outcrops. One or two routes of this new standard have appeared in the States, but the conditions of the first ascent and the protection renders them scarcely as valid as indoor climbing wall routes.

After a few more routes on gritstone are accomplished at new standards, Syrett's first real Extremes, the emphasis must shift to limestone. The rock offers the multiplicity of holds necessary for intermediate rises in standard – it is inevitable that such routes as *Cave Route* will become outstanding free routes in the next advance. When the standard has risen sufficiently the emphasis can shift back to grit which demands a much greater step to allow ascents on previously untried areas of rock.

Traditional *laissez-faire* attitudes of climbers must modify to cope with increased competition, greater care paid to choice of equipment and dress. Refinements are already evident in the more competition-conscious Valley. Chalk and protective tape on hands, benzoin and kneepads, mental build up and gear organization; all these produced by a single, central, exclusive, climbing scene breeding its own competitiveness. The gear side probably has most scope for improvement, cutting seconds off the time taken to fix protection pushes up the potential for your ultimate pitch. American 'quickdraw' slings with two krabs already clipped to the climbing rope, are already in use and more Anglicised refinements are clearly conceivable.

'Accomplished in nail boots in a snowstorm' Brown and Whillans on *Surplomb*. That kind of comment must be only a nostalgic memory; attached to a modern ascent it only proves the climber was not climbing a pitch worthy of his potential. No, warm windless days with climber in T-shirt and shorts will be the stage for his realisation of potential in the super grades.

Of one thing I am certain, we have by no means reached a flattening of the curve experienced in athletic records. Our standards have a long way to rise before the increase ceases to be significant.

See you on the 7as!

From The Leeds University Mountaineering Club Journal *ca mid 1970s.*

PART THREE

GAME ON

Captain Cool

by Geoff Birtles

I t says something about Pete Livesey that this book has a whole section dedicated to 'the inner game of Pete', which rather begs the question, just who was he?

Well, I never fully understood him back then and I still don't. He wasn't like anybody else, a man of many surprises, competitive, cunning, even secretive at times. He was Captain Cool, an outstanding athlete. But for me, above all else, he was fun and good company. I never saw him lose control, whether it was on the rock or amidst some polemic or other. Being so in control of both himself and, to some extent, those around him was important. I don't recall Pete ever picking on less talented climbers; he only wanted to take on the best.

Whilst the climbing community considered him to be a rock-climber, others looked on him as a track athlete, caver or fell runner. He seemed to excel at whatever he wanted to do and if somebody was better than him, he would find a way of shifting the odds in his favour. I think it was in a Karrimor Mountain Marathon that the rules stipulated what equipment was to be carried. A knife and fork, eh? Well, Pete soon sorted that out with a hacksaw. He actually ran the race with half a knife and fork but didn't break the rules. He was often credited with inventing training for rock-climbing, something he strenuously denied. What I think he did do though, was to bring a new attitude to training and in that respect he was a huge influence on British climbing. He once turned up at Rubicon Wall and started running up and down the path which drew sideways looks from Tom Proctor and me but what he was doing, apart from making us snigger, was what he did at race meetings – warming up.

My first recollection of Pete was when I read an article by him in a climbing magazine in the early 1970s, which was essentially a list of the hardest routes in the Pennines. To rub even more chalk into this wound he had put his routes at the top of the list and those of Jack Street and Tom Proctor, two of our great climbers of that time, down at the bottom. I remember thinking how audacious it was of him, somebody we had never heard of judging the merits of the hardest climbs in Yorkshire and Derbyshire. Although he was the new boy on the block we would soon find out just how good he was. In the meantime, he remained an elusive character to us until one dark evening when Tom Proctor and I went to Rothwell climbing wall. It was a serious place in that when you got to the top of a route, you had to traverse a long way for an easy descent. At the top of one route there was a big ledge on which I was sat when another climber appeared by my feet and introduced himself. '*Hello, I'm Pete Livesey.*' After that, I met his entourage: in particular Jill Lawrence, a climbing partner and his girlfriend at that time; Pete Gomersall; John Stanger; Steve Foster, and probably his main climbing partner, John Sheard. These were all good climbers. Jill subsequently made the first female ascent of *Right Wall* in the Llanberis Pass - no mean climber in her own right but she was typical of that group for whom Pete set high standards.

As time went by and we got used to reading about Pete on an almost clockwise basis, it occurred to me that he had a mental calendar of *Mountain* magazine's deadline dates, and as they approached, he would go out, climb a few new routes and report them. Though he never appeared to be a self-publicist when you talked to him, the news coverage he got in magazines tells a different story.

We can't talk about Pete without bringing Ron Fawcett into the frame somewhere. In early 1971, Al Evans told me about this Yorkshire lad who would be the next Joe Brown, the kind of thing we had all heard before, something to be taken with a pinch of salt. However, Al was determined to show off his discovery and that summer he turned up unannounced at my house on the outskirts of Edale with a 16-year old Fawcett and the next day I had him belay me on the first ascent of *Citadel* in Blackwell Dale near Water-Cum-Jolly. It was only HVS but as I watched him follow, I could see that Ron was indeed a very good climber, so good, in fact, that within a very short space of time he was amongst the best in the UK. Soon he would be, in my opinion the best rock-climber in the world in his time. And living in Yorkshire, right on Pete's front door, he was someone for Pete to keep an eye on. Whilst Pete couldn't out-climb Ron he could out-scheme us all. Inevitably Ron began climbing with Pete and learned the hard way. A typical ruse on a multi-pitch route would be to make sure that Ron got the easy pitches so that Pete got the glory from the crux pitches. Pete had always done his homework and, being twelve years senior, had that upper hand that comes with a significant age gap.

Back to the Peak District where Tom Proctor and myself were busy climbing new routes, especially those steep lines that had formerly been aid climbs. Whilst most of these were on limestone, the quarried gritstone edge of Millstone was rich with unfreed peg climbs, which we got stuck into without too much competition. However, that was about to change. Tom led the first free ascent of *Twikker* and whilst I was seconding and just mantelshelving on to the top slab, a complete stranger peered over the top of the crag and informed us, 'Pete Livesey has just done a free ascent of *Cave Route*!' It was as though this stranger was a messenger from Pete to announce his Gordale ascent, and this was 'Game on'.

And, game on it was. In retrospect I don't think Pete ever truly came away from the professional regime of track athletics to the rather romantic amateurism of rock-climbing. He became a predator hunting wherever there was game to be had, whether it be the Lake District or the Peak District, North Wales, France or even America. Later, I recall going down to Cheddar Gorge with Ron Fawcett to attempt a free ascent of *Paradise Lost*. We did the first overhanging pitch in the rain but got stopped in the upper groove down which water was streaming. Everybody turned up, my wife, my dog, Al Evans, a fire engine wanting to rescue us because somebody had phoned to tell them we were stuck and, well, well, well, whose car is that creeping up the Gorge? Why if it isn't Pete Livesey. He had somehow heard that we were going down to Cheddar and had driven all the way from North Yorkshire on the off chance of some carrion to be had. He was fast becoming a serial raider of other climbers' back yards.

In 1975 there was a big crowd of us northern folk down at Bosigran in Cornwall. I can't remember the route he was doing, either *Dream Liberator* or something nearby, and he had his arm stretched out full length and really high when his shoulder just popped out of its socket. He still managed to finish the route and that night sported a most peculiar lump on his shoulder that made your stomach turn. Most people would have gone off to hospital and had a month off work but somehow Pete managed to get his shoulder back into position and then went out the next day and did a new route.

In 1976, there was a large international meet at Plas y Brenin. Rather naively of me, I went to Bwlch y Moch and attempted to free a route on the *Vector* headwall along with Al Manson and Tom Proctor. We all failed halfway up but planned to return. How silly of me, Pete nipped in a couple of days later and grabbed *Cream*. Pinching my route, eh! Two could play that game.

The article below first appeared in the book Extreme Rock *in 1987.*

Stars of Peak and Pennine.
From L to R: Steve Bancroft, Tom Proctor, Ron Fawcett, Ken the Dummy, Al Evans,
Nicky Stokes, John Allen, Chris Gibb, Pete Livesey.
Photograph by Geoff Birtles circa 1977.

Livesey, Birtles and Fawcett.
Buxton Conference.
Photograph by Brian Cropper.

Left, top and bottom: Livesey and Henry Barber during the making of *American Sportsman.*
Photographs by John Cleare.

Below right: Danny Morgan on *Pepsicomane* F6c Buoux. One of the French crags initially explored by Droyer that saw a rapid escalation of sport climbing standards throughout the 1980s.
Photograph by John Sheard.

Top left: Pete still smiling despite a broken foot. At Millstone Edge Derbyshire in May 1977. *Photograph Bernard Newman*

Top right: Pete making an early repeat of Gomersall's bold E5 *Central Wall* at Blue Scar. This shot by Pete Gomersall was taken just before Livesey retired from climbing ca. 1980.

Right: A cartoon of Pete that appeared in *Crags* Magazine at the height of his influence and popularity. Pete loved to get one over, but wasn't the least bit offended when the spoof was on him.

Ron Fawcett on pitch 6 of Droyer's *Triomphe d'Eros* Verdon Gorge during the second ascent.
Photograph by Pete Livesey.

Chrysalis F6c. One of the early Verdon routes established using pre-placed bolts. Climbers Mark Radtke and Ian Cooksey in 1984. *Photograph by Adrian Ledgway.*

Necronomicon F6c. One of the early routes to get Livesey and Fawcett fired up about the scale and drama of the Verdon. Climber Adrian Ledgway. *Photograph by Mark Radtke.*

Alan Carne's photograph shows the scale of the Verdon. Climbers in red are just visible in the bottom right of the shot and are on the 10 pitch world class route *La Fête des Nerfs* F7a+.

Anglo French meet in 1976
Above from L to R: Ron Fawcett,
Pete Livesey, Gill Price, Jean-
Claude Droyer, Robert Mizrahi.
Photograph by John Sheard.

Right: Livesey's small publication
was furnished with information
gleaned from Droyer. It was
maligned for inaccurate route
descriptions but significantly, it
opened the floodgates to British
climbers.

French
Rock-Climbs
PETER LIVESEY

The magnificent scenery of the Verdon Gorge, Alpes-de-Haute-Provence, France.
Photograph by Alan Carne.

Mortlock's Arête (Chee Tor)

On a freezing cold day at the end of March 1976, Tom Proctor made what was essentially a free ascent of *Behemoth* in Water-cum-Jolly using one aid point. It had been one of the big artificial climbs of the Peak District and the first of its size and stature to fall to a wave of pure climbing soon to crash over the steepest limestone cliffs. Tom hardly needs an introduction to the climbing reader. He was one of the best British rock-climbers for ten years from the late 1960s, noted for his immense strength. An all-time nice guy; honest, quiet, unassuming, verging on the naive.

He was my regular climbing partner, or I was his, from about 1968 on and we were particularly active around 1976, free-climbing the old aid climbs. Apart from the cold rock on *Behemoth* that day we were weighed down by the stalking presence of Livesey and Fawcett prowling beneath our feet, forcing us to stay the pace. It was a significant ascent, which set the scene for a similar but greater ambition, that of *Mortlock's Arête* on Chee Tor, a mere twinkling in our eyes as the warmth of summer approached.

Chee Tor was not so popular then, a quiet venue for Al Evans and myself one Sunday. Al was somewhat overweight from the winter feast and in the circumstance I expected a quiet day pursuing a project for which success over about fifteen feet would count as rather good. The venue was *Mortlock's Arête* and after a combined effort cleaning while bouldering the start I climbed the bottom wall to a point where I discovered, beneath cobwebs, an old ring-peg, clearly of the 1962 Colin Mortlock aid-climbing era and possibly from his first aid ascent. To the left, a crack continued for a few feet and by now we had a rope on the rock. Taking it in turns, Al, by fair means or foul, placed a new peg somewhat higher and with that as security I made my way up to the obvious overhang and then onto the flake where impending old

131

age slowed my progress.

Unexpectedly, Pete Livesey appeared on the scene hungry for our meat. He was accompanied by Steve Foster, and without an ounce of sporting decency joined their unwelcome efforts to ours. The easy day became a free-for-all and the jutting flake was laybacked to a one-foot rest on the wall above. To progress, a difficult, bold piece of wall climbing was required to reach easy ground and a small tree belay, an accomplishment, which would clearly win the day, despite a second pitch.

The day was not won by any team and the climb was abandoned for another time. About 48 hours later I reckoned, from a chance remark that Pete made about one of their group having to sign-on on Tuesday morning. Al had eaten too much Christmas pudding and was too heavy for this climb and was duly sacked. What I needed was a big gun. '*Hello Tom,*' I shouted down the telephone, '*sorry to get you out of bed ... yes I know what time it is. Listen, we must climb on Tuesday.*'

Climbing of this type relies on information and 'intelligence', as in any other war. So come the Tuesday we checked with the cafe at Stoney Middleton, where it was confirmed that no Yorkshiremen had been in that day and it was unreasonable to think they would have passed this watering place after so lengthy a journey. So in confident mood we ordered food with tea to follow. Then we were off, driving down Chee Dale and along the abandoned railway to the edge of the crag. As I was familiar with the first pitch I led off and got our rope on the route. As I climbed, I doused a weeping finger pocket with a liberal dose of chalk, passed the old ring-peg and Evans's shiny new ring-peg then up on to the steep layback. '*Got it, Tom?*'

Of course he had. The route now had our rope on it and the lad had the numbers. Time for a cigarette while he sorted out some gear and tied on to the important bit of the rope, during which time I saw a movement from the corner of my eye, a lurking suspicion, a tree that moved. I looked again and Livesey's faced popped out, grinning as it does, followed by other moving trees in the shape of Jill Lawrence and Pete Gomersall and, just in case the going got tough, Ron Fawcett. The 'intelligence' was right after all, though, had they not stopped at a baker's shop and bought cream cakes the timing could have gone against us. *Cream* eh! Good name for a route. Pete laughed at the irony of it all. (Well he had no option really). Jill thought it distinctly unfunny and let Pete know how she felt. Ron twitched impatiently. They argued about whose daft idea it was to buy cream cakes while Tom climbed.

The bat and ball was ours and until we had finished play they would have to wait. Which they did. There was not a lot to choose between Proctor, Livesey or Fawcett in 1976; they were the best rock-climbers in Britain, among the best in the world in their own ways. Tom had been at it longer and had the power of Samson, Pete had the cunning of Crew, immensely fit with enough natural ability to hold his own, whilst Ron had a wild talent which engraved its own legend in due course. I had the bat and ball.

They waited. Tom unloaded the numbers, laybacked the hanging prow and stood where Pete had failed two days before. I had abseiled down on the Sunday to retrieve the runners (did I forget to tell you this?) and knew what lay before him and shouted encouragement, '*Go for it Tom, there's a jug above you.*'

He always believed me. But there was a jug of sorts followed by a desperate move, which might be easy today now that it had been cleaned. There was a distinct noise from Tom as he changed down a gear unleashing his massive strength on grass sods, hauling himself on to easy ground and the belay. I was ecstatic.

Still they waited. This was a replay of a few weeks earlier when I overheard Pete arranging to try *Behemoth* late on a Saturday night. He had good reason to feel confident then. But by midnight I was home and on the telephone, '*Hello Kathy ... yes I know what time it is ... well if he won't get out of bed tell him we've got to climb ... early.*'

She shouted up the stairs. He shouted down, '*Yes.*'

The next morning we were on Central Buttress by 8:30am with our ropes on the first runner. An amusing sight woke us up as Pete Livesey, John Sheard, Jill Lawrence and Ron Fawcett jogged down the path by the river. They waited that day and got nothing. No wonder they were looking dischuffed on Chee Tor. Vicious though it may sound we were playing by 'Livesey Rules' and to his credit he never complained, he just waited.

On Chee Tor, Tom set off up the top pitch, which was unprepared, threaded a runner round a sharp little flake and rehearsed a move into an overhanging corner. Below, Livesey piled on the pressure leading up the first pitch. Clearly there were to be no prisoners taken on this day. Prudence overtook Tom and he reversed back to my sapling. He had decided to traverse off, abseil down the pitch above and place a peg for a runner which was all very well but it left me three-quarters of the way up a cliff tied to a tiny tree with no ropes, with Indians fast approaching as the light faded.

As the action unfolded, Pete arrived at my tree and belayed. I obviously wasn't going to belay him while he tried the top pitch so he had no option but to bring up his own secret weapon, Ron, by which time mine had done the necessary and arrived back. This was a relief as I now had a rope to abseil to safety if necessary, always assuming Pete wouldn't let me use his.

While the moon threatened on the horizon, Tom returned to the pitch. Now he had a runner worth clipping and while a reach into the back of the groove was tempting, the key was a backward bending of the spine to use a tiny finger hold well out on the right wall, a high step with the left foot and sheer force upwards to small undercuts into a bottomless cleft. Above this bomb-bay was a crack, proper holds, real runners and the top. Meanwhile below I now had a lot of Yorkshire people hanging off my small sapling. And that was that. We had the day. Ron led through close behind so completing the fastest ever second ascent in near total darkness, a flashing glimpse of his tomorrow.

There was an aftermath though, an ambush for the innocent. A few days later Pete wrote to *Mountain* magazine, claimed our ascent had used dubious tactics and mischievously bagged the route for himself. Lovely boy Pete, dagger climber.

In the 1970s it became very trendy to go to Yosemite, California, which is where I went with Ron Fawcett in 1977. At Camp 4 in the Valley there was a choice group of British climbers. Livesey was already there when we arrived and, with American ace, John Long, had made a free ascent of the *Chouinard-Herbert* on The Sentinel, a major piece of rock in the valley. In the August we were there, temperatures reached 110°C and big walls were out of the question. There was nobody on El Capitan for good reason. So why, I wondered, were Ron and I getting up very early to do the *Chouinard-Herbert*? By an absolute fluke there had been a big forest fire elsewhere in California and this caused substantial cloud cover, something Ron took advantage of at a blistering pace, exploiting our two 60-metre ropes, which allowed us to make two pitches into one in places. It is a very steep wall with hanging belays in places and lurking above us, the Afro-Cuban Roof, a name that struck terror into me. Fortunately we swung leads with Ron climbing all the face and letting me have the last V Diff pitch.

All of this time, which was about five hours, we were being scrutinised through binoculars by Pete, who was doing the Merced Layback, an amusing name for lying on the beach by the River Merced. Ron and I again took advantage of the long ropes, abseiling back down the face in what seemed like 30 minutes. At the bottom, Ron coiled his rope and ran off. I thought this a bit rude but later realised that he wanted to get back to Pete as fast as he could. The competition with Pete was not confined to outsiders but had its challengers from within, well Ron anyway.

It didn't take long to get bored sunbathing on the beach, nice as it was. Just by where we lounged about there was a wooden bridge, which crossed the river, one side of which had a deep pool nearly seven feet deep. At times one or other of us would pick up a boulder, walk into the river up to chin height, take a deep breath and then walk across the river bed totally out of sight and emerge on the other side. It was light relief, which Pete couldn't share because he had a badly ripped hand that was bandaged, or so we thought. One day Pete walked over to the river, picked up a boulder, which he held with one arm, and proceeded to walk across as described above. He got round the bandage problem by holding his bad arm in the air so that as he disappeared under water, all we saw was an arm sticking out of the water steadily moving forward. He never knew when to give in.

Pete was scheming again and had his eyes on *Astroman*, one of the hardest routes in The Valley on Washington Column. For this he needed Ron but I was climbing with Ron. Pete broached the subject, suggesting we did it as a three, but I think he knew I would magnanimously step aside. Three on rope on hard, overhanging rock is not a good idea. I was a little peeved with both of them but didn't let it show, which is what sulking in a tent is all about. Anyway, they did it. Humph!

Another day Pete suggested we go to Lower Yosemite Falls, which was unusually dry. There he climbed a fine looking route called *Carbon Wall*. What Pete didn't tell us is that he had sneaked off the previous day and abseiled down it. Another cunning plan.

It was a good year to be in Yosemite as we grouped together with resident Americans such as Ron Kauk, and a group of Germans, most notably Kurt Albert. When I got home, the desire to go back was strong. And so it was that Pete's brother Alec and I decided to go back and drive across the States. Pete phoned me to tell me he was joining us, not, 'can I come as well?' One day sticks in my mind, when we went down The Valley to some cliffs by the river, where in very hot conditions Pete proceeded to climb solo up a vertical wall some 100 feet high that was covered in large chicken heads. On several occasions I saw Pete wavering about and I feared the worst but he didn't fall off and eventually he traversed across to easier ground and soloed down. I told him that I thought he was going to fall off but he nonchalantly told me, '*No, I just nearly fainted a few times in the heat.*' Pete could climb as hard solo as he could roped-up, an achievement unparalleled by any other climber I ever saw. I later discovered that the route Pete had soloed was called *New Diversions* and was regarded as a tricky 5.10.

I fetched the hire car on my own from San Francisco, an automatic limo with air conditioning, and bench seats. It was dark when I got back to the campsite but Alec was still half awake and asked me what the car was like. When I told him, I heard a groan from Pete's tent. These two were professional Yorkshiremen and they'd hoped that I would get an old banger, which needed transporting to New York for a very small fee. That wasn't my style at all. Nevertheless, we had a cruise, had a can of beer at the head of Death Valley the driest place in the USA - where it rained. Then we outwitted a Highway Patrolman who dropped his breakfast and jumped into his car to chase us but we nipped up a side road and avoided him. The free champagne breakfast at 8am in a Las Vegas casino appealed to my companions and eventually taking in Arches National Park and Zion in Utah, we arrived at Royal Robbins's home in Telluride where, though looking shocked, he kindly put us up. The next day he took us to his local crag, Crack Canyon. Being over 8,000ft, and by the road, this was an unusual place and even a Mild VS was hard going as we were out of breath. The day culminated with Pete leading a long groove with an overhanging side wall, the type you get on the West Buttress of Cloggy. Quite high up, Royal joshed with him, *'Hey Pete, why not swing out on the right (overhanging) and climb the headwall?'* (never been done before). Without blinking, Pete reached out swung across and on to the headwall, which he finished without any more runners. It was quite scary just to second.

Back home I had regular evening phone calls with Pete. One night, as I was just planning to go down to Chee Tor and do *Apocalypse*, largely because there was a jammed nut in the crux upper flake which rose to the left and where runners had a tendency to fall out with the rope drag, Pete told me he had just done the route and removed the nut by abseil because he hadn't used it. I smelled a rat and asked him if he was lying and he said he was. There was always a bit of controversy around Pete; chipped holds, or a heavily brushed *Downhill Racer* at Froggatt. He was such a good climber and amenable character that he got away with these discrepancies. Despite all, he was a loveable bloke and without doubt one of the best rock-climbers of our time.

The Circus

by Pete Livesey featuring Henry Barber

Introduction

I n 1976, leading American free climber Henry Barber was back in the UK making ascents of the latest and hardest free routes of the day. On this occasion Barber had a film crew with him. ABC/TV New York were making a series entitled, *American Sportsman*. One of the episodes was to showcase Henry Barber as the leading American climbing athlete in competition with, and alongside, as the film company put it, 'fellow Big Gun Pete Livesey'. The stage for the film was The Great Zawn in Cornwall and the focus for the documentary was to see if the climbers could make a completely free ascent of the route *Dream Liberator*.

Livesey recounted these events in his essay for the classic book *Extreme Rock*. Pete's essay is reproduced here but we have followed it with commentary from the film. The film was shot against a 'soundscape' of crashing waves and calling gulls, but in his essay Pete alludes to the fact that some of the commentary recorded on their radio mikes was deemed unsuitable for American TV, so the voice-over was recorded separately and added to the film later. The commentary has to be taken in the context that the filmmakers probably wanted to 'over-cook' the competition between the two players, but I suspect that Livesey would have resisted any scripting impositions, rather choosing to put his own inimitable stamp on proceedings. The voice-over is somewhat tongue in cheek, but nevertheless it's authentic Livesey.

Mark Radtke

Dream Liberator by Peter Livesey

The circus had arrived in town – well almost; Harris and Minks were still missing, which was surprising because they had last been spotted leading the Great Race. The circus was the ABC Wide World of Sport film crew and supporting cast. The Great Race had taken place from one location, Gogarth, to the next, Bosigran. There was a hired Transit, with a ton of cameras and Sherpas, driven by a demented Australian, a Ford Granada, with the producer, the money and the cameramen and ourselves in a racing 602cc Citroen Ami, and Harris in his van.

The Transit won, followed by the Granada and us (after draining superfluous bits of cog from the gearbox on the Severn Bridge) but there was no sign of Harris, who, although last away, was in the lead before the race had cleared the Trearddur Bay Hotel car park. We got settled in, Sherpas in the Count House, cameramen and superstars in the Miners' Arms. The superstars were there to climb *Dream Liberator* free, if possible, and get filmed at the same time. I was one and the other was 'Hot Shit' Henry Barber (called 'Hots' by most, and 'Shits' by Harris). That evening Hots walked into the bar and ordered a round of Harris's famous Strawberry Milk Shakes for everyone – pints of pink spirits at £4 a glass.

'*Put it on the ABC's bill,*' said Hots, coolly.

'*Don't have one,*' replied the barman.

'*Well, start one,*' said Hots, finalising the repartee. Not one fisherman left the pub sober or poorer that night. At midnight a call came from Harris, 'Engine seized in Plymouth but don't worry, we've got a new one and put it on the bill.'

At seven the following morning the circus rolled into action. The Sherpas rushed off to rig ropes, cameramen got into artistic moods, and the director paced up and down. Hots found a nest of baby adders which he dropped down his sock and Harris and Minks ran off to an invisible and inaccessible ledge with the camera crew's entire supply of dope. The first shots were some cinéma vérité stuff as we jogged down to the crag through the gorse, the nearest thing in West Penwith to Japanese filmmakers' grass. Hots was clearly upset and irritated by all this, he was there purely and simply to do the climb, while the other climbers were there to make as much money as possible and observe how really rich people, like cameramen, live.

We donned EBs at *Commando Ridge*, while the cameras panned furiously back and forth, from the commemorative plaque, to my EBs stuck up with Elastoplast, to the dead vipers in Hots' shoe and back to the three racks, mine, Hots' and ABC's, which I was furtively rationalising into two racks on a more or less permanent basis.

It is possible to start *Dream* from the initial ledge of *Déjà Vu*, but this avoids the traditional start coming in from below. I have noticed in sea cliff climbing that 'traditional' means getting thoroughly soaked, covered in seaweed and viciously attacked by razorbills. *Dream's* traditional start is no exception, leading off as it does from an incredibly greasy 12-foot cannonball, lodged in the mouth of the Zawn and awash for a considerable proportion of its life. The slippery, protectionless groove that follows is by far the hardest part of the route, unless one chances upon it in bone-dry condition.

Hots decided that most film exposure was to be gained by leading the top pitch, so I was allocated the lower two. I didn't care, I was too busy counting dollars and new nuts. We used the jumping start for the cameras and I grabbed the peg at the slippery end of the jump. Hot's face got deadly serious, '*Can we do the jump without the peg, otherwise we'll have to do it the other way?'* Christ what a bore, I thought, seeing bags full of dollars sinking beneath the waves.

We gained a tiny ledge with a large sea-resistant flake, just out of reach of the highest slapping waves, where one at least feels safe. On the second pitch (mine again), bold laybacking, becoming less greasy as one ascends, leads to a juggy horizontal break heading back to the arête. A long thin stretch upwards gains an appallingly rusted peg below a three-foot roof, the last aid point.

I looked at the move past the rusting relic, had half a go, thought how silly, pulled up on the peg and reached the holds over the roof. Hots was furious, never before had he climbed with one so lacking in ethics and money as me.

'You'll have to come down and let me do it,' he shouted into his radio mike, mercifully adding, *'you shit,'* which rendered the whole phrase unusable for the American market.

The roof is surmounted by means of a wonderful gymnastic move, one hand and foot leading over the roof, whereupon a mighty swinging, pushing move leaves one standing on the lead foot. Tiptoeing leads to *Déjà Vu*, then back right across blind granite cracks to the arête. Finally, a slippery finger-traverse move lands one on the tiny ledge of *Liberator's* first stance. Hots followed, free climbing the roof noisily. Having arrived at the rotting pegs of the stance, he spurned my rack of Stoppers, preferring to continue with his full range of hexentrics on bits of string, few of which fitted anything in Cornwall anyway. Above is a bold-looking overhung layback, where Hots swung brave and wild and I cringed as I imagined him crashing down into my arms on the rotting pegs and popping nuts of this serious stance. The layback gains an easier groove on the very prow of the arête. *Dream* continues up the sunny side here, whereas the final pitch of *Liberator* dives beneath a wicked-looking roof to traverse and gain a soaring flake on the darker side. Underclinging rightwards, a large triangular foothold is gained, where once stood a neat little flake, the first and only real rest on the route apart from the stances. The leaning flake above looks mean, but relents after two moves, and one can run fast up the remaining flake and finishing cracks.

It was 'in the can', as they say, so we retired for an end-of-shooting meal, to which Hots invited a coachload of female trippers as his personal guests, 'on the bill'. The morning after, we returned to free climbing *Dream* properly, before repairing to the pub for the payout. First, however, there was an end-of-film sale of the film company's climbing gear, kindly priced for them by Harris, who also bought most of it.

Commentary by Henry Barber and Pete Livesey

Pete picks up the commentary as the film captures him moving up the crux pitch of the route.

P.L. About halfway up the pitch is a little overhang to negotiate, under this is a pin which is normally used for aid. In fact, nobody has yet done it without the aid and, of course, I'll have to try it and do it without aid … because if I don't, Henry certainly will. It's kind of a competition again, but as I am leading, if I opt use the aid and Henry does it without, I'll feel as though he's beaten me.

As Pete climbs up towards the aid section and crux he explains his tactics.

P.L. The trick here is to sneak off right around the corner, around the arête onto a little hidden ledge. It's possible to take a rest here. If things get too difficult. You always think at the back of your mind, I can get out of here. I can jump into the sea and that's it, I will be free. Of course, it is not true. You do not have much chance of getting out of the sea. But it just seems to be there, it is a psychological thing I'm sure.

Pete begins to tackle the overhang.

P.L. Moving back left around the corner to the pin. I had a couple of attempts at climbing the move free but in the end, my face and eyes were all covered in sweat, my hands were covered in sweat. Chalk was everywhere and I just gave in, grabbed hold of the pin and used it to pull up and move over the roof. It is kind of a psychological relief when you grab the pin and it holds but a couple of seconds later, you know that you have given in. You have lost that particular part of the competition and you know for sure as sure that Henry will do it free. On the other hand, he won't be leading. He will be on the other end of the rope and this makes it a lot easier and you can kind of console yourself with that thought when he's powering over the roof and you think that perhaps on another day I will do it without.

Pete belays at the top of the pitch and Henry starts to climb. The commentary from Pete continues.

P.L. Henry is coming up now. He is climbing very fast which is a bit annoying, because we would like him to have difficulty on it but, of course, he knows that and so he's climbing as fast as possible.

Henry Barber takes over the commentary explaining his method for climbing the overhang free.

H.B. Climbing is an extension of walking. You also have to be concentrating on your footwork even when you're going over an overhang. If you want to take as much strain off your arms as possible, this is done by using your feet and if you can get one hand over the lip of the overhang and then get a foot over, you are immediately taking strain off the other parts of your body.

Henry negotiates the overhang using a wild heel hook and continues to reflect.

H.B. He's probably bummed out that I did the roof move without the aid, but that is really his problem. It probably has to do with the English concern and grabbiness for first ascents and for me that is really not what climbing is all about.

Henry joins Pete at the belay and sets off to lead the final pitch; Pete picks up the commentary.

P.L. It is Henry's turn to lead the last pitch now. It is very steep and each move is quite strenuous, but if you climb very fast and forget about protection, then it's a very easy pitch to do, certainly a very easy pitch to second. Henry is climbing it, but he is spending a tremendous long time hung under the roof above the stance, trying to get some protection in. I'm sure I couldn't spend that long hanging under there. Henry is strong. There's a good protection placement above him. I know it's there and I am not going to tell him because he seems to want to hang there under the roof using up all of his strength.

Henry takes over the commentary.

H.B. In a situation like this, you have a crack in the back of a corner and use a technique called 'laybacking' where you pull with your hands in a crack and push with your feet against the slab to reduce the strain on your arms and leg muscles. After the difficult layback and overhang section on the last pitch of *Liberator*, you still have to be careful. The climbing eases up quite a bit, but after you have done difficult climbing on a route of this nature you can very easily make mistakes on easier ground. Where your runners are further apart you could fall a long way.

Even though the film had been made to showcase Barber's prowess as a leading free climber of the day, Pete in his inimitable fashion still manages to spin his own take on things into his closing remarks.

P.L. I remember when Henry Barber first came over here to climb, he set out to impress the British climbers, and I am sure he would have done, but he reckoned without the great beer drinking tradition of British climbers. It is considered unsportsmanlike to go out climbing without having drunk vast quantities of beer beforehand. Henry wasn't into beer at the time, but I think he has been training since then. We notice the difference now. He has come back here and he can drink the beer as well as climb.

Original recording ABC/TV New York, transcribed and edited by Mark Radtke.

Jonathan Livingstone Steelfingers

by Pete Livesey

With a brief introduction by John Sheard

Introduction

Jonathan Livingston Seagull* was the inspiration for Pete's visionary essay on climbing development and innovation. Written by Richard Bach about a seagull learning about life and flight, and a homily about self perfection, by the end of 1972 over a million copies were in print. In 1972 and 1973 the book topped the Publishers Weekly list of bestselling novels in the United States.

The book tells the story of Jonathan Livingston Seagull, a seagull who is bored with the daily squabbles over food. Seized by a passion for flight, he pushes himself, learning everything he can about flying, until finally his unwillingness to conform results in his expulsion from his flock. An outcast, he continues to learn, becoming increasingly pleased with his abilities as he leads an idyllic life.

One day he is met by two gulls who take him to a higher plane of existence, in that there is no heaven but a better world found through perfection of knowledge, where he meets other gulls who love to fly. He discovers that his sheer tenacity and desire to learn make him 'pretty well a one-in-a-million bird'. In this new place he befriends the wisest gull, Chiang, who takes him beyond his previous learning, teaching him how to move instantaneously to anywhere else in the universe. The secret, Chiang says, is to 'begin by knowing that you have already arrived'.

The book was heralded as, *A story for people who follow their dreams and make their own rules.*

John Sheard

Jonathan Livingstone Steelfingers was born in 1973, on the very afternoon of the coffee break in which Pete Livesey wrote *The Grade of Things to Come* for the Leeds University *Climbing Journal*.

By the time Jonathan was 12, Ron Fawcett was 30, and his hands were now crippled with arthritis. Jonathan had won an Olympic bronze medal in gymnastics when he was 11 but deep down Jonathan was a climber, and he had been climbing since he was eight. What he couldn't understand was why he wasn't the best climber. How was it that all the athletes around him were peaking out at 10, 11 and 12, but the best climbers were all older, sometimes even over 20? There's no one fitter or with stronger fingers, or able to do The Move on The Wall like him.

Of course, it was the very handicap that prevented Jonathan Livingstone Steelfingers from understanding why he wasn't the best, which also stopped him being best. Physical maturity had been reached, but his mind wasn't yet able to cope with the commitment and maturity of judgment required of a top climber. He didn't realise that over 50 per cent of climbing was in the head, total mental control to drive the body in perilous situations. Oh, he was reckless all right, but that was different, useful, but not good enough to produce the mental effort required to be up there with them.

Now, if the story runs its course, by 1990 or so, Jonathan Livingstone Steelfingers will be the best. You'll see him somewhere staring intently at a piece of rock and suddenly he will disappear, only to reappear instantaneously at the top, grinning and self-satisfied at the desperate series of moves he has just done. In his head, that is.

Well, that's the end of the story, but what I'm going to talk about here are the intervening stages, the shape of climbing in the next few years.

The Grade of Things to Come was an attempt to look into the future of hard climbing, the trouble was that many of the so-called far-sighted predictions had been realised almost before the Leeds Journal appeared in print. Gordale's *Cave Route* was only a free route in the eyes of two people in 1973, but within a couple of years it was there for real. John Allen, Steve Bancroft, Al Manson, and others, were already working at grades of 6b and above in 1975. There are still Derbyshire 6bs by those teams today, despite that county's deflationary grading system; what grade they really are, I shudder to think.

But what of now, what is the state of the art today? There seems to be four identifiable areas of innovation if you like; four countries where rock-climbing is pushing forward standards in a style peculiar to that climbing scene.

In Britain there is a growing accent on the technical move; we are shifting away from the desperately strenuous and sustained climbs of the last few years. The hard new climbs now have one or two moves of absolute technical difficulty; real boulder moves, but up in the air!

By contrast, the western and central climbing areas of the USA have a sustained type of route, move after move of desperate climbing occupying the first division. Long smooth cracks where every jam is about to fall out, or very steep slabs where the tiniest of holds have to be left quickly but have to suffice for great stretches of head-spinning boldness. In Britain boldness arises from not knowing what is coming, in the States it comes from knowing exactly what you are about to receive.

France has two areas of operation. On the one hand is the very hard 'boulder garden' of Fontainebleau where the routes only last for a move or two and the climbing is safe but desperate by anyone's standards. At the other end of the scale French rock-climbers are free-climbing the fabulous long, mixed rock routes of the last few years, in which France abounds. A large number of fairly well-protected extreme pitches is the trademark of the French brand of top rock, and the quality is undeniably excellent.

The crag-sized cliffs of France have lines super-protected by big juicy bolts, with the odd boulder problem at altitude. The bolts are normally in optimum positions, and the moves are consequently of higher difficulty than the British climber may expect when 200 feet off the ground.

East Germany, and similar East European areas, have perhaps developed high-grade crag climbing in a more puritanical way than any other major climbing country. The style and equipment on the Dresden outcrops is virtually unchanged since the inception of climbing at those places, bare feet with a bolt every twenty-five feet. The climbing is hard and sustained, the falls numerous and long, but I suppose it's safe once you grow to accept several fifty-foot fliers every Sunday afternoon.

Among the other areas of top-class rock-climbing Australia and New Zealand stand out, their styles a cross between Britain and America (and their accents too. Hey there, Bruce!).

It would be pointless to say that the hardest rock-climbing in the world is in Britain, America or East Germany; the nature of the hardest routes is different, and the visiting climber invariably has problems adjusting. Generally speaking the British climber has so far had most success with the hardest climbs of other areas – the Americans have rather less success over here.

The 1970s rise in British climbing standards continues apace; each year a significant raising of the grade of new routes is perceived, and every couple of years or so a new front runner identifiable as 'the hardest route' comes along.

Interestingly enough, the current contenders are of a style new in this country but well-known in the States; long sequences of scary strenuous climbing on tiny finger holds being the main feature. *Downhill Racer* (Froggatt) and *Linden* (Curbar) on the outcrops typify this genre, though they are not necessarily the hardest examples. While *The Cad* (North Stack, Gogarth), and *Take It to the Limit* (Deer Bield), are excellent hard examples of the type. Undoubtedly the latter two are very hard and would rate in any list of the 10 hardest climbs in Britain. Yet by modern American face climbing standards they are pathetically easy. Routes like *Shaky Flakes* and *Greasy But Groovy* (Yosemite) are years ahead of the British examples.

In trying to identify the hardest gritstone routes, we come up against a scaled-down version of this international problem, different routes are hardest for different reasons. Here are three separate groups of contenders:

(A) Strenuous, sustained, protectable struggles. *Milky Way* (Ilkley), *Moon Crack* (Curbar), *London Wall* (Millstone).

(B) Serious, sustained and bold, *Linden* (Curbar), *Desperate Dan* (Ilkley).

(C) Bouldering, *Above and Beyond* (Burbage), *Profit of Doom* (Curbar), *Psycho* (Caley).

In my view group B represents the true pinnacle of achievement in gritstone climbing, though the moves in group C are harder and the routes in group A feel harder. Certainly it is the sort of climbing in group B that typifies the flavour of British hard climbing for the visitor and that for me represents all the qualities that should be found in a rock-climber. It is, of course, this kind of climb that stops the climbing wall freak dead in his tracks, tracksuit legs quaking below moves six grades easier than his gymnasium performances.

Which all brings us back to Jonathan and his head. We are already producing dozens of climbers capable physically of climbing all kinds of ridiculous problems, but the real breakthrough is suppressed by lack of trained minds. I don't mean trained by sticking dumbells on your ears; that's a dumbo's reaction. No, I mean trained like Al Rouse and Pete Minks's heads, trained to survive through the maximum amount of disorder and still produce the goods.

When these qualities are combined with a climbing wall-trained body the routes will really start to flow. American face climbing grades will appear over here but, of course, they won't be protected by bolts here as they are in the States. The moves are possible, we have the technology.

The kind of climbing we can expect in the future is already to be seen on crags like Tremadog, eliminates on eliminates, deliberately moving off the easy line for a harder move. The rock here is eminently climbable and so long as one doesn't require too much in the way of a classic line the climbing can be enjoyable, no matter how contrived it is. This kind of climbing, though, encourages the difficult move without the continuity that we expect from a 'great' climb. In other words, most of the new climbs being done and those that will be done, will not be outstanding despite their difficulty, and it is only the outstanding climbs by which a generation is remembered.

There are outstanding lines left to be done and they obviously will be done in time, but I suspect that we shall have to wait some years before the right-hand line on Cloggy's Great Wall is climbed, or the left-hand groove line above *Darkinbad* at Pentire Head. These lines could be climbed tomorrow if bolt protection were used, but then the lines would no longer be great, just a series of boulder problems.

Linden and *Desperate Dan* (about 6a and 6b respectively) perhaps today represent the grade that can be led with little or no protection, but 6c is frequently climbed next to protection, and 7a is certainly practised on climbing walls. It has been shown time and time again that whatever is possible on a top rope or in a climbing wall atmosphere, even at the limit of possibility, fairly quickly becomes the norm and is soon practised by Clive Coolhead without protection on the crags.

When Al Rouse led *Beatnik* at Helsby the moves on it were as hard as those on any climb done at that time, even with superb protection. *Beatnik*, of course, has none. Even now, if climbing wall standards could be reproduced on some of our crags, all kinds of outrageous things would be climbed. Routes would become as meaningless at Gogarth as they already are on Idwal's Suicide Wall, go anywhere with little protection but lots of holds. Probably even before Gogarth, the reasonably protected, but very strenuous walls of *Cenotaph Corner* could have had all the spaces filled twice in one generation. Gaps between *Right Wall* and the *Corner*, and between *Resurrection* and the *Corner*, now become apparent.

The blank walls crossed by *Wailing Wall* (Craig y Llyn), *The Cad* and *Take it to the Limit*, all at 6a +, and all quite bold, show just what is possible for sustained distances on tiny holds. If the near future in British rock-climbing is to have any significance then it must be from this type of route, the technical ability is already there, but what is needed is training for the head and maybe a little stamina as well. Bolt protection would wreck the climbing in our little country and we might as well start top-roped climbing competitions at the same time.

When will it happen? These are the pointers; the arête right of *Green Death* at Millstone, the wall between *Peapod* and *Right Eliminate* at Curbar. When they are done, then will follow Great Wall Right-Hand. That really will be Master's Wall.

First published in Crags *No 16 1978*

Footnote

Phil Burke climbed the wall between *Peapod* and *Right Eliminate* to produce *The Shape of Things to Come* E6 6b in 1980.

Ron Fawcett climbed the arête right of *Green Death* to produce *Master's Edge* E7 6c in 1983.

Johnny Dawes climbed the futuristic line of *The Indian Face* E9 6c to the right of *Great Wall* in 1986.

Mark Radtke.

The Understudy

by Dan Morgan

I really got to know Pete Livesey as one of his students when I attended Ilkley College in the early 1980s, but my first encounter with him was in Yosemite Valley in the summer of 1977. He was in the elite Yorkshire team that included Ron Fawcett, John Sheard and Jill Lawrence. I was from across the border and our Lancashire team comprised Andy and Paul Hartley, John Thompson and Jerry Peel. With the exception of Jerry, our ability paled into insignificance in comparison with the Yorkshire elite. In the Valley our climbing exploits remained separate, but we shared the campsite banter, scarfing for food and beer can scams as we fully immersed ourselves in the Camp 4 revelry. We watched with reflected glory, pride and a little envy, as the Fawcett/Livesey team scooped up the best Yosemite had to offer and showed the Yanks how good the Brits really were.

I knew little of Pete's professional background at this stage but his climbing prowess was, of course, legendary. When he took great pleasure in sending us off into the woods to look for his recommended classic route *Vanishing Point*, we jumped at the opportunity. We hunted high and low for the start of the route based on Pete's directions and returned late to the camp stating the obvious; it seemed to have 'vanished'. Pete was most amused by our wanderings amongst the woods in search of the route, which continued into a second day. When we finally found it and climbed it, he clapped and met us with his widest grin. We enjoyed his applause, but couldn't help thinking he was having great pleasure at our expense.

My second encounter with Pete was in 1978, on Great End Crag in Borrowdale. Paul Hartley and I were buoyed by our recent success on the Livesey/Sheard classic, *Bitter Oasis* and set our sights on another of Pete's hard classics, *Nagasaki Grooves*. Whilst sorting out the ropes at the belay ledge, below the crux pitch, a flustered Livesey joined us. He had flown up the initial pitches thinking we were prospecting a new route to the left, later to become *Trouble Shooter*. We assured him of both our objective and also of our climbing limitations, but were still struck by his proprietorial attitude, which suggested he had 'rights' over the line to the left. I was distinctly aware of his competitive and almost feudal assumptions about the climbing pecking order. We were more accustomed to being nurtured by 'senior' climbers, such as Hank Pasquill and Jerry Peel, these lads encouraged and cajoled us. With Pete we felt our inferiority, partly because he had such a formidable reputation, but also his competitive air. If we did have designs on the route to the left, I suspect we would have doffed our caps and moved off, such was our lack of confidence. It was with intrigue then, when I joined Ilkley College to see what awaited me in the form of Pete Livesey, the renowned outdoor educationalist.

Ilkley College sat on the hillside overlooking the Wharfe valley in West Yorkshire. It was a collection of annexes, old and new, attached to and surrounding a stately old building that was once a grand hotel, where people of wealth from the industrial cities of Bradford and Leeds could 'take the waters' running off the moorside. Within walking distance, arranged along the hillside, were the halls of residence, housing a number of the 1,000 or so students studying for their certificates, diplomas and degrees in a range of subjects as diverse as Home Economics, Performing Arts and most importantly, Recreation Studies.

The latter course was a recent addition to this 'liberal arts' college and had its origins in the Physical Education degree course at the former Bingley Teacher Training College, which merged with Ilkley in the late 1970s. An important component of the PE course was Outdoor Education and a number of luminaries at the time delivered these courses, they included Wally Keay and Pete Livesey. This pairing complemented each other nicely. The warm and rotund Wally was an advisor to numerous outdoor education groups, where his wisdom, knowledge and affability contributed to the early philosophies of learning through outdoor adventures. In tandem, Pete with his contribution to the performance end of adventurous activities brought a heady mix of experience, physical prowess, enthusiasm and an unconventional attitude to risk. Pete's approach to outdoor education would best be described as 'learn from experience' and be prepared to fail. Nowadays it would be termed as experiential learning and the possibility of failing, would largely be risk-assessed out of the equation.

This strong emphasis on learning by doing was the perfect platform for the cohort of impressionable and enthusiastic students who arrived at Ilkley College in the autumn of 1980, to study for their degree in Recreation Studies. Within a few weeks this enthusiasm had to be reined in, as the injury list resulting from a number of accidents on the rock faces of Ilkley Quarry and Rocky Valley, caused justifiable consternation with the tutors. No doubt they could foresee their student retention rate dropping to an alarming level. Wally and Pete addressed the assembled group, who were garlanded with plaster casts, slings and crutches. Wally preached prudence and sensibility, a 'three points of contact' approach and the group nodded respectfully. Pete, with a wry smile endorsed all that Wally said, but tantalised us with a 'fear nought attitude' and 'to make progress you may have to dyno for it' on occasion. We walked out, some hobbled, having got the mixed message.

In the early 1980s Pete was an established elder statesman in the UK outdoor education scene and known to many through his exploits, presentations, articles in outdoor magazines and (dubious) guidebooks. This notoriety was an excellent selling point for the Ilkley College degree and Pete's name was prominent in the marketing literature. His primary responsibility lay in developing, delivering and managing the outdoor pursuits programme for all four years of the course. It was difficult to discern a developmental structure to the course that would introduce, develop and synthesise the skills required to operate and lead in the outdoors. To be fair, this would have been particularly challenging, as the groups of students all came from different 'sporting' backgrounds with a range of experience.

This challenge for Pete was evident during one of our early caving forays. This took the form of a through-trip ascent of Yordas Cave near Ingleton, and the group was comprised of a real mixed bag of students, with sporting backgrounds ranging from rock-climbing to cricket. As it happened, one of the climbers was asked to follow Pete up the waterfall solo and then to rig up a body belay whilst wedged into a crevice - sort of solid. The rope was thrown down to the cricketer who was tied in by a fellow student who knew how to tie a bowline. Pete viewed the preparations from an eyrie, a little higher, where he was helping to deflect some of the water. Of course, the force of the waterfall drowned out any meaningful communication, but all seemed set as the cricketer felt for the initial holds, which despite being jugs were wet and slippery. After making little progress the holds were considered useless by the cricketer who decided to haul up the rope, making it redundant as a safety line as it looped below his legs. Despite shouts from the belayer to get back on the rock, the rope was still hauled upon and slow progress was made up the twenty feet or so. The speed of ascent decreased, as fatigue and cold fingers crept in, but he was very near the top by now and the fear in his eyes was evident to the belayer. The only recourse for the belayer was to forget the 'safety' rope and reach down, grab his hand and help haul him to safety. The wretched figure splayed across the top of the pitch panting loudly with 'wildebeest eyes'. Pete surveyed the scene, cast his judgement that it all worked out fine and shouted for the next student to tie on. The group continued to complete the ascent, with Pete out front all the way through the cave and back down to the van. There was no debrief, no reflection or comment from Pete on the ascent. The group was left to ponder the outcome and giggle at the result of our exploits. Bravado and getting away with it were prominent in our thoughts.

Pete was certainly comfortable operating with students at the extreme end of activity. On a caving trip into the Three Counties System; not a course-organised trip but one coming from students begging to be allowed to go caving with the 'Great Man'. The weather was poor and there was heavy rain forecast. Despite this, the trip was going into a part of the system that flooded to the roof, but because it was Pete Livesey the trip progressed and the group moved at a furiously fast pace. Then came a moment when Livesey asked someone what the time was and we witnessed the 'LIVESEY PAUSE', which upon reflection was him working out the vectors of the flood pulse that was in the system with the best exit route. '*Right,*' he said, '*we are going out up here, and don't bother with rigging a safety rope, just climb, fast.*' The group did as they were told, got out intact and learned an important lesson about decision-making and margins of error. In our maturing minds, he was the consummate professional outdoor instructor whose approach was one to emulate. This professionalism verged on neglect, but it could also be argued that it was the ultimate form of student-centred learning.

On the occasion of a Mountain Leader Training expedition on the moors above Upper Wharfedale, the weather was on the bad side of foul. After another wet night, morning arrived together with a barked instruction from Livesey, who was only venturing as far as to stick his head out of his tent. *'Pack up, move out and navigate to this specific spot.'* A grid reference was given to a point a good few miles away. Pete's head retreated back into his tent and the zip was firmly closed against the driving Dales rain. Because it was Pete Livesey giving the instruction (and he was not a man to be disobeyed) the group plodded off to their destination.

The group endured rain, mist, wind and inevitable delays but eventually arrived at the assigned point, suitably knackered. After a short spell, Livesey loomed out of the weather, loping along in his running shorts (with kit on back). After having gone back to his pit for an extended nap, he'd then packed up and ran with speed to rendezvous with us at the designated NGR. Call it confidence, arrogance or laziness on his part, there was no doubt the group had completed the journey through their own efforts and took pride in their abilities. What would have happened if they had got lost on the remote moors one can only speculate over, needless to say Pete was confident in his and our abilities.

As a tutor, his involvement was best described as 'hands off'. He followed the belief that meeting to monitor progress and guide achievement was excessive involvement on his part. He would arrange an initial meeting with a student, share brief thoughts in line with the student's thinking and skip beyond any discussion of technical terms like 'standard deviation', saying, 'Books should help you with that,' and dismiss the student. I recall that to obtain further tutorial support, one student lay in ambush for Pete, but as Livesey walked between college buildings he got wind of his 'assailant' and took evasive action by taking a quick detour from his normal route. It became a game of 'cat and mouse'. Pete would vary his routes from the car park to his office to avoid being caught in the open. Rather than being a nuisance, it became an enjoyable game between the two, as they stalked and avoided each other around the campus.

In contrast to my early experiences with Pete, the competitive climber, he was to many of us someone who was all about encouraging people. Encouraging is probably too strong a word, he was more about not stopping us from having adventures in the context of our own ability. Maybe he had the gift of being able to judge people's limits and offering them the choice to explore them or not, but in a non-judgmental way, or maybe he just didn't care. This was a strategy that worked really well for us in our youthful, indestructible state of mind.

As a tutor, mentor and inspirational figure, Pete was determined to do it his way. Mixing the worlds of higher education lecturer and extreme sports performer, he seemed to find the right balance. If any compromise was required, he relied upon the resilience of the students to find a way through their studies. He always left an indelible mark upon his students, not just from his reputation as a rock-climber, paddler, runner and caver, but also as an educator. His maverick approach would struggle to survive in the current outdoor education world of today with its health and safety, risk aversion and quality assurance reviews, but his philosophy still resonates and some of his students still carry his torch, albeit after completing a risk assessment form.

Acknowledgements to Iain Taylor, Andy Bell, Ian Kenvyn and Rob Gale.

Grinning

by Janine Newman

There he is, standing at the side of either the river, or the lake or the cave or the crag – grinning.

As we struggled in the cold and the wet, it was always wet, to master the intricacies of a particular activity with minimal input from him, he was grinning.

He taught us to roll a canoe in the Leeds Liverpool canal today. No warm swimming pool for us. The incentive was great, fail and bail out in the mud and slime and rat-infested water or succeed– and there he was, always grinning.

Take us to orienteer on Oxenhope Moor. We assumed in our innocence that our lecturer would have gained permission, but no, two weeks on the trot, I was returned to the Land Rover by the gamekeeper, dog and gun and Pete was there grinning. 'You're just going to have to move faster, Ja.'

Assessing us on our MLC, we were weighed down with huge sacks, wet tent, food, spare food, torch, spare torch, primus, spare primus and even a rope. We met Pete after three days and there he was in his 'Lifa' shorts with a day pack. He was still grinning.

He instilled in his students either frustration or determination. 'You've just got to get out and do it, and do it well.'

Yet when praise was given it was never forgotten. I will always remember those two words, 'Well done.'

A Long Crawl with Livesey

by John Sheard

With apologies to Tom Patey's A Short Walk with Whillans

Throughout the years of climbing together we would, from time to time, revert to what was, for both of us, an earlier passion. Adventures beneath the Yorkshire Pennines had been, for a time, an activity consuming each and every weekend. Caving with Pete had added the importance of always doing something out of the ordinary and also the extra ingredient of speed, especially when we realised the possibility of abandoning ladders and using our 8mm climbing ropes and Figures of Eight. Needless to say, thin, stretchy ropes were far from ideal and led to a number of hilarious and occasionally dangerous events. The sight of the end of the stretched rope shooting five metres back up the long pitch in *Stransgill* as he unclipped was amusing, until I realised that we were now stranded. I should have warned him that I'd only just reached the bottom with the stretch of the rope. His caustic comment on the nature of elasticity was accepted without argument as we built an enormous pyramid of boulders to affect an escape.

Sitting on ice-covered boulders in some obscure chamber in the flood prone Borehole of *Leck Fell*, gazing at the frozen water between the hanging boulders forming both the cave roof and bed of the frozen *Leck Beck*, whilst calmly discussing the next climbing project, is still memorable.

Our solo two-way traverse from *Pippikin* to *Top Sink*, at that time one of the longest trips in the UK, came towards the end of Pete's active climbing career. We drew straws for the direction of travel. I won and got *Pip* entrance, *Top Sink* exit. He wasn't best pleased at this since it meant him, by far the larger of us, having to exit uphill through *Pip* after the three and a half mile crossing, and this with his half of the ropes. In the event, he solved the problem by abandoning the lot in *Link Pot*, an intermediate system en route, sending me back midweek to recover them. He couldn't possibly do it because he was working, and anyway they were all mine. I finally got out of *Top Sink* and set off across the moor in the dark, getting completely lost in dense fog. When I eventually staggered to Bull Pot Farm I found the car had departed, together with my dry gear. Faced with a long, cold walk back to the main road in the hope of thumbing a lift, I was more than a little relieved when after the first mile I spotted car headlights approaching. It was Pete coming back to recover me. When I, with some justification, asked why he had abandoned me, he replied. '*You were so late that I had to go to see Soma in Ingleton because she would have been worried. I knew you would be all right.*' I took this to be a compliment, but you were never quite sure with Pete.

Thrutching along the rift in *Quaking Pot* with Pete stuck by his barrel of a chest somewhere behind. '*What can you see?*' he'd shouted, and after a long, complicated manoeuvre to even twist my head round in the impossibly tight passage, I'd informed him that I could see a white flowstone deposit on the wall. '*It's miles from there and gets tighter,*' was the response, prompting the end of our attempt and a slow retreat from the cave. Later I learned from Pete Gomersall that the white wall marked the end of the tight section. Livesey knew that, of course, but there was no way I could be allowed to continue if the rift was too tight for him.

At some point during these intermittent caving times news had somehow reached him, in the obscure way it usually did, that there was a major system being secretly extended in Yorkshire. Red rag to a bull, suddenly we were off again. I should have realised it wasn't going to be a normal trip when he insisted on travelling for several hours throughout the Dales in search of a wetsuit hood. He eventually found what he was looking for in the Bradford Pothole Club hut at Horton and I suppose I should have enquired why it was essential that he had one and I didn't.

I suppose another obvious clue to the fact that this was going to be a different sort of trip occurred when I asked where the entrance was. Useful to know, when the driving was left up to me as usual. *'Well, you go to Ingleton, open a manhole lid, drop down into an underground reservoir and then swim across to a bedding plane crawl.'* Nothing unusual about that then.

I should have stopped the car at that point.

Further information emerged piecemeal as we travelled in the general direction of Ingleton by a strangely circuitous route, the significance of which I never discovered. He'd heard of a secret entry to a well-known, and strictly off-limits, Yorkshire show cave which allowed, if that's the right word, access to a superb series extending, God knows how far, under Ingleborough. It seems it was the preserve of an equally well-known and formidable club called, inappropriately, The Happy Wanderers. I'd reason to believe they were not going to be too bloody happy if they found we were about to invade their secret preserve.

Apparently their technique was to enter the system by the reservoir on Friday nights, do whatever they needed to do in pushing the far reaches and exit by climbing over the turnstile at the tourist entrance before anyone was about in the early hours of Saturday morning. Fair enough, but this was a busy, late Saturday morning at the height of the tourist season and even I should have realised that the owners would be rather keen to make some money that day. The show cave would be busy and the turnstile manned. Finding the manhole wasn't easy since it involved crawling along ditches and hiding behind walls to avoid the ticket office, before breaking cover in full view of the road. Classic Livesey stuff.

The drop into the darkness of Ingleton's water supply went all right and the swim across the reservoir in wet suits was easy enough. The wet crawl that followed was okay but the water definitely got deeper, or was it the roof descending? Either way, the need for a wetsuit hood became painfully apparent as the air space shrank to a couple of inches and progress was only possible by submerging the left ear in icy water and sucking sideways through the mouth. He'd told me that only one hood was necessary. Clearly it had been intended for him as leader, the assumption being, I suppose, that I would somehow survive.

Eventually the air space improved and we crawled out of the low passage to crouch behind a scenic waterfall. The show cave lights at the other side illuminated the lower legs of tourists gazing in wonder at the cascade as we peered out from the other side, hidden by a curtain of falling water. Those lights should have alerted me to the coming problem but the numb feeling in my head from the icy water still sloshing about in my left ear prevented rational thought. After a few minutes the guide's commentary on the source of the stream was finished and the legs moved off towards the entrance and welcome cups of tea.

The lights stayed on!

Out we popped and proceeded merrily along a metal walkway suspended above the stream, heading for the fabled extensions beyond the limits of the show cave. Our enthusiasm was suddenly dented when we heard another guided party coming towards us. The lights were still on, significant this. Where to hide? Magistrates' court on Monday?

Pete was a pretty quick thinker and he already had the solution. Drop into the stream, crawl under the gridded walkway and head torches off. We lay there on our backs in the water as they walked over our heads, too intent on the stalactites to look down to where they would have seen two ghostly, partially submerged faces. Shortly after that the cave lights went out. This was obviously the key to success. Lights out, nobody in the cave, simple really.

Now we were away, strolling nonchalantly along concrete walkways, taking in the tour guide's subterranean wonders at our leisure. A bizarre free trip through this exclusive system, which we now had to ourselves. All too soon the strolling ended and leaping over the terminal barrier into the stream below we started the real caving which was my reward for gamely following the intrepid leader without the required wetsuit hood. The usual shuffling, wriggling and worrisome crawling through boulder chokes were commonplace. The swims along underground lakes in flooded passages, head torches bobbing on the water, were pretty weird until I remembered similar ventures in semi-submerged *Rowten Pot*, where I'd managed to persuade him not to free dive what had seemed to me the end of what was reasonable

Eventually we emerged above what appeared to be a massive chamber, our now weak lights vaguely picking out a boulder-strewn slope falling steeply away before rising on the far side to what I assumed to be a continuation. Two caving lights shone back at us. This should not have been happening. The Wanderers, rather sensibly, only came in during Friday night as far as we were aware. The show cave was strictly off limits to anyone other than paying customers. Four caving lights went out as we crept behind the nearest boulder.

After several minutes a shout came, '*Who's there?*'

A long pause, then, '*Who's there?*' came Pete's reply.

Silence, then again, '*Who's there?*' from the opposite side of the cavern.

'*Livesey,*' came Pete's response, followed after another pause by, '*Who's there?*'

"*Heap,*" called back their leader and the four lights came on again.

Both teams descended their respective slopes, like a scene from *High Noon*, to meet for what I took to be either a showdown or a surreal strategy meeting in an underground chamber previously seen by very few human beings.

It was quickly established that David Heap, a well-known and respected authority, was in with permission. The discussion was not easy to follow, due to the amount of cold water still sloshing around in my left ear, but it seemed that Heap had done some kind of favour in the past for the cave's owner and as a reward had been granted a one-day access to the far reaches of the system at a future time of his choosing. The almost impossible coincidence of his visit, taking place at the same time as our illicit trip, could only be explained if allowance was made for the Livesey factor.

A fair degree of sympathy was expressed for our predicament since we were now four and should have been two. We were informed that the owners suspected that cavers were somehow getting in and had asked our new comrades to keep a look out for a possible unknown entrance. Livesey came up with a plan to get us out undetected and David generously agreed to go along with it. We would return through the far reaches together as far as the end of the show cave. Pete and I would then start off out a few minutes in advance of the official party, reverse the wet crawl to the reservoir and clear off undetected, leaving Mr Heap to go out by the tourist entrance as expected, and keep faith with the owners. This solution would also preserve the secret of The Wanderers' entrance.

All went well but as we re-entered the show cave section a sense of complacency set in. Swinging easily along the narrow concrete walkway we were suddenly aware of a guided party just around the next corner and heading our way. The cave lights were still on. How could we have been so stupid? Lights on, cave in use. There was absolutely nowhere to hide now so we shambled forward to meet the guide and confess our guilt. As we met, he turned to his doting clients with an instruction to stand back against the wall and leave room for this official exploration party to pass. Muttering our astonished thanks, we squeezed by and once round the next corner made a dash for freedom.

Soon after a howl of anger echoed down the passage. The guide had encountered the following legitimate party and realised there were now two additional members who were not on the books. The owners were now obviously confirmed in their suspicion. We were in serious danger of revealing the secret and, perhaps even worse, exposing ourselves to the wrath of The Happy Wanderers, who, as previously indicated, appeared far from the jolly people their title would leave us to believe.

'They're in,' was the shout, accompanied by the sound of running feet. We took off at great speed, assisted by the comfortable concreted path and electrical illumination. It was essential to reach the waterfall unseen, dive through into the hidden bedding plane, and thereby maintain the illegal entrance. Once through the falls we paused with heaving chests having sprinted 100 metres in tight wetsuits. The pursuing footsteps approached, turned left and disappeared. Saved for the moment but if we were not to be forced to wait in the reservoir for the cover of darkness, we had to get through the submerged passage and out of the manhole before the guides reached the entrance turnstile and realised we were still somewhere in the cave.

The wet crawls were passed this time in minutes, with no thought of the numbing water and the minimal air space. Out of the manhole undetected, back along the walls and ditches, then running giggling down to the road and the parked car. A few miles later, we pulled in and stripped off dripping wetsuits before a quick visit to a local café for pots of tea, toasted tea cakes and plans for where to go climbing. It had been a memorable trip. Fantastic caving in a new system with the added satisfaction of putting two fingers up to authority but, after all, a fairly normal day in the life of Peter Livesey.

The *Paroi Rouge*

by Johnny Walker

I was only privileged to climb with Peter on rare occasions, but they are times that I'll never forget. He had that effect on you. I remember as a young man on my first climbing trip to France, we stayed at a climbing refuge in the Vercors below the huge walls of the Rocher d'Archiane. As I recall, it had rained during the morning and nobody wanted to go climbing except, of course, for Pete. At two o'clock in the afternoon, the rock had dried and Pete wanted to set off and do a route called the *Paroi Rouge*, the red face. I later discovered that this climb had something of a cutting edge reputation, but at the time was blissfully unaware of its level of difficulty. Even today it is regarded as a classic, with pitches up to a grade of F6c.

I can still remember to this day the silence which fell on the room as Pete went around looking for a 'willing' volunteer and the look of 'you're for it now' on the others' faces, as I, a naive young climber, volunteered. It was a bit of a steep and lengthy hike up to the foot of the route and Peter ran most of it with me in tow, so I was exhausted even before we started climbing. No time to rest though, off he went running out his 200-foot ropes, two pitches at a time. I could hardly pay the rope out fast enough, before it was my turn. Then it was tight rope from above and climb. I was virtually hauled onto every stance, as we climbed at breakneck speed. I was yelled at, sworn at, cursed at and told that he had 'never climbed with anyone so slow.' He led every pitch and at each stance, he just leaned over, grabbed my harness, clipped me into the belay and shot off upwards again at breakneck speed. At the top of the cliff, I just lay face down in a little patch of snow gasping for breath. The route was about 1,500 feet long and it had taken us just two and a half hours to complete. After a lengthy search for the abseil point, we started the long descent to the foot of the cliff and, finally, got back to the hut before nightfall. I read later in the climbing magazines that we had done the fastest time ever recorded for the route.

The Turd Mincer

by Peter L Gomersall

I t was 1976 and I'd been forced to take a year's sabbatical from my studies at Bingley College where I'd struck up a climbing friendship with Pete Livesey. My sabbatical had taken the form of employment at a local bath-manufacturing factory.

'*Hey Pete, do you want to meet me out at Oxenhope, I have a property I want to look at?*'

'*Sure,*' I said, and made my way out to Moorside, a single line of terraced houses overlooking Oxenhope. I pulled up next to Pete's car. The door to one of the houses was open and Pete stepped out.

'*Come and have a look. I'm thinking of buying it, it's a bargain.*'

A month or so later, he was on the phone again, '*Do you think you can get me a bath and basin?*'

'*What are you after?*'

'*Something fancy.*'

'*Well, I can have a look round the factory and see what I can get my hands on, but I don't think they have bogs, you'd have to get one to match somewhere else,*' I told him.

'*I've already had a look at what colours they do and if you can get a bath and a basin in 'autumn tan' that would be great.*'

It was 9:45pm and pitch dark as I opened the back gate of the factory yard. Pete was already waiting. '*It's this way,*' I said, and he followed, dodging in and out of the shadows to avoid the orange lights of the yard. We stuck the basin in the bath and carried it to the back of my van. A few minutes later I was clocking out at the entrance at the end of my shift and following Pete back to Oxenhope in my little green Morris Minor.

The following week I opened the door to Pete's new home to a loud, high-pitched whine and wood shavings filling the air. '*Hi Tom. What have you got there, I've never seen one of those things before?*'

'*Hey, Pete, it's a great new invention. A power plane.*' Tom Proctor was just one of Pete's accomplices in the house renovation. Terry Birks from Skipton was also in on it too, doing the plumbing and reorganising the rooms. Tom gave me a demo with the plane. '*It sure beats a hand job,*' he said with a suggestive smile.

'*So let's have a look at the new bathroom,*' I said to Pete and we trotted up the really narrow steep stairs. '*Well, that looks way better than it did at the factory. That's a mighty posh bathroom.*' I told him. We were just about to leave the room when I noticed a strange box next to the bog. '*What's that?*' I enquired. '*It's the turd mincer,*' Pete replied.

'*What do you mean, turd mincer?*' I enquired, a little perplexed.

'*Well, when you have a crap and flush the bog it all goes into the mincer and it chops it all up. It then pumps it down that little pipe.*'

'*Huh,*' I said, confused. '*Why haven't you got a proper pipe?*'

'*Well, the house isn't on the main sewer and I'm not waiting 10 years to be able to have a proper crap. I just got Terry to put the pipe out back and into the farmer's field last night under cover of darkness. The council says it will be years before the house is on main sewer and I'm not using the outhouse until then. Who's gonna know?*'

The Competitive Eating of Slugs

A letter to Alison Livesey from her great uncle Peter

Introduction by Mark Radtke

I n the days before modern telecommunications, tales and stories would often circulate around the climbing fraternity about the deeds and derring-do of famous climbers. Spread by word of mouth and embellished over pints drunk in the pub, these tales would sometimes become the stuff of climbing folklore. One such tale that was circulated about Pete Livesey was of how on one rainy afternoon in Cornwall he managed to empty a packed café of all its clientele by removing from his mouth a number of live slugs. At some point this particular tale reached the ears of Pete's niece Alison Livesey. On hearing the story, Alison then only eleven, but apparently endowed with the Livesey scepticism, wrote to Pete to check on the validity of the tale and to express her concerns about this apparent disregard for the welfare of small creatures. Pete's reply to Alison gives an insight into how his mind worked and is a great illustration of his unique sense of humour. Reproduced here with kind permission of Alison.

Pete wrote back as follows:

My dear niece Alison, I am sorry to say that much of what you have heard about your great uncle Pete is untrue. It is true that there were indeed ordinary people in my presence in that clotted Cornish café, but beyond that insignificant fact, your informant has led you astray, do not despair this often happens to children. This is what actually happened. It had nothing at all to do with slugs, I was merely offering sheltered accommodation to homeless snails, just a small part of the charitable work in which I am engaged. I do believe that others in our party were determined to undermine my humble and charitable act by turning it into a competition to see who could house the most homeless snails. I cannot say who encouraged this ridiculous competition, but he is married to a certain Mrs Cobley. As you will appreciate, I am not a competitive person, but I did through chance win the snail housing competition by housing seven snails at once. The other scores were Mrs Cobley none, Mr Cobley none, Mr Lovey none and Mrs Lovey none. Mr Lovey by the way is Steve Foster. I would hasten to assure you that full consideration was given to an equal opportunity, multi-cultural approach to this housing scheme. Four of the snails were black; three were a sort of fawn colour. All the snails were male, all the snails were female. I hope this curtails any further worries you may have.

Your great uncle, Peter.

Lime Crime

by Graham Desroy

I t was Pete's fault that I ended up in Yorkshire. His article *Castaways on a Gritstone Island* sold the place to me, especially the images of Almscliff. Once there I immediately set about making myself unpopular by not using chalk and writing a pirate guide for gritstone. The latter was born out of frustration for the absence of a current gritstone guide and I was just proving a point that even a numpty like myself could compile an update. Unknown to me there was another maverick in Yorkshire, the one responsible for my presence. One I knew only for his feats of climbing prowess, not for his belligerence to authority and the establishment. This was all to change as I continued on my crusade with a Limestone update. But the dark sorcerer had his spies everywhere and my plans were whispered through the wormholes and grikes to his lofty tower.

Ominous rumbles echoed, 'But it was my plan, my precious, my one book to rule them all.'

A summons was issued and with trepidation the young pretender found himself before the One Wizard in his Palace of Tea and Cakes in Malhamdor.

'You will pay for such insolence young Hippybit, your pound of flesh is now mine. You will be forced to complete this tome, do all the research, scribe upon the scrolls, perform the spellcheck and fund the publication. In return my name will appear on the cover scroll and I will keep most of the farthings we shall earn. And this mighty tome will be called, "*Lime Crimes*".'

'Thank you, O Great One, most obliged I am to you for your generosity.'

'Not so fast, young Nochalko Baggins. You will also perform introductory rites of instruction into the noble art of Crag Upping to my personal students of Ilkley College, on sunny days when I shall be forced to indulge in the higher levels of the same art for my own satisfaction. You will learn your place in the Grand Order of Pecking.'

And so it was with Pete and me.

The Golden Mile

by Andy Cave

The first time I heard about Pete Livesey was in 1986. I was in Cheedale with Dave Green wondering about which E5 to try. I hadn't climbed that grade before and Dave mentioned a route called *The Golden Mile*. Intrigued by the name, I asked what it signified. Being from the Bradford area and part of the Yorkshire climbing scene, Dave was well briefed.

'*Livesey really wanted to do the first ascent of this route, but he was worried his mate might do it before him.*'

'*And?*'

'*When his mate asked if he was climbing the next day, Livesey said no as he was going to Blackpool for the day. Of course he was lying. He came to Cheedale and did the route.*'

This story captured my imagination. I had no idea that such devious tactics were part of the climbing fabric. There was a charm in it all, plus the climb itself looked incredible; a smooth white wall with a small yellow thread at two-thirds height. With hindsight it was a really tough route for breaking into this grade and definitely not a normal entry level E5! Like many people, I got pumped and took a big whipper. But eventually after resting on the ground I got fired up and finished it. I should say 'savoured' as it is a tremendous climb, one of the best limestone wall routes of its grade in the country; technical, committing, strenuous and with a great route name. *Footless Crow* in the Lakes is a Livesey route I have had on my list for a long time, great name and again technical and serious, I look forward to it with relish.

In 1985, the year before, I hitchhiked to the Verdon Gorge after watching Ron Fawcett on the telly. I had a really poor map and it took three days to get there. There was little info about at that time, but Livesey's book was knocking around the campsite: a really futuristic topo at that time, opening up areas that few Brits had heard of.

It was around then, perhaps a bit later, when Livesey was interviewed at a BMC conference in Buxton. The interviewer asked him to show off some of his flexibility and I was awestruck when the guy lifted his leg and placed his foot behind his head. It was the sort of manoeuvre normally reserved for Indian yogis or Chinese circus acts. The word was that he was one of the pioneers of training in the 1970s and influenced many people, Ron obviously. Pete O'Donovan recently said he started to traverse with a weight belt after hearing Livesey was doing this. A non-climber I met through work reckoned he had seen Livesey whilst at Leeds University and said he would do some locking off on beams, slapping for a beam above. This could have been something similar to what the climbers in Sheffield had in the 1980s – a stepping-stone to a sort of campus move.

The evidence shows us that Livesey could easily apply himself to many sports, from canoeing and caving to fell running, and excelled in all of them. It is always vital to view achievements in the historical context. If you look at what he did on rock in the 1970s and remember what 99% of the world's climbers were doing at that time, then you appreciate this guy was way ahead.

My Experience of Time and Space with Pete Livesey

by Frank Kew

'Time' was a precious commodity for Pete. There was never any hanging about. In a running career, which spanned about a dozen mountain marathons in Britain and Europe and countless fell races and orienteering events, I can't ever remember arriving with any more time than to grab the gear and get to the start.

I soon learned that the trick was not to volunteer to drive (Pete didn't like being driven anyway), and to get myself fettled in the car on the way so that I could leap out ready for action as soon as the wheels stopped moving. It was the same at the end of the event; chuck your gear in the car and go.

It was the same with 'space'. Pete had a compressed sense of space. Most of Britain was considered to be no more than a day trip away. An orienteering event somewhere near Oban and back one Sunday wasn't considered worthy of comment. No need to get to Kielder (for a mountain marathon, start time 9am) the night before, just go on the day. On one occasion, Pete went from Malham to Dartmoor for the day to take part in an orienteering event. Somewhere on the M5, on the way back, he got stopped by the police. The conversation went something like this:

'Do you know how fast you were going?'

'Er, no.'

'105 mph.'

(Silence)

'Do you know I've been following you for 10 minutes?'

'No.'

'Do you know why you didn't notice me?"

'No.'

'Because you were too busy eating a sandwich whilst pouring a cup of coffee from that Thermos flask.'

Pete's command of time and space reached its zenith on a couple of weekend trips to Europe. Having finished a mountain marathon in Haute-Savoie (that morning), he navigated, me trailing in his wake, the entire Paris Metro system from south to north in nineteen minutes flat in order to catch the (last) train to Boulogne from the Gare du Nord, a feat only made possible as it didn't involve any exchange of money, because we simply leapt over all the ticket barriers.

A classic compression of time and space (this time on a 'weekend' skiing trip) involved a Thursday evening flight and piss-up in the Bar Nationale in Chamonix, skiing the Vallée Blanche on the Friday morning and somewhere else in the afternoon. The Trois Vallées area on the Saturday, Zermatt on the Sunday, Flaine on the Monday until 4pm, before a minor car shunt in the outskirts of Geneva, an evening flight to Heathrow, and a charge up the M1. At about 2.30am, I sat at home with a beer thinking 'have we just done all that?' Only a couple of days off work, but the most memorable of what we euphemistically called 'staff development' days, one of many I was happy to experience with Pete.

Eulogy on Orienteering

by Tony Thornley

I t normally takes about five years to reach the top in orienteering. It's a sport that needs a lot of experience and maybe ten years to achieve any sort of consistency. Peter won a national event, the top event in orienteering, within eighteen months of starting the sport. He topped the rankings in his age class, M45, which was and still is one of the most competitive classes, within two years. He stayed at or near the top until his illness in 1997 and won many national events. By around 1980, I think he felt he'd done as much as he could in rock-climbing and other people were starting to overtake him. Orienteering was a natural progression for him. Once again it took him to wild terrain and mountainous places. It had the challenge of independent route finding and above all, it had straight competition and that was something that Pete revelled in. He liked the head-to-head competition of the sport.

There was no doubt that his choice of event could be a little calculated. I suspect that like the way he chose his rock routes, he chose terrain that he felt he would do well at, the sort of ground he could orienteer well on, and the Lakes and the Dales became his preferred areas. To quote Pete, '*I try to avoid those races that are covered in Christmas trees and other weeds*'. I think in part, this was because he liked to see the terrain and where he was going. His wins on upland terrain in Britain, like the one at High Dam in the Southern Lake District in 1991, were often by substantial margins and earned him considerable respect from all the competitors in his age class.

He did have off days and one thing I liked about Pete was the fact that he never made excuses. I can recall one occasion when he and I drove together to Mynydd Llangynidr, which is a limestone moor in South Wales. Typically with Pete, this was down in the morning and back in the afternoon. We both had late starts and unfortunately a weather front came in from the west. We both got caught in the mist and then drizzle towards the end of the course and that slowed us down. I finished about the same time as Pete and was glad that I'd used my compass on virtually every leg of the race. At the end, he took off his pebbly glasses, which were absolutely covered in mist, wiped them, grinned and confessed that he'd dropped a bollock by not using a compass. '*Oh well, better next time,*' he said.

I do recall one occasion when he did excuse his performance and this was the Jack Bloor fell race in Ilkley. This was always a needle match between us because even though I was five years his junior he was certainly at least my running speed. On the occasion of this race I somehow managed to beat him by thirty seconds. At the finishing line he turned around to me and claimed that he had been knocked over by a sheep at the beginning of the course. This led to the famous headline in the orienteering magazine, *Rock star rammed by sheep.* Peter and I didn't see each other all that often, but we were kindred spirits. We shared the same sort of philosophy of what orienteering is about. It's about route choice; it's about running and not about hide and seek in weeds and Christmas trees. Above all it's about competitiveness, of which both of us had a considerable streak. We also shared a dry sense of humour and his was something that kept me going on wet days and in miserable conditions.

We made several joint visits to look at prospective orienteering areas in the Dales. He'd ring me up and say, '*How about a short run next Tuesday evening, Tony?*' I can remember one occasion; we went up Great Whernside to prospect it as a potential orienteering course, from the small hamlet of Coniston. It was a misty day; it always was misty when we ran together. I was out with him for about an hour and I was thinking, 'this is pretty good going over the limestone', but then we got into the peat hags and he left me inside about 500 metres. He stopped further on, turned around and gave me a minute to catch him up. '*What do you think of the terrain then, Tony?*' It took me about a minute to get my breath back. I couldn't see the terrain because my eyes were full of sweat and besides you couldn't see anything because of the mist. '*I think this prospecting has been rather a waste of time.*' He just looked at me and laughed. On reflection I think he was just trying to test his fitness out against someone five years younger than he was and someone who he thought really ought to beat him.

Pete disliked committees and the formal side of race organisation, but he could be absolutely relied on to do things and gave massive amounts of support to orienteering competitions. Any orienteering competition in the Dales during the 1990s had Pete Livesey behind it somewhere; planning events and mapping routes, which I think even he would admit I'd had to redo for him quite often. He even sheltered orienteers in his café. He always got on with people and he managed to make things work.

When I was writing a short piece for Pete's funeral oration I wondered what to wear at the eulogy. Pete always preferred the informal and sartorially I think he was the least elegant orienteer I've ever known. When I attended the eulogy I turned out in jacket and tie, but underneath I wore my oldest, smelliest and holiest Helly-Hansen. After the funeral in Skipton, rather than drifting off to the Devonshire Arms with the hundreds that had come to see him off, I went for a run in Pete's memory. As I ran up the hill to Crookrise crag, Pete was there in his old Nora Batty cast off tracksuit bottoms, and as I slowly began to tire I knew jolly well that he'd just keep going.

Travels with a Donkey

by Pete Livesey

I have always held that when I grow old I will look back with continuing pleasure at the adventures we had caving and climbing; not on the hard routes or big caves, but in the epics and adventures with vagabonds that usually had us rolling around in fits of laughter afterwards. Here are one or two such incidents.

BOOM – a plume of water shot 50 feet into the air. Kelly beamed all over his face.

BOOM – the second depth charge went off. Kelly's beam turned black as the expected trout failed to float to the surface.

'*Not enough gelignite*,' explained Kelly as he rummaged through the back of the Transit for his two cardboard boxes containing a hundredweight of high explosive. The third explosion of atomic proportions was curtailed, however, as the bushes around us swayed and parted revealing a large and heavily armed portion of the Greek Army completely surrounding our strategic position on the bridge. I suppose, in retrospect, they had a good reason to capture us; it was probably a mite thoughtless of Kelly to start dropping bombs off a crucial bridge in the military border area between right-wing Greece and lefter-than-left Albania. The other problem was that Kelly was a bandit and looked more like a bandit than most bandits. A week earlier he had disappeared into the dusty, crumbling heart of Ioannina, a mountain-backed military town in northern Greece, with five bottles of whisky. Several hours later he returned grinning all over his bandit-ridden face with a large cardboard box full of gelignite under each arm, forged permission to enter the military zone in his teeth and two full bottles of whisky still in his pockets. Again the whisky came to Kelly's rescue, though I suspect the cavalry commander was still unconvinced that everyone in Britain fishes that way.

Several hours later, we were high in the Timfi d'Oros range at the drivable limit of our van, which I thought was pushing it a bit, but then it wasn't really our van (Kelly had hired it in Salford for the day, three weeks earlier, to move his granny's effects from Dukinfield to New Mills). I actually suspect it was the first time a vehicle larger than a bull donkey had been sighted in the tiny cluster of huts that was Upper Papignon.

Here Kelly produced a sawn-off shotgun; he had vowed back in New Mills that its sole purpose was to shoot the choughs that flew about the top of the pothole we were to descend, loosening rocks on those below. Now, however, he used it effectively to round up all the village donkey drivers so that we could get our ton of gear transported up the mountain. It's a strange thing about donkey drivers that what fits exactly on one man's 12 donkeys will also fit perfectly well on another man's two donkeys, which are, of course, cheaper.

With a kind of friendly prodding action with his shotgun Kelly put me in charge of donkey management because of my previous experience. (I should perhaps mention here that the experience in question consisted of having a father who had once owned a donkey for a few months before it drank the half gallon of bright blue paint that he'd put in its field, with which to paint the fence.)

We hired and paid a Greek who promised us eight stout donkeys for the trip. The following morning he arrived with four things that resembled tatty Alsatians and a fifth animal with one ear and a splint on its back leg.

The Greek proceeded to load the animals with me supervising while the others went off to get drunk. The technique was quite simple, load the animals up with mountains of gear until their legs buckled and they collapsed, then remove one item of equipment and kick the donkey as hard as possible in its knackers to raise it to its feet again. It was barely possible to see the donkey beneath the mounds of ropes, ladders and recently acquired ex-Army tents, but off they staggered, driven forwards by a sharp 'thwack' on their private parts using a specially designed 'donkey thwacker' that all hill Greeks carry.

The donkeys collapsed at regular intervals up the hill, sometimes never to rise again, until the donkey man stopped at the halfway stage, surveyed the hillside strewn with gear, dynamite and dead donkeys and said that enough was enough, that was as far as he went.

The rest of the expedition was boring – carry all the gear up a mountain, carry it all down a hole, bring it out again, carry it down the mountain and so on (except for my illuminating experience down the hole recounted in *Crags* 19) exactly the kind of boring repetitive stuff you read in expedition books. It was on the way back that my interest in the world about was rekindled. I suppose she was in the van when we got back from the orchard we had found miles from anywhere as we crossed the Pindus Mountains. We all piled into the back, trousers and shirts spilling oranges and peaches everywhere, and were screaming off down the road before we had even noticed the beautiful, diminutive sunburnt girl sitting amongst our gear.

'*Who the fuck are you?*' snarled Kelly graciously.

'*Elizabeth,*' was the gentle reply, then as an afterthought, '*and I like screwing.*' She smiled a beckoning Californian smile at everyone but me, about whom she was obviously reserving judgment. Kelly's black eyes bulged as she unwrapped her only luggage, a sort of coloured tea towel containing a full two pound block of hashish.

The expedition drifted aimlessly and happily homeward along an undetermined and certainly illogical route as the block of happiness diminished.

Somewhere in southern Yugoslavia occurred the 'Kelly and the Giant Melon' incident. Admittedly I don't remember too much about it, although I do recall being a central character; I was still rather dazed from lack of blood and the shock of seeing Kelly auctioning two pints of my Rhesus Positive in the streets of Thessaloniki to pay for my share of the petrol.

The van screeched to a halt, the dust and daze subsiding to reveal a large field containing a large central melon.

'*Get it*,' said Kelly. As I staggered towards the melon the field got bigger and bigger and the melon began to grow. Even before I'd reached the giant, the peasants in bullock carts were beginning to take an interest in our activities. Once there, the first thing that was immediately obvious was that I couldn't even lift the thing. I beckoned for help but by the time we were struggling across the field fumbling with a melon nearly a yard wide the peasants were after us. More help! Kelly came and we ran for the vehicle, heaving the giant into the back as the show made a flying getaway.

An hour later we stopped to eat the prize; the knife wouldn't cut it and a saw only managed to win a small piece. It tasted awful but we were determined to eat it. Then Frank, *The Daily Express* man who was exceptionally clever, came back from the front for a look at the yellow giant.

'*It's not a melon*,' he screamed with delight, '*it's a bleeding pumpkin!*' Somewhere in the middle of a road in southern Yugoslavia there probably still lies 98% of a giant, uneatable pumpkin.

By the time Austria came I began to ponder why I wasn't getting my share of Elizabeth and why Kelly was getting more than his. It wasn't that she ignored me, she just observed with a strange look from a distance.

One night the team visited a disco in Spittall; I couldn't go because they'd spent all my blood money on petrol, so I stopped behind in the van. A few minutes later the girl returned with a bottle for me. She edged hesitantly closer letting her shift slide off.

'I'd like to screw a queer.' Who was I to argue? It transpired that Kelly, after he'd had his turn, had told her not to bother with me because I was homosexual and consequently wasn't interested in women. At last I had the laugh.

Four years later I found myself in a similar situation, living 11,000 feet up in the Zagros Mountains of Persia amongst the Kurds (spelt with a K, not a t). Again we were caving and I was penniless, but we had a leader who was the antithesis of Kelly; Judson was such a low profile leader that most of us never met him until the expedition was half over. I had been in the advance party dumped by bus in the desert town of Kermanshah, a genuine dustbowl hell-hole. The rest of the party were to follow when the food and other survival gear arrived by Land Rover.

Our problem in the advance party of four was quite simple; we had to get half a ton of caving gear from Kermanshah across 20 miles of desert to a Kurdish settlement, hire donkeys to get the gear to the cave entrance at 11,000 feet and ladder up the cave. Without food or money.

The first problem seemed a bit daunting. How to get the gear across the desert to the Kurds' donkeys? A promised helicopter, as expected, failed to arrive. Standing on the central island of a short dual carriageway leading out of the town, Glyn, the expedition poet from Dukinfield (I know, that's what I thought) had a brainwave. He just held out his hand and a taxi stopped.

We pointed at the four of us, the half ton of gear, then at the desert. The taxi driver beamed in Arabic and began dementedly throwing our gear into the taxi then persuaded us to climb in after it. We had just over nine pence between us; we thought it only fair to show this to the driver first, then just wait and see how far down the road to the desert this would take us.

Minutes later we were at the roadhead with ten miles of pure desert between us and the Kurds' tents. Instead of stopping, our beaming driver careered off the road into the desert with dust, sand and sagebrush flying everywhere. That taxi went in a dead straight line for ten miles over sand, dry streambeds, rocks, camel skeletons and the like to drop us at the Kurdish encampment. Off went Abdul in a cloud of dust with his nine pence, beaming all over his face.

The donkeys were there, dozens of them all controlled by one impudent little twelve-year old Kurd and his younger sister. He was very efficient, leading all the donkeys up the crag-littered mountain flank on his own after tying them all together. He tied a short rope from one donkey on to the tail of the next one and so on. This Whymper-like arrangement was to have disastrous consequences later. This little Kurd tried to swap his sister for my Swiss Army Knife, then, when that didn't work he upped his offer to his sister and a donkey. I didn't go much for that either so he stole it from me.

Well, the caving ended uneventfully with little of interest happening, apart from a ten-foot long mountain leopard jumping over John and Colin as it passed them going the opposite way on a knife-edge limestone ridge at night (what either party were doing there at that time is a complete mystery to me).

The donkeys returned for the trip down, were loaded up and tied together. At the very top of the steep south flank of the mountain the donkey Kurd decided to take a short cut across a smooth limestone slab. One donkey fell and another six went with it, donkeys and our gear strewing themselves down over hundreds of feet of hillside. The Great Donkey Disaster left much of our gear and several dead donkeys on that hillside for ever, but the Kurds just kept beaming all over their faces.

Returning to Kermanshah there only remained the most dangerous part of the expedition for me, the final meal out and booze up. It was here that Caver X made his first series of attempts to murder me. (I should explain here that he was not without motive, I did owe him £5.36 for the expedition insurance cover.)

Mister X took the expedition to a desert village meal house in the Land Rover and we ate and got plastered. This in itself was quite dangerous, to drink at all in these orthodox Moslem areas was risking being stoned by the Arabs, though we felt fairly safe in numbers. Having taken us out there Mister X decided he wasn't taking me back, but would leave me to the glaring Arabs around. I didn't fancy this so when the Land Rover set off I jumped on to the roof rack.

Halfway back I couldn't resist hanging down over the windscreen and peering in at Mister X. He was furious and immediately drove off the road into a forest of low trees in an attempt to sweep me off the roof; too drunk to argue, I got off, only to grab the towing ball on the back as I saw how close the Arabs were getting. You should try hanging on a greasy ball with your backside bouncing off the desert in the middle of nowhere, being chased by hordes of stone-throwing Arabs.

I survived, but I nearly succumbed in another assassination attempt a week later. I was sure I was in dire need of antibiotics; X, however, had padlocked the medicine chest to induce me to die. Having broken in, in the dark, I gobbled half a bottle of painkillers by mistake.

I don't think they did me any permanent damage.

First published in Crags *21 1979.*

PART FOUR

ASTROMAN

I Feel Rock - South Face of Kuh i Parau

by Pete Livesey

You've not come here for a week-end's cragging. The route is 11,000 feet up a mountain in the middle of the Persian desert, just getting there is about as difficult as getting into Yorkshire. If the inscrutable Eastern customs officers don't stop you, or the swarms of Kurdish brigands brewing up on glowing camel-shit cakes don't overpower you on the slopes of the mountain, then the 10-foot tabby cats called mountain leopards will certainly have you on top.

But the route is something else; a slender, almost vertical 1,500-foot pillar of limestone, featureless from a distance but, on closer inspection, revealing a texture like Aero chocolate. Rough little bubbles that allow you to claw the rock like a cat.

Once you've learnt the clawing technique, the climbing becomes superb, just pitch after pitch of seemingly runner-less rock, and you simply claw your way up it.

The situation is a spacewalk; 10,000 foot below, like a relief map, lies the barren, ridged desert, stretching away to the oil rigs of the Persian Gulf ghosting up from the haze.

FA South Face of **Kuh i Parau** *1,500 feet HVS P Livesey/ I Edwards 1972 Zagros Mountains, Iran.*

First Published in Crags *number 7 1976*

Cold Play

by John Barker

t was dark, it was cold, and I was stiff, tired and uncomfortable. I was perched on a cramped narrow ledge high above the valley of the Arve looking down to the lights of Chamonix twinkling far below. I had just spent the night bivi'd a few hundred feet up the *Frendo Spur* poised ready for an early start on the route. There was one slight problem. I had a Livesey on my head! My neck was aching and making me even more uncomfortable. '*Try to keep quite still, John,*' urged Livesey. '*I'm getting to a critical point.*' I was worried it would all go terribly wrong and that I would finish up disfigured or something worse. '*Steady kid, nearly there, another few seconds should do it.*' Perhaps I was going to be okay after all. '*Right, all done.*' A wave of relief swept over me. The brew was ready and Livesey could at last take the stove off my head! Yes, team Barker and Livesey were about to engage with the *Frendo Spur*.

The *Frendo Spur* has a unique attraction in that one can take a téléphérique to near the foot of its start and, on completion, a short scramble to another téléphérique from the Aiguille-Du-Midi back down to Chamonix.

My old mate Livesey had engaged me, over a few beers in the Bar National, to go, as he put it, to play in the snow with him!

'*You see, John, you're the alpinist and I'm the rock climber, so we make a good team. Pick us a good route!*' said the Great Mr Livesey. Plan A popped into my mind; it was a no-brainer, had to be the *Frendo*!

'*Right pal, a quick route and back down to the valley for afternoon...
er - beer!*' I pronounced

Livesey's alpine gear consisted of flowery shirt, a threadbare fibre
pile, an aging duvet that had long surrendered its down, and a pair of
rusty old crampons backed up by a badly battered ice axe. I couldn't
complain too much as the axe that I was using was also a rusty old
Aschenbrener that had held up a rose bush for the past twenty years
in a friend's garden.

I had been disturbed from my slumbers, during the bivi, several
times by the sound of falling rocks and ice. Livesey reckoned that it
was staff at the Midi station emptying the dustbins.

Refreshed after the foul brew that we had concocted, we were off
into the magical dawn light. Pete led off up the initial rock buttress,
which occupied the first half of the route and climbing mostly together,
belaying only occasionally on awkward bits, we gained height rapidly.
Runners were a rare luxury in any Livesey itinerary.

The sun was nearly up by the time we reached the top of the initial
buttress, and I was breathing heavily with the exertion of the pace set
by Livesey. '*You're getting old, Barker!*' said Pete. I was inclined to
agree, as I was almost five years older than him.

We sat down on the spacious ledge at the top of the buttress where
I was privy to a display of crampon fitting that would have caused
the great Heckmair to turn in his grave. The crampons were in fact
securely strapped to Pete's bendy boots. Ten out of ten! Minor detail!
I felt I'd better dispense a bit of advice '*Pete, I think the spikes are
supposed to point downwards into the snow, not upwards into the soles
of your boots.*'

'*I can see why I never really got into this snow and ice lark,*'
observed Pete.

He learns fast though does the lad. Soon we were fit for purpose
and addressed ourselves to the task in hand. The snow ridge leading

up to the final Rognon of the *Frendo Spur* is one of the purest and most finely situated that one could possibly imagine. The exposure on either side is jaw dropping and awesome. The ridge itself curves in an exquisite manner upwards towards the heavens. With a lordly wave of his hand Pete indicated this next section and said, '*After you, Mr Guide!*' I led off up the ridge keeping an eye on the 'novice', but this lad learns fast, as previously observed! We dispensed with belays and quickly gained height, covering the several hundred feet of the ridge at a spanking pace. At one point I paused and took an amazing shot of Livesey far below me, poised on the ridge, basked in sunshine. A view of him that very few get to see! I began to think he might have the makings of an Alpinist after all. Soon however we reached the rocks of the upper Rognon and the situation changed radically.

At first, steady mixed climbing, moving together, leading into the final section where more ice appeared, covering the rocks with a thin film, which made upward movement precarious, to say the least. '*I think prudence might be the strict order of the day here, Pete,*' I observed.

'*Who is she?*' asked Livesey.

'*You know, that classic Whymper quote, you prat!*'

'*It didn't do them much good, did it!*' replied Pete.

He took a reasonably secure belay; I set off, still in crampons, up the severe, steep ice-covered rocks. It was taking a serious turn for the worse from here on. I made steady but precarious progress over the next rope length and found a safe belay in a small alcove. Pete eventually joined me looking mightily impressed! '*That was worth a pint or two,*' he exclaimed.

'*Another pitch should see us out onto the final snow slope,*' I pointed out. '*I'll be out of sight around the edge of the Rognon, but I'll give three long tugs for you to start climbing*'. Off I climbed up and left-wards onto mixed ground again. Pete soon disappeared from sight.

Eventually I came out onto a 55 degree snow slope and felt happier. Not for long though. I suddenly heard a loud crunching noise and a shudder seemed to pass through the snow slope that I was on. Adrenalin coursed through my body. In that split second I thought of Pete and Bob, mates who had died on the Matterhorn in February earlier that year. I felt that the slope might avalanche at any second. I gave three long tugs on the rope and front pointed madly upwards towards the summit. The rope quickly became tight; I continued surging upwards against the pull, like Road Runner on ice. Adrenalin drove me on and upwards. I was conscious of Livesey's weight on the rope, it made no difference, I simply continued to plough upwards. I reached the point where the slope gradually ran out and the angle eased, but I still continued, until I was well back from the top of the slope on the very edge of the ridge. I buried my axe and hauled on the ropes furiously. Eventually Pete's head appeared over the convex curve of the slope, arms and legs going like windmills, ploughing up the snow in front of him, as I dragged him upwards to safety. He lay panting and gasping for breath in the snow, literally speechless for a while, and what he eventually said was totally unrepeatable.

After I explained my rather desperate actions, a mollified Pete looked me directly in the eyes and said, '*I've had enough of this playing in the snow game, let's just fuck off to the Vercors!*'

We wandered up to the Midi and took the next available téléphérique down to Chamonix. By 3pm, we were enjoying the first of many ice-cold beers and working on plan B.

We travelled to the Vercors, did lots of incredible rock routes and indirectly discovered the Verdon!

The Verdon

by John Sheard and Pete Livesey

John Sheard

The first reference in this country to the Verdon Gorge appeared in *The Alpine Journal* of 1970 when the routes of *Voie des Enrages* and *La Demande* were recorded. These climbs, made in 1968, were done Alpine style by acclaimed French mountaineers who clearly regarded the 300-metre high walls as fully justifying that approach. I'd first got a hint of the place from Al Rouse who in turn had heard a rumour from his Cambridge University days. No one we knew had even heard of the name and Pete was determined to have a look.

That look proved to be the start of many visits over the next few years as we explored, climbed and became acquainted with the style of French climbing then prevalent. Clearly there was no lack of talent in France, it's just that, possibly as a natural progression from climbing on high, dangerous Alpine routes, the use of a peg for aid or resting was seen as normal and legitimate. Pete was not about that and adopted a style familiar at home; all free if possible and the occasional peg clipped only for protection. Verdon routes at that time were largely free of bolts and were very similar to those in Yorkshire; apart from being very much longer, on better rock, subject to the romance of Haute Provence and climbed in perfect weather with the scent of wild herbs, and wine to follow.

I'm not given to record keeping and can recall little of the moves, but I clearly remember the quality of the Verdon routes and the highlights of our ascents. The unknown and scary *Luna Bong* abseil, the race up the bolt ladder on *Voie des Enrages*, and the sudden feeling of relative incompetence when Pete declared that I was leading the next pitch remain fresh in my mind. The unusual surprise of the artistic graffiti on the top pitch of *Dingomaniaque* and the magic of *Eperon Sublime*, space walking on a pillar of immaculate rock. Later, when he was not around, the technical climbing of the aptly named *Miroir du Fou*, which he would have dismissed for its bolts and ridiculous location above the road tunnel. The hard climbing of *L'Estemporanee* on the Falaise de l'Eycharme is especially memorable for the snake which came sliding down the rope on the crux pitch; I was never sure whether Pete had something to do with that. Cold, afternoon beers in the Chalet Malines when the climbing was over for the day and the speed trials could be put aside. Those are the bits which remain fresh after all these years.

Pete was so bloody fast that it was pointless trying to take the lead. Fast, but competent and safe; to try to emulate his style bordered on the dangerous or suicidal. We rarely started those long routes in the Verdon before 2pm and we'd be back in the bar at tea time. How fast we were at that time was brought home to me when years later I did *Ula* with Paul Nunn and Gill Price. We set off typically at two o'clock, but found ourselves benighted. If I'd been with Pete we'd have been in the bar for five. Even though Pete invariably led, I could follow anything that he could do. The main thing to Pete, in fact to both of us, was it remained a combined effort and definitely a shared partnership.

What also remains clear in my memory, is the first, uncomprehending feeling of awe we felt when coming round the last bend on the road from Castellane to be confronted with the chasm that split the limestone upland of Haute Provence; the Canyon of the Verdon.

Turquoise-green water, giving the name to the Verdon River, winding through blue-grey walls undercut with orange and yellow. The ensuing exploration when just finding the crag was an achievement, and the feeling, however false, that we were the first visitors into a lost land. I remember too, the occasional day when we simply wandered through the gorge probing further and further, following faint footpaths, and sometimes not.

Information was sparse; there were no camp sites, other than the overcrowded tourist ones outside the gorge area. We camped in splendid isolation in the woods at Point Sublime; an idyllic hidden site with firewood aplenty and water from the restaurant on the road higher on the hillside. We played cards with rashers of bacon as the stakes. Pete lost all his in a first half-hour of reckless betting, but still managed bacon for breakfast on every morning throughout our stay.

After the first few visits someone caught on; dug an access road, built a fireplace and an evil-smelling lavatory. It was the death of that idyll as tourists and their litter started to arrive. We moved further into the woods and met a stray American, which was unusual in those days. Eric was working in Grenoble and seemed to know the territory. He it was who pointed to the Falaise de l'Escales and the existence, if it could be found, of an abseil, which would give access to the upper cliff. In our earlier explorations deep in the gorge, we'd ignored the most impressive walls of the Verdon, assuming them to be the preserve of the aid climber. Pete pointed me over the crest of an overhanging face which we hoped was the right spot, there being no sight of an *in-situ* belay. What confidence I retained on that first descent into nowhere was the result of the knowledge that, of the two of us, he was the only one with the skill to affect a rescue if we'd chosen the wrong place.

On a future visit, at the insistence of the locals, we moved onto the football pitch at La Palud, later to become a paying camp site. In those early days the area around the village was empty. We met no climbers, other than Eric, and every day was an adventure. Find a path, descend into the depths, deeper and deeper with the certain knowledge that if it was the wrong place we were faced with a long, sun-baked stagger back up to the road. No hotels, two bars, one restaurant and a small shop where the ancient owners spoke with an accent even the locals couldn't understand. No police, since they never proceeded beyond Castellane and Moustiers at either end of the gorge, and shotguns which were the first response late at night to a traveller's knock on the door. Basque separatists in hiding, working at the bar, and Francois and his family always with a warm welcome. No wonder Pete and I, and later other climbing friends, came back time after time.

An official visit of BMC-sponsored climbers in the late 1970s, hosted by the FFM, was a turning point. Ron Fawcett, Roger Baxter-Jones, Dave Hope (always addressed by Pete as 'Bob'), Gill Price, Pete and myself were accommodated in La Palud to climb and dine with leading French activists. Our hosts saw the style of our climbing, and particularly that of Pete and Ron when they paired up to make a substantially free ascent of *Pichenibule*, probably the most important route in the Verdon at that time. It was clear that our French hosts were accomplished climbers and as their style changed in the following years, so the numbers of free routes of ever increasing difficulty rapidly followed, making the Verdon, for a time, the premier destination outside America. We learned also that Easter was not the best time of year to visit the Verdon; rain and snow were not uncommon but even that could be interesting as Pete and Ron walked the top rail of the fence around the most exposed belvedere of the gorge above the Falaise de l'Escales. A wet, slippery three-inch pipe, one eye on the tarmac road three metres below, and the other on the river, four hundred vertical metres below. Not for the faint-hearted, tourists rushed back to their cars, sheltering small children from this act of lunacy.

Later still, bolts would appear as the Verdon became, perhaps, the premier climbing destination of Europe, but by that time we were well gone.

Pete Livesey takes up the narrative

In the early 1970s climbers made a habit of fleeing the bad weather and police raids in Chamonix for the gentler, prettier and more amenable limestone of the Vercors and other big limestone escarpments in southern France. Even then there were moves afoot by both French and British climbers to attempt free ascents of traditional Alpine style routes. Free ascents were often faster than aid ascents and for once it was the French Alpiniste who was embarrassed by lack of speed on the routes.

One such 'speed' incident would ultimately lead myself and John Sheard to 'discover' the Verdon Gorge and its climbing possibilities unknown outside southern France at that time. Our journey of 'discovery' actually started on a cliff called La Pelle situated up the Chaudiere Pass above the Drôme valley. On this occasion I was climbing with John Barker and after a night and morning wine-tasting session we arrived at the foot of the Pelle at 3.30 in the afternoon. The guidebook time said 20 hours, so we figured two hours was enough – 10 minutes a pitch. After an hour we were two pitches below the top and stuck behind a French pair. They asked us what time we had started and we said, '3.30.'

'An hour after us,' they replied, disconcerted at our having caught them. The trouble was they had started at 2.30 in the morning and had been on the route 14 hours. When they realised this they let us through and later that night met us in a bar in Die where they advised us to go to the Verdon Gorge; 'Where the real climbs are.' Three years later John Sheard and I, together with the up and coming female team of Lawrence and Price, made it and so began the exploration of free climbing possibilities that would make it an area to rival Yosemite as a Mecca for visiting rock-climbers.

The Verdon Gorge is a mighty rift superimposed on to a twisted limestone landscape, 20 miles long and up to 2,000-feet deep. This place has primeval grandeur, without doubt, but everywhere the herbaceous fragrance of Provence drifts, the sun is Rivieran and old France exists; crumbling history halted. Its exploration by modern man was later, and took longer, than that of its American counterpart. Strange that, because the Romans bridged the river as it is swallowed by the gorge, and Napoleon passed by frequently, but probably hastily. The first modern exploration was made in 1905 by the renowned caver, Edouard Martel, who traversed the gorge floor, sometimes swimming or rafting beneath cavernous overhangs between 1,000-foot cliffs. More recently tourist paths, constructed by the TCF, follow tunnels and ledges to avoid the wet sections. The complete walk through the gorge is no mean feat today, though, two days and nineteen crossings of the river being required. Several escape routes now make the journey less committing, however. Abundant firewood and huge sandy cave like shelters ('baumes') make gorge dwelling a pleasure, the atmosphere and relative solitude of the gorge floor being an experience not to be missed.

Of all the places in the world I have visited, here I would be least surprised by an encounter with prehistoric beasts. Great yellow arched and pillared caves seem only temporarily vacated by something very large, a yesterday creature out nibbling a few treetops from the gorge's luxuriant foliage. How, in environmentally unconscious France, is this place still like it is? See this and you realise that Yosemite Valley really is Disneyland and not just a relative. There is no answer, but where John Muir leaves a trail of failure, the Verdon is almost without need of control and almost without blemish. Yosemite can be enjoyed but one cannot love it; an affair with Le Grand Canyon and its medieval culture is hopelessly romantic.

National emphasis in French climbing is always placed on Alpinism. Perhaps it is not surprising, then, that the English-speaking climber has not noticed a subtle tide of change in French rock-climbing circles, and is not aware of the tremendous potential for high quality rock-climbing in France. Although crag climbing takes place on all sizes of cliff, it is undoubtedly on the 1,000 to 2,000-feet high walls that France has the most to offer. Traditional areas such as the Vercors are fairly well-known to the visiting Alpinist, being an excellent bad weather retreat from the Alps. But here Alpine techniques are evident. Dolomite style routes on Dolomite style rock are climbed in Alpine fashion with the maximum number of pegs and minimum contact with the sometimes excellent rock. Some de-pegging has taken place recently, but removing twisted soft steel pegs from limestone is a laborious and rarely completed task.

Climbers from Nice and Marseilles were first to exploit the potential of the gorge in the mid-1960s. Free climbing as an enjoyable activity in itself was accepted at Les Calanques and Baou de Saint Jeannet near Nice. This attitude was brought fresh to the unclimbed Verdon, where the superb rock had perhaps inhibited artificial ascents. The outlying cliffs above the gorge were first to be explored; generally lower and less appealing than those in the gorge itself, they were, however, accessible, and the lines were obvious from the road.

Michel Dufranc and later Francois Guillot were responsible for many of these earlier lines on the outskirts of the gorge, but as yet they had not ventured into 'big momma' herself. Quite surprising, because the cliffs within the gorge are quite evidently bigger and made of better rock than those outside. The steepness and singularity of line would have been quite intimidating, however, until in the summer of

1968, northerners, Bodin, Cordier, Moch and Richard set the scene alight with the stunning *Voie des Enrages*. Hard and long, the route was sieged over several days on the 1,100-foot overhanging face of La Falaise du Duc, guarding the entrance to the narrowest and gloomiest part of the gorge. The approach involved Tyrolean traverses and lassoings to cross the river, and the climb itself was a masterpiece of route finding.

Perhaps stirred into action by the outsiders, the locals moved into the gorge and immediately came up with a superb line on what was to become the gorge's best cliff, the Falaise de l'Escales. The *Voie de la Demande*, climbed in October 1968 by Joel Coqueugniot and Francois Guillot, followed a singular and sustained crack line for 15 pitches, never desperate but always superb. The gates to the gorge were opened.

By 1970, new routes were being climbed on four separate cliffs within the confines of the gorge itself, and nearly all proved to be of high quality, on excellent fingery rock or following dramatic jam cracks.

A 'Verdon style' developed, distinct from normal French style, pegs on belays were left in place, but few were left on the pitches themselves. Nuts had appeared, were adopted as a sensible addition to protection techniques, and were found to be ideally suited to the kind of climbing the gorge had to offer. Routes were, therefore, never subjected to the gradual proliferation of pegs found in other areas of France. Protection, both pegs and nuts, was generally used to rest on, apparently without prejudicing the 'freeness' of the climb. Even this tactic has been called into doubt in the last couple of years, however, with increasing interchange of ideas between French climbers and those to the west. It is the French themselves, of course, who deserve the credit; their adoption in so short a time of an essentially foreign style of ascent is a considerable achievement. It is to be hoped that visitors are aware of this and do not, by their actions, aid degeneration into over-pegged routes.

The real boom year for the Verdon was 1973, with literally dozens of new routes going up and a further six cliffs opened up for exploration. Fewer sections of pure aid appeared on new routes and the sections of V and VI multiplied. The occasional aided *tour de force* appeared but these routes usually inhabited the few areas of bad rock, leaving aesthetic lines for free routes, like *Luna Bong, Necronomicon* and *Triomphe d'Eros*. Peculiarly British techniques of abseil descents to garden and inspect routes have been used on one or two of the latest high standard routes. At the same time first free ascents of the slightly older climbs are being made and, perhaps more significantly, are being acknowledged.

The current scene is one of a climbing area with some 150 foot long climbs, mostly of a quality that would ensure a 'classic' tag elsewhere. Comparison has to be made with such Californian classics as *East Buttress* and *Direct North Buttress* on Middle Cathedral Rock, *North-East Buttress* on Upper Cathedral, or *Astroman* and the *Chouinard-Herbert* at the upper end of the grade. In every case the Verdon routes compare well; the quality of line and the enjoyable nature of the climbing seem, in fact, to give them the edge over many Yosemite counterparts.

New routes like *Pichenibule* and Jean-Claude Droyer's *Triomphe d'Eros* sport unrelenting quality and sustained climbing, much of it at 5.10 level with the occasional 5.11 crux. Virtually free ascents (one or two points of aid) of routes like *Peril Rouge* and *Voie du Roumagaou* provide sustained 5.9 experiences with the odd 5.10 move to overcome previously aided sections. Fanciful route names, common for decades now to English-speaking climbers, are being used in the Verdon; another sign of the area's divorce from the traditional French Alpinism.

Luna Bong, is a powerful diedre line with an unbroken bulging

The magnificent nose of El Capitan, Yosemite Valley.
Photograph by John Sheard.

Left: This photo by John Sheard shows the rock architecture of Yosemite Valley. The Royal Arches are in the foreground. Washington Column and home to *Astroman* is the defined pillar in the centre of the shot.
Photograph by John Sheard.

Below:
Pete Livesey seconding the *Enduro Corner* pitch during their one day ascent of *Astroman* in 1977.
Photograph by Ron Fawcett.

Top: Ron Fawcett out foxing
Livesey by stringing two pitches
together to ensure Pete ended up
leading the dreaded *'Harding Slot'*
pitch.
Photograph by Pete Livesey.

Right: Pete heading up towards
the *'Harding Slot'*.
Photogtraph by Ron Fawcett.

Left, top and bottom: Geoff Birtles and Ron Fawcett waiting for the train, Yosemite 1977.

Below right: Gill Price and John Sheard in Camp 4, Yosemite Valley 1977.

Photographs by Geoff Birtles.

Livesey Soloing *New Diversions*, Yosemite Valley.
Photograph by Geoff Birtles.

New Diversions guidebook description: *"One of the harder and more classic 5.10a climbs anywhere. The climb is sustained from bottom to top and involves truly wild and committing moves. At the crux, tie off and wrestle large spaced-out knobs. They're positive but it's not obvious how to use them. This climb definitely favours the taller leader. The anchor is slightly sketchy slings wrapped around the base of a block. Save a 4" piece to back them up. Most climbers rappel from here with one 60m rope to the Burst of Brilliance anchors or with two 50m ropes to the ground."* Not Mr Livesey, he continued to the top and then climbed down the slab to the right.

Left: John Sheard climbing *Wheat thin* 5.10c, Cookie Cliff, Yosemite.
Photograph from Sheard collection.

Below:
The Brits doing the Merced Layback, Yosemite Valley 1977. Pete Livesey, John Sheard, Jill Lawrence, Gill Price, Alec Livesey. Ron Fawcett on the lilo.
Photograph by Geoff Birtles.

Pete Livesey on the classic *Crack–a-Go-Go,* Cookie Cliff, Yosemite, mid 1970s.
Photograph from Ken Wilson collection

Livesey's magnificent 1974 route *Right Wall* E5 6a, Dinas y Gromlech.
Climber Martin Atkinson.
Photograph by Bernard Newman.

600-foot crack up its centre; it provides the normal descent route to reach the foot of routes leaving the Terrasse Mediane. Four or five airy swinging rappels from a ledge twenty feet below the plateau, mostly using horizontal trees as stances, lead one on to the terrace just right of a little pillar.

Luna Bong starts up the pillar but soon enters the magnetic crack line, which it follows at 5.8 and 5.9 for four sustained pitches. The fifth pitch follows the crack to its abrupt end at a three-foot roof. You are stuck on poor jams on 5.10 ground below the roof; the next move straddles the border of the improbable and the impossible. Three feet above the roof a pine tree corkscrews outwards. A dynamic lunge from an undercut incredibly ends up with a hand closing satisfyingly around the corkscrew. Feet fly off, a horizontal bar move and that's it. Ten more feet and the top.

While mechanically jamming up the lower pitches of *Luna Bong*, we could not help noticing the steep slender pillar on the right. The odd bit of threaded tape told us the route had gone, but the climbing looked so enticing we couldn't forget it.

A year later, with Ron Fawcett, I was abseiling down *Luna Bong* to the traverse line at the top of *Luna Bong's* second pitch that led to the rib. Our French guide, Bernard Gorgeon, sat chuckling on *Luna Bong*. The route, *Necronomicon*, he said was V and free. The climbing was incredible, exposed wall climbing that only Verdon limestone can offer. I found myself splayed out on the rib involved in hard 5.10 thinness trying desperately to make it look like 'V and free' for the watching Bernard; no way. For 100 strenuous feet it was 5.10 and solid, passing peg-scarred holes from the only previous ascent. I kept shouting: 'V and free' at the delirious Bernard, who had tactically declined to follow the route, saying we were too slow.

A tiny foothold at 160 feet was the stance. Ron followed finding it as 'V and free' as I did, then whooped his way up the other 150 feet of this incredible rib. Screaming, 'V and effing free.' He made an ungradable lunge from a position built on one hundred 5.10 moves. I would swap a dozen *Great Walls* for a rib like that to beanstalk out of Snowdon.

Later we free climbed the Jean-Claude Droyer classic *Triomphe d'Eros* with one 5.11 pitch and several of 5.10. The last pitch was 5.10 and climbed a super sheet in the same vein as *Necronomicon*. 'Five and free,' we proclaimed mercilessly at the top.

Extracts from articles which first appeared in Mountain *61 1978 and* Crags *24 1980, edited by Mark Radtke.*

The First French 7a

by Jean-Claude Droyer

I n the years following my discovery of climbing in Great Britain in October 1973, I felt that I knew Peter Livesey even though I hadn't actually met him. Pete wasn't at the 1973 BMC meeting, the event that was to have such a major impact on my life in making me realise that free climbing was the way forward for the sport. At the time I was avidly reading *Mountain* magazine, to find objectives for my future trips across the Channel. And it was thus that I discovered Peter Livesey, his characteristic face and silhouette in the photos, and his action and performances in the text. I read about his first ascents, *Right Wall* of Cenotaph Corner, *Footless Crow*, *Wellington Crack* among others, these routes were my dreams and inspired me to progress. *Mountain* also revealed his training methods and 'tactics' used to make these first ascents, some of them very controversial. A pioneer often draws the wrath of more traditional climbers, but it seemed to me that Livesey was breathing new life into a British climbing scene that was perhaps lacking in inspiration in the early 1970s. Months passed and I made two or three trips to Britain to practise using nuts 'clean climbing', but I did not get the chance to meet the man himself. In France I actively sought out free climbing that would push the level of difficulty both on my local crags (Saussois and Burgundy) and elsewhere, in particular at Buoux, and in the Verdon. 1976 was the year of the first 6c in France and the following year, the French Mountain Federation (FFM) decided to organise a French-English climbing meet in the Verdon Gorge, then in a golden era. And who was to represent British climbing at this event? Peter Livesey himself, along with a young climber who Pete had taken under his wing, Ron Fawcett.

It was in Paris, at the FFM offices that I finally met Pete and he was exactly how I had imagined him, athletic, enthusiastic and full of energy. Although Pete had already visited and appreciated several French crags his excitement at going to climb in the Verdon with the best French climbers was obvious. I too was happy to be sharing climbing time with the best of British climbing. At a time when a free climbing ethic, which avoided the use of any form of aid, was cause for much incomprehension and scepticism in France, Pete Livesey was a passionate ally for the cause. We left for the Verdon with Gill Price and John Sheard in the English clan.

Obviously Pete's objective was to try to free climb the prestigious routes that had originally required some 'peg-pulling' or aid. After warming up on one or two classics, he and Ron chose to try *Triomphe d'Eros* on the Falaise de L'Escales and, as I had done the first ascent, I was to accompany them (with Robert Mizrahi). The two Brits overcame the obstacle with mastery and, inspired by their example, I also managed to do it free. They also freed *Solanuts*, far from easy.

That evening English and French climbers talked passionately and free climbing was often the topic of conversation. Of course, I had been promoting free climbing for a while in France, but because of the north-south rivalry, and also it must be said, the pretension of the Marseille and Auxois climbers, who thought all the southern crags (including the Verdon) belonged to them, I was mainly preaching in the desert. The 'southerners' were more inclined to be convinced by the English arguments, especially after their astounding Verdon demonstration. Pete and Ron's high point was to free climb *Pichenibule* (except, of course, for the overhang, still futuristic for 1976); with the hardest pitch yielding to Ron's determination.

Livesey's presence at this French-English meet in the Verdon was a major factor in helping other climbers realise the considerable potential for free climbing offered by the Escales cliff. From 1980 the optimism of the English, resolutely sporting, influenced future first ascensionists who started to believe in the possibility of numerous new routes, often bolted from above. Pete and Ron's example was also a source of inspiration and motivation for Patrick Berhault, who had left his mark on the Verdon at the end of the 1970s. And for *Pichenibule* the circle was completed when Patrick freed the famous overhang at the beginning of 1981.

But Livesey's influence outside Great Britain was not limited to the Verdon. In the Dolomites for example, he was also at the origin of the freeing of some of the traditional routes on Tofane and the Cima Scotoni. In 1977 he left Le Saussois, which he'd particularly wanted to visit, after making a substantially free ascent of *L'Ange* and also convinced that the adjacent *L'Echelle* overhang could be free'd. Following his visit I was sufficiently encouraged to make the first free ascent of *L'Echelle*; the FIRST French 7a. The pace accelerated in 1980 as Jacob Laurent made a free ascent of *L'Ange* at F7b.

Unfortunately, I did not see Pete again for many years. He did not attend the big festival in Konstein, Germany in the spring of 1981, the first public event dedicated to sport climbing, and it was Ron Fawcett I met there. The same Fawcett who, profiting from Pete's drive, continued to considerably push the limits of difficulty, in particular on the English limestone crags at the heart of the island.

Despite the passing years, the memory of times spent with Pete did not fade and that is why in 1994, on a climbing trip to Yorkshire limestone, I was determined to visit him. Pete and his wife were running a café in the village of Malham, not far from the crags, and our meeting was a special moment for us all. Pete had not climbed for several years, but he still ran, a sport he had always pursued; he congratulated me on having done some of Malham's star routes. Pete seemed very well, but it would be the last time that I saw him.

Kindly translated from French into English by Sharon Horry

I Feel Rock - L'Ange (The Angel)

by Pete Livesey

I f you think you've ripped off the French in Chamonix, then it's only fair to let them do it to you, they've got a special place for it, the Saussois.

It's just Stoney Middleton with French-speaking routes; sort of smoother, more subtle, more elegant. The French will laugh at your efforts to climb the routes in English. You see, the French still regard a fifi hook for a rest as free climbing, while you end up with dislocated fingers after failing to make decent hooks out of them. It's worth being sandbagged to climb in English, though, just for the experience of swinging up highly overhanging and improbable walls on superb hidden fingerjugs, or to be confronted suddenly on an overhang with a thread that you can crawl into for a rest.

L'Ange is the ultimate test of these techniques; nowhere is there a poor hold, just steep sustained strenuosity up a highly improbable line. Protection is superb except at the start of the overhanging section, which is de-pegged. Thirty feet above and fifteen feet out in space is a large jugular thread, ready threaded.

Just rush up this technical steep bit until good holds start you curving backwards up the roof. In such a haven of runners, that section is truly exciting. Next come two or three resting pegs, though it could be done without if you hadn't been to the pub the night before. That's the other place the French are out to rip you off, but we beat 'em.

When the landlord realises you're English and not just noddy

Frogs, he produces a free round of strong green liquor from a bottle wrapped in a towel. When you've drunk it, he whips off the towel to reveal a pickled python, and you're supposed to rush off to be sick.

Not so our team. The landlord's jubilant garlic grin turning sour as Sheard ordered two beers and another round of snake juice, s'il vous plaît. The angel, it seems, is no match for the devil.

Le Saussois, Yonne, France 250 feet, XS (E3 with three aid points on roof)
FFA Jacob Laurent

First Published in Crags *number 7 1976.*

Only the Best Route in the World

by Pete Livesey

I t was just after midday, temperature touching 110 degrees and no shade. White bleached rock and a few scrawny ebony-hard manzanita bushes with nowhere to go, nothing to do but tear at passing legs. Yesterday had been 110 degrees as well, and as far back as I could remember it was the same; but today I was happy. Unable to talk, with a throat like the cracked, flaky bark of yellow pine, slithering blind and carelessly down dusty gullies, but I was very pleased with myself, and a little bit with Ron as well.

It was over; *Astroman*, we'd done it. It was the best, better because I was quite unprepared for its architecture and uncompromising colour scheme applied to perfect rock. Clean cut and glassy yellow, rippled but smooth.

In the spring of 1973 big walls were still big walls in Yosemite, with all the hauling and aiding that goes with it, but the concept of a free big wall route was alive in Camp 4 and, more particularly, in the 'Stonemasters' camp site. The Stonemasters were a predominantly Los Angeles group of high school drop-outs, with a few PhD students for class. Torn souls living in two worlds; chocolate milk for breakfast, immediately followed by vast quantities of various illegal substances.

But they could climb, and the East Face of Washington Column was surprisingly the big wall they chose to do. Surprising, because it was so much steeper and more horrendous (an American word meaning anything) looking than the other possibilities, such as the

South Face on the same mountain, the North West Face of Half Dome or the *Chouinard-Herbert* route on The Sentinel. But the East Face was undoubtedly the best line, an uncompromising series of cracks shooting straight for the summit following a recess in a magnificent overhanging prow.

John Long, Ron Kauk and John Bachar sieged the first free ascent; yo-yoing was employed. But the result was a route so incredibly sustained that it was incomparable with any other existing route. At a time when there existed only fifteen 5.11 pitches in the Valley, *Astroman* (as it became known) in its fourteen pitches, had no less than six of 5.11 and five of 5.10.

Over the next two years the route had three more ascents, all employing seconds who jumared rather than climbed, but the last two of these ascents, in the spring of 1977, were remarkable in that each took only six hours. However, Ron Kauk and John Bachar, the two leaders, had prior knowledge of the route, which must have aided their considerable achievement.

The summer of 1977 found Ron Fawcett and me eating sherbert ice cream down by the river most days; it was too hot for much else. Some days Ron was missing, that was when he was out stalking nude female sunbathers. His technique was as polished as that of any naturalist, starting out 200 yards away in the morning he would edge imperceptibly closer, inches at a time. By noon his hot breath would be wafting around her nipples. Around the middle of the afternoon he'd shout, 'Ow do,' in her ear, a greeting completely unintelligible to most young Americans, whose entire vocabulary consists of the phrases, 'Oh really', 'Right on', and the occasional, 'Have a good day', when real oratory is called for.

I know it sounds a bit like John Wayne, but neither of us spoke about doing *Astroman*. We just knew it was there and we had to do it, until one day we just got together and set off. We left in the evening to walk up to the foot of the face and bivvy below it; a dawn start on the rock was essential to avoid as much of the midday heat as possible.

We stocked up at the village store with six packs of beer for the evening meal and six packs of Seven-Up for the dawn start, and caught the bus to the Ahwahnee Hotel below the Royal Arches. The bus was full of incongruous dinner-jacketed or long-dressed people going to dinner in the colonial opulence of the Ahwahnee. At least we felt more suitably dressed for a change, sawn-off jeans and rock-tattered vests being much more suited to scuffing around the valley floor dust than white dinner suits and striped dresses with stars in your hair.

A mile of trail led towards the face; halfway along in gathering dusk Ron spied his tea, a half-eaten melon lying in the dust. He ran for it only to find himself racing three cuddly little bear cubs for the same prize. Ron's fatherly instincts took over and he made to stroke the tiny two hundred-weight balls of fur that gobbled his melon. Now, I'd read all the anti-bear pamphlets and I knew that it was not very wise to get between a mother and its cub, let alone three cubs. I'd also seen the sky darken as a huge black mother bear lumbered up to Ron.

The cubs shot off and ran up the nearest tree they could get their paws around. Mother bear hunched for the attack, but Ron, with superb presence of mind and one eye still on the melon, held up his hand and said, '*Nay lass, it'll be reight*.' This seemed to impress the bear, which wandered off to find the tree containing its cubs, content to live with the intruders.

Half an hour later we reached the foot of the face, identified the first pitch and lit a huge illegal bonfire to ward off noises in the forest. After two cans of breakfast, which did nothing to relieve my dry apprehensive throat, we were off into a superbly clear-skied dawn. Today would be very hot. We carried only a rack of nuts, two small water bottles and some Elastoplast tape in case our hands got too battered. We soloed the first pitch, a long 5.7 affair that headed towards the start of the line proper. Now underneath it, we could appreciate the steepness of it all. Minor roofs from a distance turned out to be gigantic ceilings, through which *Astroman* slides carefully yet directly.

Roping up, we had the usual indecision about who should have the first lead – all a bit false, really, because we both knew that each of us would end up with three 5.11 pitches. The aim was really to see who could get himself the 5.7 chimney pitch on the fourth lead, the only easy pitch on the route. I let Ron have the first lead, a 5.10 layback pitch, which he climbed fluidly in a little under five minutes. I followed, pleasantly surprised at the ease of the climbing but it was only supposed to be 5.10, and we were good at laybacks anyway. It did ease the tension somewhat, however, and we could almost look forward to what was coming.

Mine was the first 5.11 pitch, a short 30-foot affair to gain a pedestal below a soaring crack-and-groove line. Now 5.11 in Yosemite to me means either just getting up by the skin of my teeth, or falling off once or twice trying, or not doing it at all. But fingertip laybacking is my scene so I launched up the thin peg-scarred crack ignoring the protection peg at the foot of it. Twenty seconds later I was clipping into the peg and grinning nervously at Tap (Tap was Ron's name for the summer, but it was only wise to use the name when one was out of reach). Another couple of attempts and I was up on the pedestal; quite strenuous but not really desperate.

'*Easy, Tap come on,*' said I, out of reach with 30 feet of crack too narrow for his banana fingers between us. Ron climbed, avoiding most of the crux by gigantic reaches, but having trouble where the crack just would not accept even a small portion of his fingers.

Above, a perfect corner containing a perfect one and a half inch crack speared upwards for a full rope length. Gently overhanging, it gradually changed colour as it rose from a glaring yellow to a rich red, but the rock itself was uniformly hard. Several *in-situ* pegs interrupted the absolute commitment and finality of this lead.

Ron took off, and for fifteen minutes laybacked and jammed his way to become a dot at the top of the groove. Two of the *in-situ* pegs had been loose, carelessly tossed away by Tap, and another two had come out and slithered noisily down the rope to rest on lower nuts. So much for morale boosting *in-situ* protection.

Seconds after Ron had fixed his hanging belay, he lit up in a blaze of colour as if his halo had become incandescent. The sun was up, and fast creeping down the face to meet me halfway up that totally energetic pitch. The temperature rose immediately and drastically. At the belay we tied our thick shirts into knots and tossed them off. Mine floated 500 feet gently downwards to land inches from our bivvy gear; Tap's landed in a spiky tree 100 feet up the face.

The chimney pitch was beautiful, not one of those gripping smooth back-and-foot chimneys from the 1920s but a pleasant cool interior covered in giant jugs and perfect little jam cracks. Over all too soon.

Ron was off again, missing the belay and running two 5.10 pitches together. Towards the top of his 220-foot lead, at the second 5.10 section, and it really was 5.10 this time, Tap came to an impasse. (Notice how it's always 'Tap' when I'm winning). Understandably perturbed that I hadn't been belaying him for the last sixty feet because I was climbing, he couldn't work out how to negotiate a section of flared flake stuck on the wall.

I fished out the topo, saw that it was only 5.10b, shouted up that I could see how to do it from here. All he had to do was chimney it, it looked easy. After much derring-do and soul-searching he chimneyed the awful flake to reach a little stance. Seconding, I reached the flake, soon realised it was manifestly impossible to chimney, only a fool would do that, and promptly laybacked it quite confidently.

We were needing a drink after each pitch now as the temperature rose with us. Ancient Mariners of ascent, each the other's Albatross. As if to add to the general atmosphere of heat, the meadow and forest next to Camp 4 had burst into flame, stampeding wildlife and lunchtime lovers towards the river. Multitudes of immaculately uniformed rangers milled about ineffectually while a handful of climbers and hippies efficiently dealt with the blaze. But from above we just saw and smelled the pall of smoke as it lingered itself across the valley, trapping and magnifying the sun's heat.

Now, of course, my careful pitch planning was askew, my lead a steeply overhanging crack at 5.11 funnelling into the depths of the famed Harding Slot, nearly free at 5.9 on the original aid ascent of this route, it now looked manifestly un-five-nine-ish. For a start, it overhung twenty feet or so, coming out over our heads at a crazy angle. Ron looked contented, I sweated upwards, cunningly avoiding the 5.11 crack by bridging the groove it was in. And so into the Slot, nine inches wide, it was thirty feet of hard labour gained in instalments of less than an inch.

Breathing out coincided with upward movement; breathe in to jam. The Whillans harness, a trusty friend (though don't tell Troll or they'll want to use my photo in adverts) was now making progress impossible. I managed to wriggle out of it and clipped it and my climbing ropes to a sling across my shoulders. I couldn't really have fallen very far if I'd tried. I popped out on to a beautiful ledge and, hidden from Tap, took an extra large swig of water.

Ron forced himself upwards into the Slot. I could hear him talking to it. '*Yer little bastard, yer little bastard,*' he said repeatedly, accusing Harding's poor little Slot. But the Slot kept grinning and if anything, narrowed, because Ron couldn't move. He wanted to be sick, but couldn't because he was too constricted. '*You'll have to slide out and hand over hand up the outside,*' I shouted triumphantly.

Ron slid downwards out of the bomb bay, simultaneously spewing into mid-air as he penduled out into space. In a second he was with me, not amused. He recovered and led what seemed to be a very hard 5.11 layback pitch next, long and tiring, but perhaps we were tiring as the sun strengthened. More drinks, but not enough left for you to drink enough to last for a pitch.

My pitch next, first a 5.11 mantel-shelf, the idea is too absurd to comprehend, there can be no such thing. And there wasn't, just one tricky mantel move with rests above and below. A couple of tries and easily done; perfect protection. The thin crack was hard, though. Sweaty slick, my fingers kept curling the edge of a peg to retreat a move. Eventually I did it, having laced the crack with all my small nuts, I was moving well. But above, previously out of sight, the crack continued thin and hard for fifty more feet. A peg at twenty and fifty were the only biscuits to go for, but go I had to; it would be my last hard lead on the route, so it was worth expending all on it. Belayed. I couldn't talk, a mouthful of water and I managed a grunt to Ron.

The next two pitches would have been beautiful, had it not been for the heat and our condition. Perfect flakes and fist cracks followed corners, wearing through giant roofs for two 5.9, or easy 5.10 pitches, our assessment of grading was by now quite subjective.

A long ledge in the shade below the last pitch. Ron's lead, 5.11 face climbing, poor protection in complete contrast to the well-protected cracks below. Can't talk now, no water and our throats have had it. Ron dithers up and down from a climber-splitting pinnacle below the hard stuff. There is protection, a large angle stuck out a long way filling the only foothold and above, out of reach, bashed-in nuts and a peg. More dithering. I suggest he allows his foot to slip down on to the peg where the hold should be. He does and he's launched upwards, committed to the face. A roof after forty feet seems to lead on to a blank headwall, but a good hold under the roof allows Ron to stretch right past the headwall, all four feet of it, to perfect holds on ten feet of slab and abruptly to the top. A tree. Hot smoky breezes.

Yes, that was only the best route in the world.

Washington Column, East Face

V, 5.9, A3 Warren Harding, Glen Denny and Chuck Pratt, July 1959. About ten days spread over a year were spent on this formidable, overhanging wall. Fixed ropes were placed over the entire route. The first continuous ascent took two days and was made in 1962 by Royal Robbins and Tom Frost.

Yosemite guidebook (1971), describing Astroman *in its original state.*

First published in Crags *12, 1978.*

Cleckhuddersfox One - Camp 4 Nil

by Ron Fawcett

first met Pete via John (Doc) Hammond. Doc was a teacher at my school and was one of the old time 'good guys' who was getting fed up of being terrified whilst seconding Pete on his early new routes in Langcliffe Quarry. The rock at Langcliffe is what you might call a bit disposable and Pete's new routes were more akin to tottering death traps than actual rock-climbs. I remember early pictures of Pete from that era, thick woolly socks, canoe helmet and his big hair sticking out from underneath. Like Pete, I wore the thick woolly socks back then, but in those days it was a means of padding out badly fitting rock shoes. I loved his anarchic attitude towards the 'old school' climbing clubs of the day and his ability to use them when it suited him. He was the nearest thing to a hero I ever had, but I'd never let him know.

We climbed wherever there was rock, from the Dales to the Lakes, Wales to Cornwall, Verdon to Yosemite and most places in between. Pete was ultra competitive in whatever he did, yet there was always this casual air, it wouldn't have been cool to look as though he was having to try too hard. Of course, back then there were no mobile phones, we didn't even have a home phone. Pete would pole up at my house in his MG, his only concession to a modicum of style (he later owned a Lotus too), he would charm my mother, '*Ooo what a lovely man,*' she'd say. She really loved him, if only she knew what he was getting her lad into. He would manically drive us here, there and everywhere to pick off what was newsworthy, always an early repeat, second ascent, aid reduction or new route and it was always done with a caveat, '*That was a piece of piss.*' I remember him giving me some words of wisdom, '*It's dead easy being a hero in your own backyard kid. It's much tougher making it in the wider world.*' It was like his mantra and that stayed with me forever, what a fantastic legacy.

In the early 1970s we'd all read about this rock-climbers Mecca in the good old US of A, in *Mountain* magazine number 4, but our trips to Yosemite in those days were never really planned, that would have been too easy, it was just a matter of turn up and go climbing like any other trip. Brits had climbed in the Valley before us of course, but they'd adopted the aid climbing style and followed the tradition in which many of the classics had been initially established. In Pete's mind this was simply 'cheating, kid'. Like all of his derogatory comments, calling aid climbers cheats wasn't handed out with malice, but more to see what sort of response he got; it was all part of the psychological game that he was so good at playing. His gaming also extended beyond the climbing and formed part of our lifestyle on trips away. On one of my early visits to the Valley I bumped into Pete in Camp 4, the usual climbers' hang-out. He was with legendary American climber John Gill and, as was typical, had all the financial and domestic affairs in camp covered, which amounted to capitalising on whatever scams could be devised. For example, if you signed up for the mountain rescue team you could camp for free. The mainstay of his sustenance was a big bag of dehydrated curry, which he'd purloined free of charge from the outdoor education department of Bingley College, where he'd just started working. He occasionally took pity on me dossing in the dirt and would hand out a portion of his curry, but this was usually as a bribe with some ulterior motive or other. I didn't care as I was always starving hungry. In fact, the only times I wasn't hungry was when we went scarfing for food. In its easiest form this meant going to the café and simply finishing off the oversized portions that greedy Yanks had failed to complete. When we were really desperate we adopted more extreme measures; a gang of us would enter the café and when the owner disappeared to the bathroom we'd cause some fracas or other, which usually meant the café was emptied of diners and loads of untouched food was left on the tables. What were we supposed to do, leave it to be thrown away?

I have fond memories of the routes we did together during this era, early ascents of many 5.12s. Routes like *Hangdog Flyer* and *Crimson Cringe* were real cutting edge back then. We also did mega classics like *Nabisco Wall*. It was ironic that Pete's real forte was vertical face climbing on small holds, coupled with crap rock and poor protection, the exact opposite to the style of climbing that Yosemite offered. Despite this Pete did many first ascents in Yosemite, and I was lucky enough to be involved in several.

As well as the climbing, what sticks in my mind more than anything were our japes down at the river where we lay in the sun, ate ice cream and basically had fun. One of Pete's party pieces was to pick up a large rock and walk across the river. Nothing special about that you may think, except that the river was ten feet deep. He'd usually do this when unsuspecting tourists were sharing our little piece of heaven. As you can imagine, with the majority of Americans appearing to have no sense of humour, or comprehension of a bit of Yorkshire dialect, they were left, shall we say, a little bemused. Occasionally some hunk would try to impress his 'gal' by emulating Pete's extraordinary feat, usually with dire consequences like dropping the rock on a foot, or suffering a near drowning as they ran out of puff mid-stream. Of course, this would leave us in convulsions of laughter. The onlookers were often shocked by our behaviour, how could someone get such amusement at the expense of someone else's torment? What they didn't get though, was that in reality, we laughed the loudest at each other and more often than not, that was when we were on the rock and the stakes were high.

Pete got on with everybody in Camp 4 and made some lasting friendships with the locals, who often distanced themselves from 'outsiders'. Even American 'hot shot' Henry Barber was regarded as an 'outsider', and the Yosemite crew took the piss out of him mercilessly. I was young and gormless and never really understood all the 'politics' that were going on around me. On one of our trips we heard that Henry had just done the second ascent of *Butterballs*, a superb finger crack that had been first climbed by 'the godfather' of Yosemite, Jim Bridwell. I seem to think that Bridwell had frigged it a bit on the first ascent, but by all accounts Barber had made a pretty good job of it on his repeat. Pete just had to do it. All the information we had was that the route was on The Cookie, a brilliant crag down the valley, so we got the thumbs out and started to hitch a lift. Back home this was my usual form of transport, but to Pete it was quite a novelty. I recall that on this occasion we were picked up by a pair of local climbers. As always when in need, Pete was charming and chatted away to the guys who were en route back home. They asked us about our plans and I could see the perplexed expressions spreading across their faces as Pete said, '*Oh we're going to do* Butterballs.' I could see them thinking 'Who are these two bullshitters?' Back then, Brits were a rarity in the valley and here we were, a couple of fruitcakes. Our two hosts tried to explain the severity of our proposed route, but Pete just laughed them off, saying, '*It'll be a piece of piss for Tap here.*' Tap was his stateside nickname for me, but most Americans never got the joke.

As was usual we had no precise idea of where the route went, so we just looked for a hard looking crack. '*That'll be it,*' said Pete pointing at a thin-looking seam. I was always gullible and had complete trust in the man. '*Get up there,*' he said. So I did. My memory of the route was of hard, not overly well-protected climbing. Pete threw the odd comment up like, '*Stop messing about*', '*Stop being a wuss*', and, '*If Henry can do it, it should be a piece of piss for you*'. I remember getting really high on the route, very near to success when a couple of guys came round the corner and asked us what we were on. '*Butterballs*,' replied Pete.

'*Err, no it's not*,' said one of the Yanks, '*Butterballs is up there*,' he continued, pointing to high up on the *Nabisco Wall*.

It looked like a path compared to the crack I was currently on. Pete ordered me down. Even though the sun was overhead and it was about 100 degrees there was no slacking, we still had to bag *Butterballs*. Pete hurriedly set off up the trilogy of pitches that make up *Nabisco Wall* leaving me with the crux *Butterballs* pitch. As we climbed a crowd gathered to watch these 'limey upstarts' who had the audacity to try their hardest route. As ever Pete played to the audience, placing minimal protection on what was a really well-protected pitch, leaving me to get stuck into the meat. *Butterballs* suited me perfectly and felt easy, so like Pete I also placed minimal gear, but to be honest, with the archaic gear we carried then, that was the best way to attack these pitches. Just climb. Many years later I learned that the crack I had attempted and so nearly succeeded on, later became one of the first 5.13s in the States; this was when there was less than a dozen 5.12s in the entire country. I should have stuck at it; hindsight is a wonderful thing.

Pete wrote some fantastic articles about his climbing and travels, and one of his best in my opinion was his piece about our repeat of *Astroman*. I have such great memories of this. The bears, the heat, and I did not stand on that peg on the last pitch, you rascal. We were the first team to use really long ropes back then when most folk used 120 or 150-foot cordage. On *Astroman* we used 200-foot long ropes, which enabled us to do less pitches and climb really fast. Pete had a little hand-drawn topo of the route, which he kept to himself and in his usual cunning way had worked out that if I led the long *Enduro* corner pitch, the dreaded *Harding Slot* pitch would also fall to me.

As we drew close to the obvious cleavage I managed a monster pitch, which meant that Pete got the infamous 'Slot'. It was probably the only time I ever got one over on the old fox.

The Camp 4 locals loved pointing us at the various latest test-pieces that had been put up, obviously hoping that we'd fail, but Pete would always return to camp with his usual appraisal, '*Piece of piss.*' We both loved climbing on Middle Cathedral; the granite was rougher than the rest of Yosemite and actually had face holds as well as greasy cracks. The Camp 4 hot shots had just put up *Space Babble*, a long and bold route up the face left of the *Direct North Buttress*, as usual the local gurus told us that this was the route to do, so off we went hitching down the Valley. When we got to the base of the route Pete informed me that he'd forgotten his harness and that I'd have to lead it all. Being young and daft I had no problem with this. Our description of the route amounted to 'climb the big blank wall left of *Direct North Buttress*'. This covered acres of featureless rock, but we were so confident in our abilities we just set off up what we considered to be the most logical line. We were a few pitches up when the quiet serenity of the Valley was broken by howls and screams coming from the forest. 'Wolves or bears,' declared Pete. Being of farming stock I knew it wasn't either, not that I'd ever encountered any of these critters in the Yorkshire Dales. In fact, it turned out to be the first ascensionists who'd come down from Camp 4 to try and freak us out. Not a chance, Pete just shouted down, '*Piece of piss this, when does it start to get hard?*' We always did our bit for Anglo-American relations. Pete even relented and decided to lead a pitch, it was the easiest bit of the route but it didn't matter a jot, we'd done the second ascent of another mega classic and once again the score card back in camp read:

'Cleckhuddersfox One - Camp 4 Nil'.

All this feverish activity came from Pete's ability to network with the best from around the world. He knew what routes were hot, where the gaps were and, most important of all, how to get one over on the locals. This was all done with a most casual air and the suspects never knew he was gleaning amazing knowledge that was truly global. In a pre-internet world that was something else and another facet of Pete that set him apart.

I Feel Rock

by Pete Livesey

Moratorium, El Capitan, *Yosemite Valley, 560 feet, XS (E4), P Livesey/ T Jones, 1975.*

El Cap's *East Buttress* route starts high above the Valley at the end of a ledge system on the mountain's right flank. It's a beautiful sun-baked route on a bulging rounded buttress of fine weathered yellow rock. If you're waiting there to start the route, it's slow because there are usually several Japanese teams hurling themselves at the first pitch like demented bananas. So have a look over the end of the ledge. Below, in deep-contrasted shadow, is a tremendous corner sweeping down for 600 feet. Continuous, with smooth wide walls, one overhanging and one just leaning back, the hair-like corner crack makes no secret of its challenge.

If you're into laybacks, then this is it, you've found it at last, the spiritual home of laybacks, whence came all the other little laybacks in the world. In all this climb's length there is just ten feet of bridging on the second pitch, the rest is just pure ape-like joy in every conceivable kind of layback position.

The start is ten minutes from the road and blatantly obvious. Senses are immediately stirred by the incredibly harsh light-and-shade chequerwork of the corner's beautiful slabs, features obliterated by deep black shadow on brilliant sunlit stripes. It's hard to be single minded enough to concentrate on the first pitch of laybacking, but there it is, there's no other way.

234

Laybacking is a strangely committing kind of climbing. It always feels like that's it, once you start. You just stand there looking at it, building up for a rush, and although you know the crack will take good protection, you can't see where to put it once you're arched up in a layback position. There's always a tendency to get going and forget the protection: As some would say: 'Just layback and enjoy it.'

Reeds Pinnacle Direct, Yosemite Valley, 280 feet, XS (E1)

The first pitch is a wicked curved slash like a sabre scar, but it's just my size. Forty feet up, twenty feet to go, and I put a chock in. Hand jam size, number 9, pick it out on a tatty white tape and throw it in. I threw it in, it went right in, two feet in, krab and all, out of reach. I was broddling round with my longest wire, and was just pulling the tape out, when I saw one of those sights you just don't want to believe or accept. In the crack behind the nut was a hand, yes a hand. It still had chalk on, and grubby fingernails.

Not only was the sight of a hand completely unacceptable to me, but also it was dragging the nut away, my nut, into the depths of the mountain. I instinctively let go of the tape, and I remember thinking that dozens of climbers have probably lost their hands that way, but to let it have the nut and clear off. At the top of the pitch I grabbed the tree, tied on and checked to see if my feet were still there, you never know with hands in cracks what they're after.

Behind the tree was a perfect dark chimney parallel to the cliff face. Creeping out of the base at ground level was a giggling Yank with my nut.

The next pitch looked potentially even more horrific. A slab of rock weighing a few million tons had split, leaving a curly crack, then one side had slipped a couple of feet so that the curls on one side were out of phase with those on the other. Could it be a giant American meat grinder?

Our fears were allayed. The crack proved to be perfect jamming, just throw a fist or a finger in, and let it slide down until it jams. Easy, just like that for 120 perfectly vertical feet.

The last pitch was another leap into the unknown. Run into the back of a 20-foot wide cavernous chimney and bridge out of its roof, funnelling up into a narrowing fissure, squeezed out into space on a fist jam; layback and mantelshelf on to it, another jam for fingers only, and grab the top.

Lunatic Fringe, *Reeds Pinnacle, Yosemite Valley, California 200ft, XS (E2), Barry Bates, 1972.*

Barry Bates's routes are all alike, sort of thin cracks that split smooth walls with no footholds.

Having fingers the same shape and consistency as Chouinard 5.5 Stoppers is a distinct advantage on these routes. For the rest of us, it's just a 150 feet exercise in every conceivable kind of finger jam, finger layaway and half-a-hand jam. Feet are a kind of embarrassment: there appears to be nowhere to put them, and if you start worrying about it, your hands fall out. I finally worked out that the best scheme was to hide them away underneath your knees and hope they'd get up the route on their own.

It's not a straight-in crack. It's angled slightly and this makes the climbing a little easier, all kinds of peculiar finger jams surprisingly sticking in place.

The rock is magnificent, even for Yosemite, one of those routes where you get back down and say, 'Did I do that? Let's do it again.' But you don't, because somewhere in your inner mind is a subconscious but compelling chink of cool beer cans - or half a gallon bucket of sherbert ice cream, if your name's Ron Fawcett

Regular Route, *Fairview Dome, Tuolumne Meadows, California 1,500ft,* *HVS.*

To the unsuspecting British climber the High Sierra is unbelievably beautiful. Gentle forest trails and the occasional road wind across an 8,000-foot plateau, dark sweet-smelling pine alternating with areas of sun-bleached bare granite, acres of glacier-scoured rock sprouting the occasional lonely, twisted Jeffrey Pine.

In the distance are a dozen or so domes of brilliant white granite rising in perfect curves from the forest. The tallest is Fairview Dome, an 1,800 feet sweep of granite, perfectly circular, with curves that ensure its place as the most perfect and biggest breast in the world. There's no way you can drive past without fondling its smooth slabs.

So gentle at first that it's easy walking; almost imperceptibly steepening until the slab is a steep slab and friction is not enough, and the eye is drawn to the line, the only line, a pencil-line crack creasing the surface of that cuppable tit. Find the line, follow it, and be drawn through the slabs to the wall, through overlaps and roofs, the line still faithfully leading to the only possible finishing point on this mountain.

Higher, the walls gradually curve back again, easing off for three pitches before the last final thrust of what one can only call a nipple, whether it looks like one or not.

Do you know what it feels like to sit up there on the biggest tit there is, looking down on a pine-crested woman with eleven more tits all around you? Outasight, man.

First published in Crags 7 1976.

With 'God' on My Side

by Nicho Mailänder

The Christian-Kehrer coach from Cologne seemed stuck for good in the hairpin. 'No trouble, no fuss – just take our bus!' From light summer dresses and tennis shirts, arms are excitedly pointing up the pass road. But the driver of the opposing bus from Roma just shrugs his massive shoulders gesturing backwards towards the long line of cars winding out of sight into the mountain forest at the next bend. *'Scusi signore, vadi in dietro per favore!'*

A flourish of trumpets signals retreat to the last passing bay. The space above the asphalt strip is filled with a veil of thin, grey mist condensed at the exhaust pipes into little dark clouds, which are distributed in the scanty larch forest by the insetting updraught.

The legendary King Laurin couldn't have meant to cause this kind of mess back then when he cursed his Rosengarten Mountains never to bloom again. They are looking down at us through the trees, rather pallidly due to the black diesel fumes ejaculating from the MAN coach while it inches past its Latino opponent. We turn up the side windows and, with a slipping clutch and the smell of burning graphite rubber in our nostrils, stammer our way along the road through Vallonga and Chiusel, up to the Karerpass.

Of course, all this is Pete's fault. He is sitting beside me grinning, thriving on his reputation as the 'ugliest climber in England'. He never gets the corkscrew ringlets of his half bald-head off the pillow before nine o' clock. And after that only if somebody holds a mug of Twinings under his flat nose. Then he likes to stuff his scrawny body for an hour with white beans, sticky toast bread and Heinz Spaghetti before he starts leafing through Walter Pause's *Extreme Alpine Rock: The 100 Greatest Alpine Rock Climbs* book. *'Isn't there any proper climbing in the Dolomites?'* he asks.

'What do you mean? The Messner Route on the North Face of the Second Sella Tower yesterday, wasn't that "proper" climbing?'

'Easy rubbish!' Pete pushes his receding chin forward in a gesture of defiance. For almost ten years, his status as the best British climber has not been seriously challenged. His friends call him 'God' in ironic respect.

Suddenly he stops turning the pages. *'This looks good. Where is it?'*

I peer over his shoulder. *'You're crazy! The* Hermann Buhl Memorial Route *on the Rotwand is VI, A2. It will never go free.'*

'We'll see!'

Half a mug of Darjeeling is chucked into the Alpenrosen, a lump of sick looking beans into the garbage, the grimy sleeping bag into his tent. Three quarters of an hour later, our Opel Kadette is overheating on the congested road to the Karerpass. It is eleven o' clock when we cram our climbing gear into the packs at the station of the funicular.

With the pack on my lap I recline in the swaying seat of the ski lift. It seems to be taking us directly up to the Rotwand, which looks like a plastic laminate kitchen table tilted upright. Rising 400 metres above the scree, the reddish-yellow colour of the rock signals that it is scarcely touched by water. If you look at it closely, however, structures emerge; the 60-metre high buttress at the bottom, no problem, but then the heat is turned up in the thin crack through an overhanging fracture leading up to the grey ramps, which continue diagonally to the right. The 90-metre shoulder crack above is clearly visible, which is followed to the piton ladder at half-height and above it nothing but unstructured blankness until you reach the terrace below the summit overhangs. Late in the summer of 1958 the Dresden sandstone aces, Lothar Brandler and Dietrich Hasse, undoubtedly among the best climbers of their time, struggled up this wall in almost four days; three bivouacs, some of them in hammocks, 180 pitons, bolts and wooden wedges, hunger, thirst, and danger. For about ten years the *Hermann Buhl Memorial Route* was reserved for the best but somehow pitons started to sprout in sections Brandler and Hasse had overcome by hard free climbing.

As an aid route, the Brandler-Hasse on the Rotwand was degraded to a strenuous but relatively trivial trade route. According to our Pause prayer book, the climbing time is twelve hours, using etriers, and all the other aid climbing tricks of the trade. But Pete, the old rascal, has pinched my little rope ladder from the car and hidden it somewhere in the mungo pines close to our tents. In his vocabulary 'aid climbing' is a cuss word. If he can't get up a piece of rock just using his hands and feet, Pete prefers to abseil off and spend the rest of the day lying in the sun with a mug of tea or a bottle of vino rosso. Why did I ever get involved with this madman? I know too well that as soon as his shredded running shoes touch the ground he will take off on the trail to the Cologne Hut at marathon speed. There he will open the throttle and bluster up the steep talus to the start of our climb, at a nauseating rate, just another one of those merciless cockfights, but my only chance to kill him. There is no disputing that Pete climbs in a league of his own, but I have always managed to beat him up the steep screes, a starting shot. Feeling the suspicious look of the ski lift attendant on my neck, we turn a small concrete building and take off on the horizontal trail. The feet are accustomed to their work and have no problem finding the best hold on the stony mountain path; packs thumping against our backs counter the rhythm of running.

I've been up to this craziness much too long to chuck my rucksack down the next scree gully, lie down in the sunshine on one of the pleasantly warmed boulders and let the psychopath from Yorkshire go off on one of his infamous solos, but the emerging listlessness is irresistible. My legs start hurting, become heavy and slow. Pete looks back and takes off triumphantly; I let him go. For a week now it has been the same every day. Livesey never could be number two. But I also have profited from Pete's ambition and enjoyed being connected to his drive. A long time ago, at the age of sixteen, I had struggled up the famous Pilastro on the Tofana di Rozes in ten hours. A free ascent in about a third of this time was thought impossible. Last week, the lads from Bludenz didn't believe their eyes when Pete calmly climbed out the first roof on underclings without even hesitating a second. A little later I bridged up the inside corner to the second overhang, found another good undercling, the fingers locked off in the crack splitting the roof, allowing the other hand to reach for the jugs just above the lip. A heel hook, a mantel and, 'Off belay!' Above the overhanging chimney, where Hermann Buhl once upon a time spent an exhausting afternoon, my snivelling appeals just succeed to keep the crazy Brit from coiling the rope. Two hours later he is snoring in the afternoon sun on his stained foam rubber mattress.

Early the following morning, at the ungodly hour of 'half-eight', the team of Amazons connected to Peter and myself starts stirring in a spirit of euphoric restlessness quite hard to endure. Jill and Liz are going for the first all-women's ascent of the *Lacedelli Route* on Cima Scotoni. The description in the guidebook seems to have animated their imagination, '...After ascending some 15 metres, you reach a vertical wall. This is climbed utilizing pitons, etriers and a double shoulder stand, before performing a difficult pendulum to the right...' Actually, Pete is only interested in the first pitch, reputedly strenuous and at that time still waiting to be freed.

Our resistance is in vain; in a sleepy stupor we are transported over the Falzarego Pass into the Abtei Valley. There we have no other choice but to follow in the footsteps of the weaker sex to the start of the famous *Lacedelli Route*. Here we meet Franco Nero and Titi Capone. They look like a mixture of a Yosemite climbing bum with Blackbeard the pirate and an Amazon parrot. Shoulder long pitch black hair, wild growths in their faces, Franco is clad in canary yellow gym pants, Titi in toxic green ones; their psychedelic shirts would have sent hardened acid heads groping for the wall.

'*Hi*,' says Pete and sits down grinning. Our competitors offer a friendly greeting. Two hours later we have stopped laughing. We are still sitting below the first pitch while our ladies are chasing the birds of paradise. Up there a concept of the universe seems to be falling apart, Jill's attempts to pass the Italian gentlemen are triggering panic attacks: '*Dai Titi, dai! Velocita!*'

Eventually, the war between the genders moves on to the second pitch, so Pete starts climbing. He is crestfallen to use one peg for resting and awards the pitch the new grade, 'DD', desperately difficult.

In the meantime, the race between the Anglo-American women's team and the Romanic mountain heroes has escalated to total war. We decide to bypass the champs de guerre keeping a respectful distance. Titi Capone, the guy with the poisonous pants, is shaking his way up on lead with a single 9mm rope. The line, that looks as if it had served Noah to anchor his Ark on Mount Ararat, curves up from the 'belayer' with at least ten metres of slack. Titi Capone, the Amazon cockatoo, is frantically trying to get away from Liz, who is challenging to pass him. Madonna!

We find a sunny spot on the second terrace, sounds of battle drifting up from afar. Suddenly, there is a terrible panting and crashing in the gully below us. Titi and Franco come into sight, climbing un-roped. Slightly battered, but with a victorious look in the eye and chests swollen in triumph, they bid us goodbye and disappear into the exit chimneys. Despite my sulky mood, a smile spreads on my face when

I think of our two Italian friends while I am stumbling up the talus to the base of the Rotwand. Pete is already waiting nervously for the first person narrator to take up his part again in the story.

Of course, it would have been below our dignity to rope up on the first pitch, graded IV in the topo. With a dry mouth, I hastily clamber past a few pitons left by more safety conscious predecessors. Under an overhanging crack, lined with pegs, we switch from our running shoes to EBs. I'm barefoot while Pete has two pairs of socks, allegedly to protect his delicate toes. I tie myself to a bunch of pitons and prepare the double ropes to belay Pete up the first crux pitch. It is hard to understand how he does it. Where others dither for hours in their etriers, he bridges and jams his way upwards at an unimaginable speed, now and then clipping into one of the numerous pegs. It takes him less than ten minutes to get up this pitch, the Americans would have graded at a solid 5.10. Following with the pack, I can't help marvelling at Pete's ability to combine minute points of contact into climbing sequences as the chalk marks clearly show where he touched the rock. I hand over the pack and, pulling two official pitches together, climb up diagonally to the right, reaching the beginning of the shoulder crack. Both of us are in top shape, my weight is down to 59 kilos. It is pure pleasure to blast up this off-vertical crack, splitting a blank wall on good jams and holds as if nothing could stop us. The pitons beside the crack seem anachronistic and absurd. One and a half hours after leaving the ground we are at half-height of the wall. Looking upwards, our climbing euphoria evaporates instantly. The crack runs out in a seemingly blank 95-degree shield of rock. Hasse and Brandler must have spent several happy hours here, persuading their smallest pegs to stay in contact with the tiny holes and minute cracks in the 12-metre high wall that looks as if it was made out of high grade concrete. Below us, the face drops off about 200 metres. The boulders down on the ground, as large as houses, look as if they belonged to the miniature scenery of a toy train. Little stones we send into space never touch the wall.

'*Watch me, Pete!*' Using tiny protrusions, pencil-wide ledges and little holes, I sneak up towards the right, legs bridged far apart to keep the centre of gravity as close as possible to the wall, outsmarting four pitons before the going gets really tough. There is a little diagonal hold up on the left, but I need both hands to hold on to the one centimeter edge I have manteled through on. Putting my left foot on a protuberance, three fingers of my left hand are just starting to curl on the hold, when the toe pops off the smear sending me flying into fresh air. I find myself five metres below swinging from the ropes, a gleeful grin at the belay. Up on aid to unclip the gear for a second go. Soon I find myself in the same position as before following gravity. My forearms are getting pumped, heavy breathing. But this time the rubber sticks to the smear. The handhold is small but sharp, so I can clip the next peg on counter pressure and start scanning the rock above with my right hand: smooth, smooth, smooth, smooth, nothing!

'*Tension!*'

I slump into the ropes. It's over. My strength is spent. Pete also gives it a try, but to no avail. Reluctantly, we cope with the seemingly blank piece of rock in the style of the first ascensionists. We manage to climb the upper part of the wall free, but it takes every ounce of our mental and physical stamina. All pitches are similar, steep, technical, fingery and improbable. The wall ends abruptly; a final vertical move delivers me onto an almost horizontal flowery meadow. But nothing of rest and savouring the sublime grandeur of the peaks. '*Let's get out of here, man, I need a beer.*' Impatiently, the amateur climbing bum, in his civil life lecturer at a teachers' college in northern England, switches from his smelly EBs into a pair of dilapidated Adidas fell-running shoes and shoulders his hastily coiled rope before he storms off down the grassy incline with the marmots scurrying for cover, without even a warning whistle.

Accounts of ascents made in the Italian Dolomites in 1979.

Note. The girls referred to in the article are Jill Lawrence and the late Liz Klobusicky, talented American rock climber, Alpiniste and Himalayan mountaineer

Shalom

by Dennis Gray

I n May 1980 Pete Livesey and I were invited, via the famous Wingate Institute of Physical Education in Tel Aviv, to organise an instructor's course in Israel on behalf of the Israel Alpine Club. The Club's Secretary, Sam Rosen, had studied in the UK, during which time he had climbed regularly in North Wales and the Peak District. He closely followed British climbing developments, so Livesey was a name known to him before our arrival. A colleague of mine, the Principal of the Carnegie College in Leeds, Clive Bond, had previously lectured at the Wingate Institute. He was also at that date the Chair of the British Society of Sports Psychologists, of which I was a Board member, and I was therefore able to find out from him how sport was organised in Israel, and the role of the Wingate Institute within that. I had also previously been to the country in 1968 and made some friends there. The raison d'être of the course was to develop a cadre of rock-climbing instructors in Israel to cater for the growing number of people wishing to take part in the sport in that country. The intention was that the qualified instructors would be fully up to the standards set in other countries.

By May 1980, Pete and his coterie of friends had introduced British rock-climbing to a totally new concept in fitness training. He was himself a typical example of the dedicated, trained and super-fit sportsman. He was almost uniquely fitted to apply his concepts within the sport of climbing because of his previous sporting associations, and his academic training. So far, so serious, but we were not in retrospect all that serious. Witness the terrifying games of rollerwall we used to play under Pete's direction at the Leeds University Climbing Wall, and the terrible mickey taking of one another that we used to indulge in. Typical of this was that as Pete was tall, powerful and bespectacled, with unruly, unkempt hair, and was not a dedicated follower of sartorial fashion, he only climbed so well because he was so ugly. This was, of course, tongue in cheek, and as the first time Pete and I had ever met, I was resting on a sling, trying an early repeat of a route at Malham in 1965, he was quite able to counter such calumnies with verbal ripostes of his own.

Arriving at Heathrow to fly to Ben Gurion airport with El Al, we ran into a serious problem. This airline, with good reason, has the most intense security of any, and they would not let Pete board because the photograph in his passport did not look anything like him. We argued and argued, but time for take-off was fast approaching, and though we had a letter of invitation from the Israeli Federation they were unmoved. Fortunately I remembered that I had a copy with me of the latest edition of *Climber* magazine, then the BMC's official organ, and in that Pete had an opinion column, with his picture at its head. I pulled this out and showed it to the guards, and they took it away to be investigated. Then with just minutes to spare they let us onto the plane. Livesey pretended to be hurt by all this anti-attention, and so the purser listening to his protestations brought him a free half bottle of scotch. Which then had him chuckling for the rest of the flight.

After a round of meetings and socialising in Tel Aviv, including a night at a very lively disco, whilst staying with Sam Rosen and his family, we travelled to the Wadi Amud Valley. This is set above the Sea of Galilee and we were quartered at a nearby kibbutz, eating our meals with its members. We also had to rise at the same time as them, which was at 5am, for by mid-morning it was too hot to climb.

The Wadi Amud cliffs of sound limestone are much the same in scale as those to be found in the Yorkshire or Derbyshire Dales, but the most impressive feature in the valley is a free standing pinnacle called the Amud. This is about 200 feet high, and overhanging on its shorter side, which abuts into the steep slope of the dale. On our first visit Pete and I both solo climbed up the long side of the pinnacle, which turned out to be technically harder than we had expected. We then sat wondering on its summit if the rope we had carried up with us would reach the ground if we abseiled off down the short overhanging side.

'*Only one way to find out,*' decided Pete and off he launched into space. It did reach, just, with a wild swing in to grab a ledge set above the sloping ground. I had stupidly left all my equipment on the ground, and had to abseil classic fashion to follow him. The last sixty feet, spinning through the air with the rope running round my thigh and through my bare legs (we were only wearing running shorts and T-shirts in that great heat), left me with a high-pitched voice and a rope burn which took some weeks to heal.

The first morning of the course we met up with our would-be students at the mouth of the Wadi. They appeared to be a real cross section of Israeli society, with some students from Tel-Aviv University, a professor from Jerusalem, a housewife from Jaffa, a Colonel who was the head of their paratroopers and some kibbutzniks, plus several younger climbers. Many of them had undertaken long journeys by public transport to be present, such was their enthusiasm.

Pete's and my job was to note their technical proficiency and comment on their suitability to become rock-climbing instructors. Once the course started it was all action, with climbing from six in the morning until midday, when a halt would be called for lunch and a rest in the shade out of the crushing heat of the sun. Another two or three hours in the afternoon completed the day. As the week progressed, the more I liked and admired Pete. He was no show-off, neither did he strike you as being outstanding immediately, but he was solid and really knew technique and rope-work intimately. The Israelis were very impressed with his attention to detail and we had to point out that some of their belaying and security methods were not recognised as safe practice. They took this criticism with good grace, and accepted they all needed more experience before they could run climbing courses on their own. When it came to enthusiasm and application however, our charges took some beating, and some mornings we would do five or six climbs before lunch then three or four more in the afternoon, some of them multi-pitch.

High up in the Wadi was a mirror-shaped wall of perfect, steep, grey limestone, about eighty feet high, set above maybe 120 feet of easy rock. It was concave with a shallow groove running up its centre, and it had been top-roped innumerable times, but no one had dared to lead it for there was no protection on the top wall. A fall from it would have had dire consequences. One lunchtime Pete slipped away unnoticed and, wearing only a pair of shorts and his rock boots, in the searing heat, he had climbed the easy first section of this challenge before we spotted him. As he traversed out across the concave upper face, solo and with no protection of any kind, we spied him and a buzz of excitement went round our circle sitting in the shade below. I hardly dared to watch. He had no idea how hard this climb might be, and was now apparently stuck in the middle of the face. But no, after a few moments carefully assessing the problem, he began to move precisely and confidently, in complete control. Move then followed move, climbing quickly he soon reached the top of the pitch; we all cheered. A brilliant on-sight first ascent behind him, he later assured me it was, *only about 5b*', but I was not to be deceived by this and later that night, in a bar on the shore of Lake Galilee, I bought him a large whisky to celebrate his ascent. A Yorkshireman buying a fellow Tyke a whisky is almost unheard of, so you might guess how impressed I was by this feat, especially as it was carried out in the heat of the day.

Living on the kibbutz was an almost unique experience, and it gave Pete and me food for thought. In the evenings we would sit in our accommodation discussing all that was happening around us. I was impressed by how Livesey was so keen to enquire, to find out what made the kibbutzniks so willing to live as they did, and what their motivations were. We spent quite some time over meals in the refectory discussing their lives, their hopes and fears, and finding out about their backgrounds, for many were not native to Israel.

In this experiment in socialism everyone owns everything. The children are brought up communally and everyone shares in the chores of cleaning and cooking. Besides agriculture, kibbutz usually also include some form of manufacturing within their sites, and the one Pete and I were staying on had a small metal fabrication plant. In our discussions with the kibbutzniks one man struck me in particular. He had been a famous portrait photographer in Switzerland, but now he worked as a labourer in a banana plantation on a trial basis to assess if he and kibbutz life were mutually acceptable. If he proved himself to the other members, by dint of hard work and self-sacrifice, he would be set up with the best photographic equipment and be able to, once again, use the skills that had made him famous in his earlier career.

He invited Pete and me along to his accommodation after supper one evening for a drink. We spent quite some time poring over his photographs that he was keen to show us. His colour work was good, but his black and white portraits were masterpieces.

'Don't you feel that eighteen months working in a banana plantation is a waste of your life and skills?' we demanded of him.

'No, not at all. It has taught me many things, and if I am to live the rest of my life here on this kibbutz I must earn my place like everyone

else has done,' he replied.

At the end of our course Pete and I bade farewell to our newfound climbing friends. When we returned to the UK we were able, via the BMC's International Committee, to invite some of them to come to the UK the following year to undertake an instructor's course at Plas y Brenin.

With Sam Rosen as our guide we then travelled around the country for a while, visiting the Dead Sea, Jericho and, finally, Jerusalem. Pete acted like a young boy again once immersed in the Dead Sea; we just could not persuade him to come out of the water. He could not get over the fact you could just lay in it, floating about, and be able to read a magazine as you did so, and not sink beneath the waves, however hard he tried.

Sam proved to be a really sociable guy and Pete and he became good friends. We would sit over beers in the evenings discussing climbing and climbers, and the difficult political situation in his country. Sam's two sons were then still young, but he was worried about what the future might hold for them, and he was very much on the liberal wing of Israeli society, keen for a peace to be concluded with the Palestinians and his country's neighbours. You cannot visit Israel and not become involved in such discussions, boring, as they may seem to most young climbers.

At our last destination, Jerusalem, inevitably we met up with some local climbers, including the professor who had been on our course. Just outside the city walls is a small but sound limestone cliff, which I had been to on my own in 1968. Pete solo climbed almost every existing route on the crag and even pioneered one or two new climbs, but got stuck on one problem and, despite repeated attempts, could not solve it. Several years later at a BMC Youth Meet in the Peak District, a brilliant young climber from Israel, Joav Nir, quizzed me about our visit. And I asked him about the climb that Livesey had failed on. '*Yes we have now climbed the route that he could not climb,*' he reported. '*We have called it,* Peter Could Not Climb It.'

This really made me laugh, for I guess such is the fate of every leading pioneer of every generation in our sport. It is still as true today as when Mummery first observed many years ago, 'Today's impossible climb is tomorrow an easy day for a lady'.

To have been with Pete on that visit to Israel was a rich experience for myself. Obviously I knew him reasonably well before we left the UK, but this cemented a friendship that was to last until his tragic death in 1998. Later we were both members of the Plas y Brenin Management Committee and we used to drive to these meetings from West Yorkshire to North Wales together on occasion, discussing everything that interested us.

To say that Pete was an outstanding figure might read as cliché, but his achievements speak for themselves, which may seem worthy to a new generation although to some of them perhaps somewhat dull. He was almost the archetypal Yorkshireman, not easy to impress. Accompanying Livesey was never dull. And although like many other outsiders, he was to be eventually embraced by the establishment, he remained at heart a true son of Huddersfield where the folk are renowned for their plain acting and speaking. He did have a wicked sense of humour. Witness in one of the TV climbing series, Chris Bonington seconding Pete, shouting for, '*Tight*', and Livesey pretending to mishear and give him, 'Slack', whilst making a cryptic comment, direct to camera, concerning the alleged effectiveness of the rope.

Climbing-wise Pete was a pivotal figure who did much to raise the standards of rock-climbing in the 1970s but more than that he was a good communicator, especially with students as our trip to Israel exemplified for me. And some of his writings are still read, especially his amusing articles, my own favourite being *Travels with a Donkey*.

He remains an influence still widely felt in the UK and amongst the climbing communities of several countries. I know the climbers in Israel that he met feel likewise, and Sam Rosen recorded this fact many years after Pete's death in correspondence with me, he declared that '*He was really an outstanding figure and I feel privileged to have known him*'.

Legacy of a Leader

by Mark Radtke

pushed my shopping trolley down the aisle of the supermarket, regularly consulting my grocery list in an effort to make the weekly chore as efficient as possible. My eight-month old daughter Lauren kept herself content by chewing the ears of her yellow bunny. I emerged from the confines of the baby food aisle to be confronted by Pete Livesey and his wife Soma. It was an incongruous, but not uncommon, meeting place; I'd often bump into the Liveseys in Morrisons as they stocked up on grocery supplies for their café in Malham. I never considered myself close friends of the couple, but I'd known Pete for well over a decade and whenever we met he'd always take time out to chat about the one thing that we had in common, climbing. Today wasn't an exception. As was customary, we stopped to pass the time of day. Pete was always eager to catch up on recent developments, despite having stopped climbing himself some years earlier.

'*What've you been up to?*' said Pete, which was code for a whole range of things including; how are all the lads, what new routes have you been doing and what's happening on the scene.

'*Oh, this and that, you know the usual sort of stuff,*' I replied. '*Anyway how are you?*' I enquired politely. I knew that Pete had been ill.

'*Pretty good after some of the damn treatment I've had. I'm back running and feeling pretty fit,*' Pete said full of enthusiasm and with a beaming smile. I looked him up and down. He looked strong and fit.

I always got the impression that he towered over me whenever I was in his presence, an illusion I think, probably born out of his charisma and the awe in which I held him. Pete then diverted his attention to my daughter. '*And who's this pretty little thing, can I pick her up?*' He reached down and lifted Lauren from the shopping trolley and cradled her, a giant of a man with a babe in arms. As he and Soma cooed over my daughter he looked directly into Lauren's smiling face and said, '*Always make sure that your daddy looks after you.*' I choked a little at that. Pete handed Lauren back, we said our goodbyes and disappeared back into the maze of consumerism. It was the last time I saw Pete Livesey, within two months something that he could no longer outcompete got the better of him.

Livesey had already bowed out of mainstream climbing just as I was getting well and truly hooked, although he maintained an active interest in climbing and regularly reported new developments in a monthly column called *Rock Scene* in *Climber* and *Rambler* magazine.

The limestone country of the Yorkshire Dales had been an adventure playground for me in my youth even before I started climbing and the Gothic architecture of Gordale Scar held particular magnetism for me; I loved its scale. As a novice climber I was drawn back to Gordale, which was a little illogical since it really doesn't lend itself to the beginner, but despite this I had great experiences on obscure routes like the vegetated but compelling *West Face Route* and the bizarre and appropriately named *Darkness*. I'd even done a new route in the gorge within my first year of climbing. During those early years I'd also spent time learning my trade on the more diminutive crags known as the Stoney Banks up the valley from Gordale. In 1984, in the company of Adrian Ledgway and Chris Frost, I'd added a number of half decent new routes to Low Stoney Bank. I later found out that on one occasion whilst out running, Pete Livesey had observed us in action on the crag and had been quite intrigued to see new route action taking place on what at face value looked to be quite a loose and unstable crag. He reported these developments in his *Rock Scene* column even publishing two crag photographs to illustrate the action. I think it must have been a 'slow news' month in Yorkshire in April 1984. I was quite surprised when some time later as we called into Livesey's café for a brew we were greeted by a mocking Pete. *'Are you lot going grubbing around on that pile of choss up from Gordale.'* I was surprised that he recognised us, let alone knew what we were about. It was typical Livesey; he always seemed to have his finger on the pulse of what was going on.

Whether grubbing around on a pile of choss actually struck a chord with Pete I'm unsure, but from that time on he always took more than an active interest in what we were up to whenever we met. My enthusiasm for Gordale never waned until an accident there in 1995 nearly put an end to me. Up to that point I had worked my way through the routes and grades learning the secrets of the crag as I went. Livesey routes were always highly prized: *Face Route* for its position and historic significance; *Jenny Wren* just for the adventure; *Mossdale Trip* for the sheer mental commitment required. Perhaps the fact that Pete always had the time of day for me was, in part, down to the fact that he knew how much I relished the Gordale adventure.

Jenny Wren was first climbed by Pete Livesey and John Sheard in 1971. Unlike some of the aid routes that Livesey was attacking around this time, *Jenny Wren* followed an intricate line unique to itself. It was 200 feet long and meandered across the left wall of Gordale Scar in three exposed pitches. The line could be traced from the safety of the gorge floor, but once you set foot on the route it was apparent that the challenges ahead were hidden from view. At E5 6a it was probably the hardest free route in the country in 1971.

John Sheard recalls events from the early 1970s.

Routes like *Face Route* and *Jenny Wren* are no big deal today, but back then it was real cutting edge stuff. The leap in standards that we made by climbing those routes was also unfortunate in a way because it caused Pete a lot of controversy, people just wouldn't accept that he'd done these things free. Pete was very strong and fit from his athletics days, but he could execute a move without protection in the most trying of circumstances and that set him apart.

I think the Livesey mind might have deduced an interesting concept with his ascent of *Jenny Wren*. He'd produced a fine climb that lacked any discernible line. At that point in history climbers were largely conditioned to look for more obvious lines, usually defined by cracks, corners grooves, arêtes etc. With *Jenny Wren*, Livesey and Sheard moved away from this pre-conditioning and had the vision to see that if a series of features on a large face could be linked together then it would produce an almost imaginary and more ill-defined line. The only problem with this was that the areas of rock between these features often looked blank and devoid of protection. Face climbing of this type required a bold approach with good route finding ability. Livesey had both these qualities, but when prospecting new routes he would often pre-inspect the line to stack the odds in his favour. This did lead to a degree of some criticism by some observers, but as John Sheard points out below, a Livesey pre-inspection would pale into insignificance compared with what a lot of modern day activists do.

'*On* Jenny Wren *he abseiled the route, felt a few holds and then said to me, "It's too hard for us, but we're going to do it anyway" and he then led it in immaculate style.'*

From an interview with John Sheard in 2012

I think Livesey applied this concept to his groundbreaking ascent of Right Wall in 1974. He could visualise distinct features dotted up the face and realised it was just a case of linking these together with a bit of bold climbing. It seems a trivial concept today, but back then sinuous face climbs of this type weren't the norm. There were exceptions of course, routes like *Suicide Wall*, *Vector* or *Dream of White Horses* were cryptic in line, but the climbing on these routes didn't look as extreme as the 'lines' that Livesey started to visualise. Routes that Livesey produced like *Jenny Wren* at Gordale and *Central Wall* at Kilnsey, or *Right Wall* on the Cromlech in North Wales, epitomised bold climbing and difficult route-finding at its best at that time.

Another route in a similar vein was climbed by Livesey and Jill Lawrence in 1977, and once again it was at Pete's old stamping ground of Gordale. A bit of history gives a brief insight into the inner mind of Livesey. In the late 1960s Pete was at the height of his caving prowess and was instrumental in exploring the notoriously flood prone Mossdale Cavern system. In 1967 fate played a hand that may well have saved his life. As we have already read in Part One of this book, Livesey opted for a climbing trip to tackle the Troll Wall in Norway with John Stanger rather than pursuing further explorations of the Mossdale cave system. On June 24th, a team of ten cavers entered the system, but after several hours, four members of the party decided to retreat and returned to the surface. Shortly afterwards Mossdale Beck, swollen by rainfall, burst its banks and flooded the system, drowning the six cavers who remained underground, all friends of Livesey.

Ten years after the 1967 caving tragedy, Livesey concluded his search for adventurous wall climbing on Yorkshire limestone when he climbed the poignantly named *Mossdale Trip* in remembrance of

Pete on the first ascent of *Cream* E4 6a, Tremadog in 1976.
Photograph by Al Evans.

On *Gates of Delirium* E4 6a, Raven Crag, Thirlmere during the second ascent. *Photograph by Pete Gomersall.*

Above: Livesey with legendary American pioneer Royal Robbins in Crack Canyon USA.

Left: Outside the café in Malham.
Photographs by Geoff Birtles.

Above: Livesey with bouldering ace Al Manson.
Photograph by Geoff Birtles.

Left: The Gomersall and Livesey partnership.
Photograph by Bonny Masson.

Above left: The slab of *Downhill Racer* shortly after Pete's ascent. He was accused of over-zealous wire brushing by Peak activists.
Photograph by John Woodhouse.

Above right: Livesey climbing the bold *Downhill Racer* E4 6a Froggatt Edge, during filming for *Rock Athlete*.
Photograph by John Sheard.

Left: A picture of Pete that appeared in *'Private High'* the satirical back passage of Birtles' unique *Crags* Magazine.

Right: Livesey where he liked to be: 'at the front of the pack'. Taken during a local Yorkshire Dales fell race after Pete had retired from climbing circa mid 1980s.
Photograph kindly supplied by Lionel Sands seen here wearing number 4.

Below:
The award ceremony after winning the 1981 TV series 'Survival of the Fittest' against a competitive field of world class sportsmen.
Photograph by John Sheard.

Pete Livesey on the first ascent of *Carbon Wall* (now known as *Shadow Wall*) 5.11a, Lower Yosemite Falls in 1977.
Photograph by Geoff Birtles.

John Sheard repeating Livesey's Yosemite route from 1973 *Maxine's Wall* 5.10c.
Photograph from Sheard collection.

The Golden Mile E5 6b, Chee Tor Derbyshire. This Livesey classic marked his departure from competitive climbing in 1980. Climber Graham Hoey. *Photograph by Ian Smith.*

his friends who'd died. At E6 6b, *Mossdale Trip* epitomised what Pete stood for as a climber. It was a bold undertaking with only marginal protection in its first sixty feet, the rock is friable adding to the adventure and the route culminates with a vicious crux at about eighty feet. Success depends on a cool head and a calculated approach. In my opinion *Mossdale Trip* is analogous to *Lord of the Flies* climbed two years later by Fawcett. The rock types and settings are poles apart, yet the voyage that the climber undertakes, on both, are very similar. When I led *Mossdale Trip* myself in 1989, (the same year incidentally that I led *Lord*), it had only been repeated by about ten people, unlike *Lord* that had become a well trodden classic. Like most of Livesey's routes, *Mossdale* left a lasting impression on me.

In 1991 I climbed a companion route to *Mossdale Trip* up the wall to its left. It wasn't on a par with the quality and difficulty of Pete's route, but it climbed similar terrain and required a similar bold and cautious approach. I called the route *The Living Dead Extensions* after a squalid series of rarely explored passages at the deepest extremities of Pen y Ghent pot. I named the route in Pete's honour. I had the pleasure of pointing the line of my new route out to Pete when he was out on one of his training runs through Gordale. When I told him what I'd called it he just gave me a wry smile.

I give the impression that Livesey's routes are all about bold adventure and cryptic line, but this is not the case. Many tackle blatant challenges and feature exacting moves. The peg-scarred and previously aided line of *Wellington Crack* required a new sort of technique. In 1973 finger jamming of the type required to climb peg scars was in its infancy and was the sort of challenge that Pete relished. His landmark route *Footless Crow* on Goat Crag, climbed in 1974 at E5 6b, featured powerful technical moves through unrelenting steep ground. *Lost Horizons* on the East Buttress of Scafell has purity of line. Whatever the style of climb I think most people would comment on the excellent quality of the Livesey route; they are always memorable.

Johnny Walker related an amusing little tale to me, which gives an insight into either how Pete perceived some of his own routes, or was able to promote them. Johnny was talking to Pete when their conversation turned to Goat Crag in the Lakes, home to two of Pete's great signature routes, and Pete suddenly said: *'Goat Crag is a load of rubbish.'*

'Well what about your routes Bitter Oasis *and* Footless Crow,' asked a somewhat confused Johnny Walker.

'Ah well you see Johnny, Bitter Oasis *and* Footless Crow *are not on Goat Crag they're in another world,'* said Pete without batting an eyelid.

Johnny was just dumbfounded.

In my eyes Livesey was a natural leader. In the early 1970s he had the vision to see the appeal of the 'totally free' approach to rock-climbing. He understood how to apply training and athleticism to make that vision a reality. He had courage, both in his own convictions and in the real sense when moving into previously uncharted territory under demanding conditions. He had goofy looks, yet oozed charisma and was able to attract talented climbing partners who shared his vision and were inspired to achieve great things themselves. Fawcett and Gomersall both fitted this mould and perhaps this is where Livesey made his greatest mark. Not so much in the routes that he left himself, but in how he inspired his followers and how they in turn inspired a whole generation. In this way he continued to be instrumental in climbing's evolution even when he'd stopped. He led the way showing what was possible, but it took an even stronger and fitter Fawcett to finally dispense with the remaining aid points on the *Cave* routes in Gordale, and the superb *Doubting Thomas* and *Mulatto Wall* at Malham. From a platform of possibility created by Livesey, Fawcett went from strength to strength and achieved groundbreaking things on the rock that made people look and listen.

Lord of the Flies was a natural step forward for Fawcett. For the time it appeared as an audacious piece of wall climbing, set on a perfect stage, the iconic Dinas y Gromlech. The drama and historic significance of the ascent were all accentuated by Perou's filming of *Rock Athlete*. This meant that *Lord* became the Golden Fleece and prize for the climbing elite in the early 1980s, which continued to perpetuate the penchant for hard trad in the UK. Perhaps none of this would have happened without Livesey and the loosely connected cohort of stars that he inspired. As Livesey bowed out, focus on the limestone of Yorkshire and the Peak continued on eliminating aid from steep artificial lines. More climbers with exceptional abilities were operating on the scene. Inspiration, competition, and sometimes jealousy were all thrown together in the melting pot, and this meant that the climbing bar would be raised fast and high over the next decade.

During the 1970s, Pete Livesey and friends exported their free climbing ethic to France. He is often credited with introducing the concept of free climbing to the French but, in truth, pockets of French climbers had recognised the challenge and value of free climbing for years. Parisian climbers had practised free climbing on the sandstone boulders of Fontainebleau since the early 1900s. Perhaps a more realistic perspective would be that during the 1970s, Livesey acted more as a catalyst for the move from 'cragging as practise for Alpinism' to 'totally free' as a means to its own end. He was also a very fast climber, applying track and field mentality to rock-climbing and obviously deriving pleasure in knocking hours off typical ascent times for long multi-pitch routes. This must have sent out strong messages to the Alpine traditionalists. Livesey's totally free approach was demonstrably a purer, faster and arguably safer method of attacking multi-pitch routes. During his early explorations in the south of France he met the extremely talented Jean-Claude Droyer. As we have already heard from the man himself, Droyer not only shared Pete's enthusiasm and vision for free climbing, he was inspired by him. Like Livesey he was a change agent and his new methods met some resistance from his countrymen, yet he was undeterred and led by example, establishing the country's first 7a in the style that would later be defined as the Red Point by the late great Kurt Albert. Jibè Tribout credits Droyer as the inspiration behind his own rise to climbing greatness, together with that of others such as Le Menestrel brothers and Alain Ghersens.

As sport climbing gained impetus and blossomed in the late 1970s, in France new routes of immense quality and difficulty were opened up, illustrating what was possible and this was regarded as massive progress. The French led the way, but the Italians, Spanish and West Germans followed suit. In 1980 Livesey published an unassuming little guidebook called *French Rock Climbs*. The content of the book was largely based on information gained from Droyer. This little book, although criticised at the time for inaccurate route descriptions, contained just enough information to entice British rock climbers away from their traditional Alpine destinations and get them to crags like the Verdon Gorge, Le Saussois and Buoux, and that was it. For many, once they'd sampled the culture and nature of climbing on these crags and witnessed what the French were doing from a 'free climbing perspective' their own attitudes were changed. Brits also started visiting other countries where the great quality of sport climbing could be enjoyed. It was only a matter of time before another 'next generation' would import the continental approach back into the UK.

In 1982 film maker Sid Perou produced a documentary called *The Fingertip Phenomenon*. It was a natural extension to Sid's successful series of TV programmes called *Rock Athlete*, which had featured Pete Livesey and his close climbing associates expounding the challenge and appeal of 'free rock-climbing'. *The Fingertip Phenomenon* painted a picture of modern rock-climbing against a canvas of the Verdon Gorge in the south of France. Its stars included Ron and Gill Fawcett, with Jerry Peel to support Ron on some of the harder climbs, and Chris Gibb in charge of sound recording. When the film was broadcast on UK television I watched it in awe and knew that I had to climb there.

As we have seen in previous essays in this book about the Verdon, early routes were climbed ground-up and followed natural crack and chimney lines very much in the Alpine style and tradition. On early visits to the Verdon, Livesey and Sheard climbed these lines 'fast and free' making ascents of routes like the 15-pitch long *La Demande* in under two hours. Even today for an accomplished party of two it would be a hard time to beat. In between these natural crack lines are acres of smooth grey limestone. From a distance the rock looks blank, but nature has worked in the climber's favour. Acidic rain over the millennia has dissolved little pockets into the carboniferous limestone that accommodate fingers and toes perfectly. In certain areas these pockets are present in sufficient numbers and adequate combinations that they can be linked together for hundreds of feet. When Livesey, Sheard and friends started making visits to the Verdon, local climbers, inspired by the 'totally free' concept, had begun to realise the potential of these pocketed faces and soon started establishing new routes, equipping them from above by abseil. In this way climbers could be quite selective in their choice of line. Venturing onto these faces meant that features in the rock affording natural protection were often absent so the use of pre-drilled expansion bolts was the logical way forward. The appeal of these new routes revolved around several compelling factors; perfect rock, athletic movement, fantastic exposure and difficulties, which the up-and-coming rock athlete could test and measure their performance against. The tiny snowball that Livesey had been so influential in creating grew at an understandable rate.

When I first visited the gorge in the spring of 1985 I only had a week and had compiled a hit list created from what I'd seen on *The Fingertip Phenomenon*, the contents of Pete Livesey's article in *Mountain* 61 and the inspiring poster image of Ron Fawcett on the route *Necronomicon*. Livesey, Sheard and Fawcett definitely played an influential part in my own journeying into France and Europe and I suspect that many others of my era would say the same. When I was researching this book project, having lost my own copy of *French Rock Climbs* by Peter Livesey, I ordered a second-hand copy from Amazon. Inside the cover it bore the name and address of Sheffield's Paul Mitchell; it was dated September 1981. I have no doubt that this is the same Paul Mitchell, renowned Peak activist, new router and friend of the remarkable Steve Bancroft.

During the 1980s I had many visits to the Verdon, they were great times spent in fine company. In those days La Palud was a simple rural Provence village surrounded by lavender fields and still free from any of the trappings that its popularity would eventually encourage. There were two bars, a restaurant, a tobacconist, a bakery and a local shop. A simple campsite at the top of the village provided our home. It was run by an eccentric farmer called Jean Paul. If proceedings ever got a bit rowdy or out of hand Jean Paul, in true Wild West fashion, would emerge from his house, shotgun in hand and let off a couple of barrels into the air to quieten things down and let people know who was the boss. I think that my own experiences were not too dissimilar from those described by Livesey in *Mountain* magazine published in 1978, with one exception, the scene.

La Palud was buzzing with climbers from all over the world. Development in the gorge was at its peak and 'the scene' felt fresh, with a real spirit of pioneering adventure about it. It was commonplace for regular guys, like us, to brush shoulders with some of the world's finest. Jean-Marc Troussier and Patrick Edlinger from France, Beat Kammerlander from Austria, Christian Griffiths from America,

Stefan Glowacz from Germany and, of course, home-grown talent in the form of Simon Nadin, Paul Pritchard, Mark Pretty, Craig Smith and Chris Gore to name but a few. The list of highly influential rock-climbers visiting the Verdon during this period could go on and on.

Talk in the bars and on the campsite often revolved around who had done what and which were the latest must-do routes, everyone enthusiastically sharing info and waxing lyrical about this route and that. Further details could be obtained by consulting a newly published guidebook to the Verdon, together with the new routes book, both of which were kept in the bar. In this way, people built up their 'hit list' for the trip. The Verdon experience always took you on a mental journey and a day in the gorge was guaranteed to leave your body flooded with an intoxicating mix of endorphins. At the end of the day this heady mix was usually fuelled with copious quantities of cold beer and warm red wine. Groups would gather together around camping stoves, eating and telling stories long into the night.

Looking back, the mid 1980s Verdon scene was pretty unique. Different nationalities were literally thrown together in a couple of small bars and on a tiny campsite. Different attitudes, styles and approaches to climbing were debated in the bars and demonstrated with some audacious ascents on the rock. Some climbers came for the sheer adventurous nature of the place, but it was also a forcing ground for pushing standards and not just the grade. Some extraordinary feats were accomplished; like Philippe Plantier's free solo of *Les Frères Caramels Mou*, which featured F7a climbing with hundreds of feet of space beneath his feet.

The Verdon definitely opened up people's imaginations and broadened their horizons. I am sure visiting climbers of all nationalities took new ideas, attitudes, and beliefs back home with them, with influential consequences. Sport climbing arguably had some of its roots in the 'totally free' ethic espoused by Pete Livesey, Jean-Claude

Droyer and those who followed, like Fawcett, Berhault and Edlinger, who took up the flame and continued to champion the free climbing cause.

Ironically it was the birth of 'sport climbing' that was one of the reasons Pete chose to bow out of rock-climbing with his Derbyshire test piece and limestone classic, *The Golden Mile* in 1980. Pete was always driven to raise the game, for him rock-climbing standards were judged by a combination of speed, technical difficulty, being able to operate coolly under physical pressure and most importantly of all, adventure. During the early 1980s hard rock-climbing standards were defined more than ever by the strength and technique of the athlete and this could really be perfected when climbs were protected by reliable gear. By 1983 the magic grade of F8a was established on the French crag Buoux by Edlinger. In the UK, limestone became the arena where the sport climbing elite battled for the records. By 1980 I think that Livesey probably realised that his own predictions in his visionary piece of writing, *The Shape of Grades to Come*, were coming to fruition. A new game was emerging, and in a game where stronger and fitter meant best, it was obvious that he couldn't compete in such an arena. Pete saw this coming well before sport climbing was legitimately recognised in the UK. His own prodigies in the shape of Fawcett and Gomersall were graphic proof of this, so he decided to bow out gracefully. I don't think it was the inability to compete that was the sole determinant of his decision to retire from climbing. I think he also believed that sport climbing lacked an intrinsic component of the game, the element of adventure. This is brought home to me when I recall a vivid conversation with Pete back in 1984 in his café in Malham. On that occasion my good friend Adrian Ledgway and I shared a coffee with Pete before an excursion into Gordale.

'*Are you going up to Gordale again,*' Livesey enquired.

'*We are,*' we stated in unison.

'*And what are you going to do this time?*' he continued.

'*We thought we'd have a go at* Jenny Wren.'

Pete came over and joined us at our table. '*You two like your adventure, don't you?*' He then continued on a different tack. '*Have you heard about that young kid down in Wales. I believe he's just done a new route at Pen Trwyn. I heard that he put seven bolts in seventy-foot of limestone. What do you make of that?*' Livesey was referring to a climb called *Statement of Youth*, which had just been done by a young rock-climber called Ben Moon. The way that Livesey emphasised, ' seven bolts in seventy feet', suggested to me, that he thought these bolts somehow undermined or discredited the route. The name, however, appeared to have a powerful underlying message. It wasn't just a throwaway name, it appeared to be deliberately conceived very much like the route that it described. To me, it suggested that Moon was sticking two fingers up at the old guard and saying, 'Here I am, I'm here to stay and this is what the future looks like'.

'*Mmm, seven bolts does seem a bit excessive,*' I agreed, '*but it's still reckoned to be desperate, it gets E7.*'

Livesey concluded his ethical line of questioning with a matter of fact conclusion, '*Well, personally, I can't see how a seventy-foot climb with seven bolts in it can be graded E7.*' Of course the 'E' grade was used in the UK to roughly define three elements within a climb; its technicality, how sustained it was, and importantly, how run-out or serious it was. In Pete's mind I'm sure that, 'seven bolts in seventy feet', completely removed the intrinsic and important element of risk. He redirected his attention to Ledge and me, and with a grin said, '*Well you'll not find any bolts on* Jenny Wren, *so don't fall off.*'

In 1984, just four years after Pete Livesey had retired from competitive climbing, Ben Moon had established the UK's first 8a protected entirely by pre-placed bolts. It modelled what was being done in the sport climbing idiom in mainland Europe. A new generation of rock athletes were emerging who would continue to shape the sport of climbing. Like Livesey, these athletes trained hard. Naturally, people became fitter and stronger and this continues to be reflected by the standard of sport climbs being produced across the globe today and also in the styles that these routes are climbed. The modern rock-climber's aspiration surely has to be for the 'on-sight flash', and some truly remarkable advancements and achievements are being realised today. The importance of purity of style was something that Livesey himself expounded, but sometimes failed to live up to.

Pete was an exceptionally driven individual. His hunger to be first or fastest in the competitive field of cutting edge climbing sometimes meant that in his own mind, 'the end result sometimes justified the means of getting there'. This is relevant to one or two of Pete's new routes, where he employed 'unethical' tactics to climb them free. His route *Claws* at Kilnsey Crag in Yorkshire is a good illustration. It stands as a fine climb, yet it is marred by a series of chipped holds on its second pitch. . Chipping holds, resting on gear, soloing with back ropes were occasional practices used by Livesey, which sometimes meant he courted controversy. This led to accusations of double standards, but these actions must be observed in the historical context in which they were set. It was a period during which the climbing bar was raised significantly and continually. These actions promoted important ethical discussion, which, in a way, galvanised people around the principles that continue to guide the development of climbing today. Livesey's legacy of training and athleticism has also been translated into the bouldering arena where phenomenal things continue to be achieved. As Livesey predicted, sport climbing, like other athletic disciplines, continues to illustrate what a climber can achieve with raw talent and a dedicated training programme. To date the acceleration of standards achieved in sport climbing and bouldering has not been mirrored in the traditional crag climbing arena. This is understandable given the risks and high stakes of pushing the frontiers of adventure.

Significant bold climbs continue to be made, but not on the same scale and rate as in the sport and bouldering facets. Livesey's bleak predictions about the doom of traditional climbing have proven incorrect however. I wonder whether living in Malham and being so close to one of the stages for the bolt revolution polarised his views. Trad climbing remains alive and well in the UK and there are many who value and embrace the diversity of climbing from bouldering to Himalayan mountaineering. This said, I do believe that a naïve and small minded movement exists who would like to turn rock climbing into an accessible risk free arcade game for the masses.

On the bigger cliffs, groundbreaking speed and solo ascents of hard traditional multi pitch routes continue to push the frontiers of possibility. As we have seen, Livesey was a champion and pioneer of both these approaches, but more importantly he led the way at crucial periods in history. His ascent of *Astroman* with Fawcett coincided with their friendship with John Long and crucially the genesis of the Stonemasters group, who would go on to redefine rock climbing standards in America. This was all coincidence, but still an important part of Livesey's influential reach. Remarkable speed ascents continue to define climbing standards for some. Look at Ueli Steck today and his speed records in the Alps and Himalaya, and the American Alex Honnold and his superlative solos in Yosemite. If Pete had been alive today I think the competitive athlete in him would be suitably impressed.

As mentioned earlier, Livesey's early explorations of the crags in France and his 'totally free' ethic had brought him into contact with the like-minded French pioneer, Jean-Claude Droyer. Competition and mutual respect between the two revealed to them just what could be achieved in the free climbing arena. Moving fast and free, these guys must have felt they were breaking record after record when compared with the traditional peg and aid ascents typical of the day. This in itself must surely have fuelled their intrinsic motives and personal drive; in turn their achievements inspired a new generation of rock athlete and sent out clear messages to the old guard that fast and free was a better and purer form of climbing. These events heralded a change in the hearts and minds of climbers across Europe. Some people have accused Livesey of being a self publicist. He certainly knew how to influence and make an impact, but I think Fawcett's wry observation '*He knew what routes were hot, where the gaps were, and most important of all, how to get one over on the locals*', is a more realistic reason as to why he left such a lasting and powerful impression. I think history shows us that Pete's positive impact in climbing massively outweighs his minor flaws. Free climbing principles demonstrated to such great effect by Livesey initially in the UK, but then on the big limestone crags in Europe and the granite walls of Yosemite, continue to be fundamental to our approach to rock climbing today. The route and discoveries made along the way are as important as the journey's end.

The Circle is Closed

by John Sheard

What shaped Pete's attitude to climbing can be seen, in a way, by what happened after we put the Verdon firmly on the climbing map. More campsites appeared, hotels were built and climbers from the UK poured in, encouraged by Pete's little guidebook. Flawed but effective, it was the instrument which opened Europe to UK rock-climbers. The tide was turning and it was time to start thinking of moving on to other nearby destinations; always with the lavender-scented air of Provence, the shimmering clarity of the limestone scenery, the shady plane trees and the Gauloises smell of welcoming French cafés. But most of all, I think, it was Pete's need to be out there in front, one step ahead, looking for the next adventure. New routes in the Verdon were becoming as difficult as any around: bolts would proliferate and climbers would avoid the river approaches in favour of abseil descent from the crest to do two or three pitches. Times were a-changing. Yes, time to move on.

The climbs in southern France were by no means the end of Pete's affair with climbing. Other major routes were to follow in the UK, Yosemite and the Dolomites, but around 1980 even though he was still pretty much at the top of his game he made the deliberate and conscious decision to quit, at least publicly At thirty-seven he probably recognised that age was not on his side, there were an increasing number of younger climbers who must inevitably surpass the standards that he had set. Many in his position would have quietly retired from the limelight but continued, as many have, to climb routes, which were challenging and new but no longer at the cutting edge. That he enjoyed climbing and all that went with it was never in dispute, in fact, he quietly went about doing what he had always done, having adventures, revelling in the wonderful freedom of the outdoors, and meeting respected friends, ancient and modern. But there must have been more to it than that. Why did he apparently turn his back on a game he had, for a time, dominated; why cease to practice and participate only as an armchair pundit and commentator?

At his memorial, when family, friends and colleagues turned out in celebration of a climber's life filled with achievement and fun, Geoff Birtles presented a perceptive line when describing Pete's sudden explosion on the climbing scene, 'There was a game on'. I hadn't appreciated the significance of those few words at the time, but on later reflection the true depth of that comment struck home and is perhaps at the heart of why he left climbing with apparently still so much to offer.

Pete's understanding of what constituted a 'game' was not that generally accepted by most of the Western world, which requires rules, governance, referees, structure and often the ubiquitous strip. Hence he was able to say (June 1991), '*Climbing does not slot neatly into play, games, other sport activity or contemporary recreational circles. It is essentially non-competitive (in the generally accepted sense), anti-social, not based on uniform or team rules and giving freedom of action and ability to do your own thing*'. He knew what he was talking about, having walked away from athletics after narrowly failing to win the 'game' at the Three As Steeplechase at the White City in Manchester, and had worn the green LIVESEY vest when he competed in Survival of the Fittest in New Zealand.

Pete's game was one of the mind. Pushing the known limits; rationalising what could be done with indifferent protection; playing with the media; part self-publicity, part discovery; testing the limit of acceptability and then exceeding it; provocatively testing everything that was accepted as the norm in teaching, climbing, society, friendships, commitment, life and, ultimately death. Emphatically not what can be done by those who accept rules, conditions, standards and regulations.

His last Derbyshire route, *The Golden Mile*, in July 1980, seemed to mark his increasing disillusion with the path that recent climbing was taking. He used his monthly column in *Climber* and *Hillwalker* to advance his unease at the ever-escalating introduction of organised competition and bolt protection, seeing both as a negation of all that was vital and essential in climbing. His pessimism led him to the conclusion that adventure was being stifled and that the future of world rock-climbing was being jeopardised in the interest of safe leisure for all. In his words, '*The complete asphyxiation of the breath of adventure*'. He saw sport-climbing resulting in the elimination of risk and that this would impoverish climbing and indeed sow the seeds of its destruction. It had nothing to do with real climbing and, therefore, nothing to do with mountaineering. It was worthy but separate and sterile. This new game was not one that held any attraction for him. There was nothing there that interested or motivated him. Time, therefore, to leave and find a new game, as simple as that for a man who knew his own mind and was not given to compromise.

'*Tether the horse before it has time to bolt!*' was his whimsical advice, to be followed shortly by his tongue-in-cheek farewell to a game he predicted would become ultimately dominated by Olympic hopefuls training for media glory. '*I am retiring to become a professional athlete and sport climber. I don't climb much these days, 100 routes a year, mainly in trainers. Don't like gritstone, never have, can't see any reason for not bolting it. Rock-climbing is now a separate activity, a pariah in mountain activities. It has nothing to do with mountaineering, Alpinism, fell running or big wall climbing. There is no interweaving of activities. Sport climbing is simply mastering moves. I haven't the remotest inclination to join this band of climbers, nor have I anything against what they are doing. The BMC has made two big mistakes. Firstly, getting involved with access, and increasingly playing the role of policeman. Competition is the second. The BMC should take the position that Mountaineering is what they are about, and have nothing to do with sport climbing. Other problems are on the horizon with access and professionalisation. Anyway, I don't care – bye!'*

Pete was undoubtedly visionary as can be seen in his articles, *The Grades of Things to Come*, and, *Jonathan Livingstone Steelfingers*, but his pessimism (or was it just a provocative and timely warning?) has perhaps proved to be ill-founded. I suspect he would have been relieved had he lived to see the state of play today. Younger climbers on our crags taking calculated risks undreamed of in the 80s. Bold new rock-climbs being pushed out on serious and remote mountain walls in the Livesey tradition. The adventurous are still with us, even though dwarfed in numbers by the thrill seekers in the leisure centres.

Limestone saw the first appearance of Pete as a new force in climbing, it also provided his swan song; the circle was closed and he exited when still at the top of his game having made an impact that ensures his place as one of the all-time greats. I believe he would have been justifiably proud at the continuing respect shown for his achievements, and relieved that the tradition to which he subscribed has quietly survived.

APPENDIX

Chronology

Significant Events and Dates

1943   Michael Peter Livesey born in Huddersfield on 12th September.

1957   As a member of Longwood Harriers Livesey achieves top rankings in junior cross country events.

1960s   Takes up potholing and rock-climbing and earns a reputation as a courageous caver. Visits Norway on caving trips.

1965   Invited on the Karst Hydrology Expedition to Jamaica and spends six months exploring and mapping the Quashies River System.

Tries and fails to climb *Vector* (E2 5c) at Tremadog.

1966   Develops as a skilled canoeist and is earmarked as potential member of the national slalom team by the 1968 Olympic Selection Committee.

1967   FA *Douk* with John Stanger, Livesey's early new route climbed with one point of aid now E3 5c.

Caving expedition to descend Provatina on the Greek/Turkish border. Reported as world's deepest shaft at 411m by expedition leader Ken Kelly. (Pete later based some of his humorous writings on these events. Also covered with great wit by Jim Eyre in his book *The Cave Explorers*.)

Second ascent of the *Rimmon Route* on the Troll Wall, Norway with John Stanger. New route on the South Face of the Bispen, Norway.

1968	Early repeat of *Extol* (E2 5b). Livesey starts to develop his climbing skills in earnest.
1969	Caving expedition to Epos in Greece with Jim Eyre.
1971	FFA *Face Route* (E3 6a) Gordale with John Sheard. FA *Jenny Wren* (E5 6a) Gordale with John Sheard; possibly the hardest route in the UK at that time. (These routes are dismissed as implausible by some members of the YMC. They remain in denial of Livesey's abilities.)
1972	*Adjudicator Wall* (E3 5c) Dovedale; second ascent. FFA *Clink* (E4 6a) with John Sheard, Trow Gill. FFA *Flaky Wall* (E4 5c) with John Sheard, High Tor. FFA *Central Wall* (E4 6a) with John Sheard, Kilnsey. FA *Doubting Thomas* (1 pt) Malham FFA by Ron Fawcett in 1979 at E5 6b.

FA *Fine Time* (1 pt) Raven Crag, Langdale (FFA Pete Botterill 1979).

Reduces aid on *Rebel* (to 4 pts) with John Hammond, Gordale (FFA Ron Fawcett in 1978 at E5 6b).

Schmuck Kamin (Austria); third British ascent of this long multi-pitch route on the Fleischbank East Face climbed with John Sheard.

FA South Face of Kuh i Parau Zagros Mountains of Iran 1,500 feet (HVS) with Ian Edwards.

Cruel Sister (E3 5c) Pavey Ark, second, partially aided ascent with Ron Fawcett.

1973   FFA (almost) *Deliverance* (1 pt) Gordale with John Sheard (FFA by Dougie Hall in 1982 at E5 6b).

FA *Limehill* (E5 6a) Malham with John Sheard.

Livesey makes the first of several visits to Yosemite and comes away this time with the FA of *Maxines Wall* 5.10.

1974   FA *Wellington Crack* (1 rest) Ilkley. Livesey later returns with John Sheard to climb the route clean at E4 5c.

FFA *Footless Crow* (E5 6b) Goat Crag with Robin Witham.

A phenomenal effort at the time and a clear demonstration of how much Pete had raised the game.

FA *Bitter Oasis* (E4 6a) Goat Crag with John Sheard.

('*Well the thing is Johnny,* Footless Crow *and* Bitter Oasis *are not on Goat Crag, they're in another world.*' Livesey in conversation with Johnny Walker several years later.)

FA *Eastern Hammer* (E3 6a) Gimmer Crag with Al Manson.

FFA *Hardline* (E5 6a) Heptonstall with Al Manson.

FA *Right Wall* (E5 6a) Dinas Cromlech. A stand-out route on a historically significant crag.

FFA *Zukator* (E4 6b) Tremadog with John Sheard.

FA *All Quiet* (E4 6a) Almscliff with Al Manson.

FFA *Nagasaki Grooves* (E4 6b) FA Dry Grasp (E4 6a) Borrowdale.
(Both climbed solo with a back rope system which drew some veiled criticism from the locals.)

The Cumbrian. The first ascent by Paul Braithwaite and Rod Valentine used 3 pts. Livesey made the second ascent with Al Manson and claimed the FFA, but initially failed to disclose that he'd taken one rest. Eventually freed at E5 6a by the Berzins brothers in 1977.

(A classic line that sparked up controversy between the various protagonists as they levelled criticism at each others' style of ascent.)

Livesey's second visit to Yosemite. Climbs with Ron Fawcett and leaves with FA of *Crack A Go Go* (5.11c) and FFA of *Bercheff-Williams*.

Pete in collaboration with Dave Nicol and Keith Nannery publishes a 'home produced' topo guide to Yosemite. A futuristic approach to climbing guides at that time.

Returns from America in September and joins Bingley College as a lecturer in outdoor education.

('*Having Livesey on your staff was like having Nureyev in your ballet company!*' The late Tom Price and Dean of the College.)

1975   FFA *Eroica* (E2 6a) Pentire Head with Jill Lawrence.

FA *Arries Ook* (E4 6a) Almscliff with Ron Fawcett.

FA *Acid Test* (E4 6b) Giggleswick with Jill Lawrence.

FFA *Fingerlicker* (E4 6a) Tremadog with Jill Lawrence.

FFA *Great Arête* (E4 6a) Lech Dhu North Wales with Jill Lawrence.

FA *Beyond the Fringe* (E5 6a) Ilkley with Jill Lawrence.

Cave Route Right-Hand Gordale. Livesey and Fawcett combine forces to climb this spectacular aid line free. They significantly reduce the aid, but have to resort to three rests such is the sustained nature of the climbing. Still a tremendous effort. Fawcett returns in 1982 and finishes the job off producing a couple of Limestone masterpieces with CRRH and CRLH.

FA *Moratorium*, El Capitan, Yosemite Valley with Trevor Jones.

Baffin Island trip, Livesey and Lawrence climb the West Face of Tirokwa, 48 pitches, grade 5.9 with two points of aid in a record-breaking 15 hours.

1976   FA *Bastille* (1pt) High Tor with Jill Lawrence (FFA Mike Graham 1978 at E5 6b).

Filming with Henry Barber for the American TV series, *American Sportsman*.

FFA *Liberator* (E3 6a) Great Zawn with Ron Fawcett.

FA *Cream* (E4 6a) Tremadog with Ron Fawcett.

Mortlock's Arête (E4 6a) second ascent.

FA *Claws* (E5 6b) Kilnsey with Jill Lawrence. Pete chipped a series of holds on pitch 2, but maintained that the quality of the route outweighed the minor discrepancy of the chips.

FA *Foil* (E3 6a) Dinas Cromlech with Jill Lawrence; a good find by Livesey.

FA *Lost Horizons* (E4 6a 1pt) with Jill Lawrence. Once again Pete attracted criticism from local activists about his style of ascent, pre-placed protection and peg for aid (FFA Bob Berzins 1982).

Livesey makes first visits to the Verdon with John Sheard and friends.

1977   Joint BMC/FFM meet in the Verdon with John Sheard, Ron Fawcett, Gill Price, Dave Hope and Roger Baxter-Jones. They make free ascents of routes like *Necronomicon* (E4 6a/F6c) and *Triomphe d'Eros* (E4 6a/F6c). Livesey and Fawcett make a substantially free ascent of *Pichenibule*. (Possibly the birth of what would evolve into modern sport climbing. Certainly a key catalyst in its evolution. Like-minded French climber, Jean-Claude Droyer, is inspired by the style of the ascents.)

FA *Downhill Racer* (E4 6a) Froggatt, Pete receives criticism from Peak activists for 'over enthusiastic' wire brushing.

FA *Mossdale Trip* (E6 6b) with Jill Lawrence (Gordale) a Livesey masterpiece.

FFA *Blitzkrieg* (E4 5b 6a) Raven Crag, Thirlmere with Pete Gomersall.

FA *Peels of Laughter* (E5 6b) Raven Crag, Thirlmere with Pete Gomersall. Gommy led the route first, but Livesey recorded the climb as 'First ascent, P Livesey & P Gomersall, alternate leads'.
(As Gommy later said: '*Nice reporting for a one-pitch route.*')

Livesey makes a further visit to the Verdon.

Livesey's third visit to Yosemite. Makes a one-day and early free ascent of *Astroman* (5.11c) with Ron Fawcett. Livesey and John Long make the FFA of the *Chouinard-Herbert* (5.11c) and Livesey makes the FA *Carbon Wall* (5.11a) Lower Yosemite Falls.

1978   FA *Das Capital* (E6 6b) Raven Crag, Thirlmere with Pete Gomersall.

FA *Wailing Wall* (E4 6a) with C Crawshaw.

FFA *Snowdrop* (E4 6a) Clogwyn yr Eryr with Pete Gomersall.

1979   Livesey teams up with Nicho Mailänder for FFAs in the Dolomites and Switzerland including the mainly free ascent of the *Brandler-Hasse* on the Rotwand.

FA of *Purr Spire* (E5 6a).

FA *Zero* (E6 6a) with Jill Lawrence.

1980   FFA *Oriole* (E4 6a) Clogwyn yr Eryr with Pete Gomersall.

FA *Golden Mile* (E5 6b) Chee Tor with Alec Livesey.

FA *Musical Women* (E5 6b) with P Gomersall.

The Rock Athlete series is screened on national TV. Footage features Livesey climbing *Wellington Crack, Face Route, Downhill Racer* and training on indoor climbing walls.

French Rock Climbs is published. The first British guidebook dedicated purely to the rock-climbs of France.

Pete retires from competitive rock-climbing, but keeps in touch with climbing, reporting developments through his monthly magazine columns throughout the 80s and into the 90s, (*Rock Scene* in *Climber* and *Rambler* and the *Pete Livesey Column* in *Climber* and *Climber and Hillwalker*).

1981	Meets his future wife Soma.

His interest turns to his track and field roots and he starts competitive fell running and orienteering. He enters his first Karrimor International Mountain Marathon (KIMM) and is placed 9th in class B.

1982	Moves to Mallham village and later sets up the café.

Lime Crime is published, co-authored with Graham Desroy.

He continues to compete in the Karrimor International Mountain Marathons.

KIMMs with date of race, race class, distance height of ascent and placing:

1982 B/60KM/1800M/9th
1983 A/54/KM/3600M/26th
1985 A/65KM/4600M/10th (1st Vet.)
1988 A/59KM/2650M/16th (2nd Vet)
1989 A/67KM/3800M/12th (1st Vet)
1995 B/56KM/2200M/43rd

1983	Pete gets first place in HTV's *Survival of the Fittest* competition.
	(This was an adventure sporting challenge in which a field of eight top athletes competed in a series of endurance challenges in Snowdonia over a period of a week. The show was filmed and broadcast on national TV. Fellow competitors included 400m hurdles champion and multi Olympic medal winner David Hemery, Olympic Judo Champion and gold medal winner Neil Adams, world's strongest man Geoff Capes and English rugby union international Roger Uttley. The event became international and Livesey took part in the New Zealand event.)
	Tai Livesey is born.
1984	Climbs *Footless Crow* with Chris Bonington and their ascent is filmed as part of a new TV series. The programmes are screened on national TV and a book of the series is published.
1984 onwards	During this period he competes in many national fell races and orienteering competitions with regular podium places. He enters two Raid Francital races in the Alps and takes 3rd place both times in Class A.

1997   Pete retires from Ilkley College. Continues
             running and maintains his number one ranking
             in the M45 class of orienteering. Soon after is
             diagnosed with pancreatic cancer.

1998   Dies at the age of 54 on 26th February.

             *'Don't let the buggers start talking about me
             when I'm gone.'* Pete's last words to John Sheard
             shortly before his death.

Significant Solo Ascents

Pete was an avid soloist, and made many solo ascents during his career including significant ascents of multi-pitch routes overseas.

Below are listed some of his significant FIRST solo ascents.

Route	Grade	Crag	Length	Date soloed
Steeple	E2 5b	Shelter Stone	240m	1973
Blind Valley	E3 5c	Ilkley	18m	1973

(*Blind Valley* was also a FFA solo)

Nagasaki Grooves	E4 6b	Great End	100m	1974
Dry Grasp	E4 6a	Upper Falcon	50m	1974

(*Nagasaki Grooves* and *Dry Grasp* were FA solos in which Pete employed a back rope system.)

Lord of the Rings	E2 5b	Scafell	345m	1975

(Complex route-finding on this 14-pitch route. Soloed trailing a rope.)

Holocaust	E4 6a	Dow Crag	70m	1975
Sidewalk	E2 5b	Dow Crag	90m	1975

(*Sidewalk* was soloed in descent.)

Silly Arête	E3 5c	Tremadog	40m	1975
Kafoozalem	E3 6a	Great Zawn	36m	1976
The Ghost	E2 6a	Great Zawn	36m	1976
Eroica	E2 6a	Pentire Head	64m	1976

(*Kafoozalem*, *The Ghost* and *Eroica* were all soloed around the time that Pete was filming with Henry Barber. Barber was also an avid soloist and word would have definitely reached his ears about these solos.)

Route	Grade	Crag	Length	Date soloed
Old Friends	E3 6a	Stanage	18m	1976
Grand Alliance	E3 6a	Black Crag	70m	1976
Green Death	E5 5c	Millstone	20m	1977
Fern Hill	E2 5c	Cratcliffe	18m	1977
Five Finger Exercise	E2 5c	Cratcliffe	20m	1977
Darius	E1 5c	High Tor	50m	1977
Great Wall	E4 6a	Cloggy	70m	1978

The Tick List

A legacy of great routes – Pete's Top Thirty British Classics

	Route	Grade	Quality	Crag	Location
1	*Das Capital*	E6 6b 6b	***	Raven, Thirlmere	Lakes
2	*Mossdale Trip*	E6 6b 5c	***	Gordale	Yorkshire
3	*Footless Crow*	E6 6b	***	Goat Crag	Lakes
4	*Peels of Laughter*	E5 6b	***	Raven, Thirlmere	Lakes
5	*Deliverance*	E5 5c 6b 6a	***	Gordale	Yorkshire
6	*Golden Mile*	E5 6b	***	Chee Tor	Derbyshire
7	*Claws*	E5 6a 6b	***	Kilnsey	Yorkshire
8	*Right Wall*	E5 6a	***	Dinas Cromlech	North Wales
9	*Limehill*	E5 6a	***	Malham	Yorkshire
10	*Jenny Wren*	E5 6a	**	Gordale	Yorkshire
11	*Hard Line*	E5 6a	**	Heptonstall	Yorkshire
12	*Nagasaki Grooves*	E4 6b	***	Great End	Lakes
13	*Lost Horizons*	E4 6a	***	Scafell	Lakes
14	*Blitzkrieg*	E4 5b 6a 5c	***	Raven, Thirlmere	Lakes
15	*Bitter Oasis*	E4 6a	***	Goat Crag	Lakes
16	*Central Wall*	E4 6a	***	Kilnsey	Yorkshire
17	*Downhill Racer*	E4 6a	**	Frogatt	Derbyshire
18	*Fingerlicker*	E4 6a	***	Tremadog	North Wales
19	*Wellington Crack*	E4 6a	***	Ilkley	Yorkshire

	Route	Grade	Quality	Crag	Location
20	*Great Arête*	E4 6a	***	Llech Ddu	North Wales
21	*Cream*	E4 6a	***	Tremadog	North Wales
22	*All Quiet*	E4 6a	**	Almscliff	Yorkshire
23	*Arries Ook*	E4 6a	**	Almscliff	Yorkshire
24	*Snowdrop*	E4 6a	**	Clogwyn yr Eryr	North Wales
25	*Dream Liberator*	E3 6a 6a	***	Great Zawn	Cornwall
26	*Eastern Hammer*	E3 6a	***	Gimmer	Lakes
27	*Face Route*	E3 5c 6a	***	Gordale	Yorkshire
28	*Foil*	E3 6a	**	Dinas Cromlech	North Wales
29	*Eroica*	E2 6a	***	Pentire Head	Devon
30	*The Diedre*	E2 5b 5b	***	Kilnsey	Yorkshire

Grade Comparison Table

British Traditional Grade	American Grade	Sport Grade	Some Livesey Benchmarks
5a E1 5c	5.10a – 5.10c	5 – 6a	
5b E2 6a	5.10c – 5.11a	6a – 6b	*The Diedre* E2 5b 1972
5c E3 6a	5.11a – 5.11c	6b – 6c	*Face Route* E3 6a 1971
5c E4 6b	5.11b – 5.11d	6c – 7a	*Central Wall* E4 6a 1972 *Nagasaki Grooves* E4 6b 1972 *Wellington Crack* E4 5c 1974
6a E5 6c	5.11d – 5.12c	7a – 7b	*Jenny Wren* E5 6a 1971 *Limehill* E5 6a 1974 *Right Wall* E5 6a 1974
6a E6 6c	5.12c – 5.13b	7b – 7c	*Footless Crow* E6 6b 1974 *Mossdale Trip* E6 6b 1977 *Das Kapital* E6 6b 1978
6b E7 6c	5.13a – 5.13d	7c – 8a	
E8	5.13 – 5.14	8a – 8b	
E9	5.14 – 5.15	8b – 8c	
E10	5.15	8c – 9a	

A Short Treatise on Training

by Pete Livesey

Before I start with the main point of this article I'd like to look at some ethical considerations, such as why is it necessary to train, or can one still enjoy climbing without training? One could climb at one's own level for instance and still push very hard but never train at all. But some people do train, some people do want to train, and some people have always trained. It seems to me there are three possible reasons for this:

Some intrinsic self-fulfilment motive, in which one wants to test one's own limits to the logical maximum and to do that, of course, one has to train – a laudable motive but not, I fear, the popular reason for training. Most likely, I suspect, is a desire to excel at the activity in a competitive way – that is, in relation to others and, perhaps, thirdly to achieve and further team, club or national standards. (The latter reason seems particularly prevalent in snowy mountaineering.)

All in all I don't think that refined and single-minded athletic training should sit comfortably in an activity like climbing, whose most highly prized attributes are ideals that seem to be the antithesis of training. Wherever we finally take a stance it should be said that although training may be a part of climbing, it must never be a compulsory or an essential part.

I'd like to counter any anti-training arguments with a few words in favor of training for climbing – reasons why it might not be so bad after all. Firstly, climbing will only retain interest if standards continue to rise. Improved gear, etc, would only mean too many people climbing at a top standard, and consequent boredom – a state reached in French rock-climbing a few years ago, where, because of the style and use of equipment nearly everyone could climb every route. We need mental and physical advancement to ensure a receding horizon to head towards – for some of us that horizon may be receding a little too quickly for comfort.

Secondly, one should never deny that climbing is physical and that much of the inherent pleasure is distinctly physical. That pleasure is almost certainly heightened by a sense of physical well-being, or perhaps even athletic competence; fitness training of some kind is the way to heighten or ensure that experience.

Let me now dispel two popular myths – those of training being a new thing to climbing and me being the inventor or instigator of it. At the end of the last century O G Jones pumped iron through city winters to prepare himself for Lake District summers; early expeditions prepared themselves for the mountains by running and other forms of flagellation, developed to the ultimate by later stars, who spend the winter in ice-boxes playing with their Birds Eye peas. My only contribution to training was to use the knowledge available at the time and apply it to rock-climbing specifically and probably in a more systematic way than before. With hindsight and more knowledge I now realise that most of my methods were wrong or inefficient and just a few, by dint of luck, were right.

Surprisingly enough, considering that so much of it goes on, our knowledge of training is amazingly naive. It is only in certain individual Olympic events like athletics and swimming that the art of training is at all developed. For instance, fitness training amongst professional football clubs is quite basic and probably highly inefficient considering it is a multi-million pound industry. In climbing we have the well-documented activities of one flawless superstar who reputedly performs 200 press-ups three times a day – I hope he enjoys it because it's certainly not doing his climbing much good.

Training is an activity directed towards improving one's level of performance in a chosen activity and the problems of training lie in discovering the most effective means of achieving specified results. The exact nature of the activity is crucial, as will become obvious later, but it should be stated here and now that climbing is not one activity but a diverse range of activities whose only common factor is the participant, who is normally characterised throughout the range as the drunken loony. The activities of bouldering and snowy mountaineering are so distinct that I can think of no common aspects in the way one should train for such activities. I am reminded of one Bernard Newman who once spent the whole summer in the Alps training for his winter season on the Leeds climbing wall. As to performance, just what is performance in bouldering or crag climbing or mountaineering, and what are the constituent abilities one brings to this performance? Perhaps more important, what abilities and in what proportions should they be brought to ensure best performance? How many of us divvies have ever sat down and thought: *'Why am I a divvy at rock-climbing?'* or *'Why didn't Chris invite me on that 'soooper' trip to China?'*

We are divvies because of some shortcoming in one or more of the following: the physiological – consisting of strength, endurance and flexibility – or the psychological, which for convenience we can separate into motivation, and what could loosely be called self-control.

Finally, the area of motor-skills – though this is really a part of the psychological, but it is useful to consider it separately. These are the constituent parts of performance in either bouldering or snowy mountaineering, but for either activity the answer to the question: 'How much of each is required?' will be different. I can't answer the question except in generalities by saying that successful performance in snowy mountaineering probably has a much larger psychological component than does bouldering, and conversely bouldering performance has strength as a major constituent. It is no use, therefore, doing endless strength training when strength accounts for only 10% of total performance in the activity. The amount of training of one type or another should bear some relationship to its proportional value in the total performance. If, however, you are very weak at one particular aspect then it is that aspect which will be improved most easily by training. There is unfortunately a great tendency in sportsmen, and climbers seem to be the same, to train at what you are good at regardless of whether it is efficient or not, because it feels good and you are motivated – it is, however, much easier to improve performance in a component in which you are only 50 per cent efficient than in one at which you are 95 per cent efficient and it is, of course, especially valuable if the former component, the 50 per cent efficient one, is a large constituent of overall performance.

I suppose the major and crucial concept in training is that of specificity, a concept common to all constituents of training. Simply, this states that the more specific to the activity your bit of training is, the better, or put another way, the best training for bouldering is bouldering and the best training for climbing rotten snow is climbing rotten snow. But there is a little bit more to specificity than that. There could be several reasons why it is impractical to train for bouldering by bouldering. One may be that training on boulders does not meet any of the other requirements of efficient training such as the possibility for overload or the ability to continue for a given length of time before finger-ends wear out. The other much more likely reason is that it's pissing down outside. So if we have to train on another lump of environment than the boulder itself, and this could be a climbing wall, house wall, or little-related situations such as running and weight training, then we must look to the wider meanings of specificity.

Weight training may develop strength, speed or endurance but it should be developing the same kinds of strength, speed and endurance that are required in the activity and in the same proportions. A snowy mountaineer, for example, may require 95% endurance and 5% speed/strength energy development, whereas a crag rat may require 80% speed/strength energy and 20% medium duration energy. On the psychological side it may be possible by training to gain increased confidence in anxiety-provoking situations, but again there may be a greater or lesser degree of specificity required. It is no use becoming supremely confident in situations of interpersonal danger (though this might be useful for the pub afterwards) if you still turn into a dithering wreck after reaching an altitude of eight feet in a situation of physical danger.

So let us recap now. There are three constituents of our performance and, therefore, of our training: the physiological, which includes strength, speed, endurance and flexibility; the psychological, which includes motivation and self-control and, finally, the area of motor skills. In pursuing all these aspects of our training we should work towards as much specificity as possible. Henry Barber once failed to make the second ascent of *Foops* in the Shawangunks, so he hung about on a rope photographing and measuring up the crucial section, which is a 10-foot roof, went home, built the whole lot out of wood in his cellar and trained all winter on it until he could float up it.

'We tend to concentrate very hard on the task in hand as we become anxious, but then when anxiety turns to fright the main task turns from what we should be doing to that of flight or saving our skins.'

Let us look briefly at the individual components of training and how best to achieve improvement in them:

The physiological, and significantly I start with this because so much is known about physiological training and much less about other aspects. Strength and endurance are concerned with muscles and their energy supply. Strength can be increased by training more muscle fibres to work at once and strengthening individual fibres, while endurance is also affected by the energy supply to the muscles. Both aspects are trained in a similar way and there need be little distinction between them. The basic principle is that of overload, and overload means working the muscle near its maximum for as long as possible and training effect is only achieved when this is happening. When the muscle is cruising there is little or no training effect. Lots of overload in a short length of time is achieved by doing repetitions of the action with something like 70 per cent of the maximum load possible for one action. The usual kinds of repetition are done in bunches of six to ten with three sets. This is really talking about weight training or move training on a climbing wall, but is translatable into mountaineering terms by doing sets of uphill runs at near-maximum speed. If we are talking purely about muscular strength and endurance then half an hour's training three times a week seem the optimum amount. However, there are other factors such as standard of performer and habituation to the stress situation which normally demand that better performers train much more often than this and for longer. It should be noticed here that there is a commonly held but mostly erroneous belief that endurance training which gets the heart pumping away is actually improving the heart and cardio-vascular system in general. This is not so; cardio-vascular training is for the greater part only effective on the limbs which are involved in the training; lots of running training, therefore, isn't much good for endurance work which uses the arms. Flexibility has been the underdog in most physiological training schedules but it seems as though it might be very important at the more gymnastic end of the climbing continuum. If you have a given strength in any one muscle the range over which you can use that strength is governed by the total range over which the particular limb will operate. If the limb's total range (in a specific way, of course) is increased, then the range over which maximum strength can be used will be increased. Furthermore, and perhaps more important, the fundamental movements involved in climbing demand a greater range in the limbs for effective and efficient progress to be made. So much strength can be conserved by being able to step from hold to hold rather than making six scrabbling moves between each foothold relying on the arms for support. It is, in the main, flexibility which enables this efficiency of movement. Flexibility is quite simply increased statically by working the limbs over a gradually increasing range without bouncing the body weight on them. It is improved less satisfactorily and less safely in a dynamic way by using a bouncing action of the body to momentarily increase the range of the limb.

Psychological – I have no idea how one increases motivation, except that it will come naturally with visibly improving performance in other aspects of training. It is, of course, related to self-control in that increased motivation is an incentive not to be overcome by fear when more than a foot from the last runner. Control of anxiety or fear, which is probably what we are talking about when we talk of self-control, may be improvable and is obviously significant in rock-climbing performance. We do chicken out of moves that we are physically capable of doing. It is unlikely that one's inherent predisposition to be anxious can be changed all that much but what we can do is become very familiar and happy in the situation which causes the anxiety – in other words we are not triggering our potential to become anxious or frightened. This is known as habituation. Despite the familiarity we will still become frightened in certain situations. Experienced performers tend to displace the feeling of fear to another time away from that time required for the execution of the task in hand. In this way the fear does not interfere with the physical performance. Another phenomenon which occurs is that we tend to concentrate very hard on the task in hand as we become anxious, but then when anxiety turns to fright the main task turns from what we should be doing to that of flight or saving our skins – a situation that most of us have experienced from time to time. The problem here is that the centre of our attention is focused on to the wrong thing; deliberate thought or concentration can in time enable us to focus on the correct task, that of doing the climb.

Motor skills – in many ways learning or improving of motor skills should be carried out in situ, on the boulder or mountain, because there we meet the exact kind of rather open-ended skills demanded of us in climbing. I don't think it's necessary to go out and consciously do skills training – once you have learnt the skills you won't improve them much anyway and it's probably better just to let it happen in situations which can't be used for other kinds of training, and then just think about climbing with style (or whatever you like to call it). As a counter to this it might be said that the cliff itself is not a good place to learn skills because there are too many distractions and it is an anxiety-provoking environment, neither of which are conducive to the learning stages of a skill. Obviously boulders or good climbing walls are the best places to do skills training.

Conclusions

That just about covers the various aspects of training for climbing. I haven't prescribed any training schedules because these must be individually tailored to the needs of each climber, so that any specific aspect of a specific activity can be improved upon. As far as the would-be trainer is concerned the main problem lies in analysing just which bit of the activity it is that he needs to train, and perhaps even more difficult, just what is the nature of that bit of activity? This can be illustrated by comparing, say, the climbing of a 50-foot gritstone pitch and the canoeing of an 800 yard stretch of white water – both take the same amount of time and use the same muscles with the same amount of maximum strength being exerted, but they are still very different physiologically. The canoeist uses his strength continuously over five minutes whereas the climber tends to use his strength in little bursts of 20-30 seconds with half-rests in between. The two sets of actions, therefore, require different kinds of training. Once someone sorts out exactly what is required of the various activities involved in climbing, the rest is easy.

First published as 'You Too Can Have A Body Like Mine' *in High No. 24 November, 1984.*

Contributors and Characters

Henry Barber

Henry was born 1953 in Boston, Massachusetts and developed into a leading rock and ice climber in the 1970s. Known by the nickname 'Hot Henry' he was a prolific first ascensionist and free soloist. He was one of the first American rock climbers to travel widely to climb in different countries and became one of the first "professional" American rock climbers, supporting himself as a sales representative for outdoor equipment companies including Chouinard Equipment and Patagonia, and by giving lectures and slide shows. He was one of the few climbers of his era to actively seek and use media attention. His repertoire of moves, creativity, and problem-solving abilities and his tremendous self-confidence and mental control, set him apart from his contemporaries. Henry Barber was an early advocate of clean climbing, using only nuts for protection, before the era of spring-loaded camming devices that made protecting cracks without pitons feasible. Like Livesey, one of Barber's specialities was doing the first free ascent of established aid climbs. Barber was a prolific soloist, specializing in on-sight solo ascents. In 1973, Barber soloed the *Steck-Salathé* Route on Sentinel Rock in Yosemite National Park. The solo ascent, done on-sight and in 2½ hours, brought Barber to prominence as a leading rock climber. Henry's biography *On Edge: The Life and Climbs of Henry Barber* was written by Chip Lee and published in 1982.

John M Barker

John Barker was a member of Bradford Pothole Club and focused on caving for many years, exploring most of the known Yorkshire systems. His earlier interest in climbing was later rekindled after reading *Conquistadores of the Useless* and accounts of Bonatti's amazing exploits, causing him to specialise, for a time, in aid climbing on the main limestone cliffs of Yorkshire, bringing upward progress on virtually non-existent placements to a fine art.

John met Livesey, Sheard and Barraclough in the 1960s and that led to an accelerated learning curve to the higher levels of extreme rock climbing, including early free ascents of *Mammoth* and *Rat Race* with Livesey.

He visited the Alps in 1969 where his first Alpine route was the *Walker Spur*, followed by the *Route Major*. He subsequently became known as the 'Climbing Policeman.' Livesey often joked about using a policeman for aid if needed.

John eventually left the Police Force, and almost inevitably became a student at Bingley College; later pursuing a long career in teaching along with the completion of many seasons in the Alps, climbing most of the Grand Courses, including: *Central Pillar of Freney*, second British ascent of *Croz Spur* on the Jorasses, north face of the Matterhorn, *American Direct*, *Bonatti Pillar* and north face of the Dru, *Brandler-Hasse* on Cima Grand, and solo ascents of *Sentinel Rouge* and *Pear Buttress* on Mont Blanc.

John Barraclough

John grew up in Bradford, West Yorkshire … in a pub! By the early 1960s, he was knocking about with a group from the Topic Folk Club. They had regular weekend camping trips, using public transport of course, to any village with a hostelry that didn't mind being taken over on a Saturday night for singing. On one such weekend his brother tied him onto a rope thrown down a route at Wimberry Rocks by a total stranger who shouted, *'Have a go mate!'* So began his rock climbing days, which lasted until about 1970. In that decade, Barraclough climbed at home and abroad, got into mountaineering and skiing, and teamed-up, for a year or two, with Pete Livesey. He worked for the MA (Mountaineering Association) in London for a year, did a degree at Bradford University and spent 1969-1970 on Barbara Spark's Outdoor Education course at Bangor University. After that, jobs in education, marriages and 2 sons, meant that climbing had to take a back seat, although he continued to enjoy some scrambling and the occasional easy winter route. *'I think the mountains in winter garb are simply superb and soloing is maybe the sport of the gods.'* He retired to Snowdonia in 2000 and embarked on renovating his cottage. *'Although I have not done any serious rock climbing since the early 70s, a continuing love and appreciation of the great outdoors together with the many important friendships I made continue to sustain me as the challenges of later life take hold.'*

Martin Berzins

Martin Berzins was part of the vibrant new wave climbing scene that centred around Leeds University in the 1970s. He started to make his mark repeating hard routes of the day and became an active new-router particularly on Yorkshire Limestone and in the Lake District with routes like *Ringwraith* E56b on Scafell in 1977, *Wise Blood* E6 6b and *Dominatrix* E6 6b at Kilnsey, *Blue Angel* E7 6b at Blue Scar, *Angel Heart* E7 6a on Pavey Ark, *Siege Perilous* E7 6b on Scafell East Buttress in 1992 and the 'bucket and pail' routes on the North Buttress of Dove Crag, including *Vlad the Impailer* E7 6b in 1990. Martin remained active in the UK climbing scene until he moved to America in 2003 where he is a Professor of Computer Science at the University of Utah. He still climbs new routes, often while discovering and developing whole crags in the mountains and deserts of Utah, with others equally obsessed by the lure of the unknown and the solitude that accompanies it.

Geoff Birtles

'I began climbing at Stanage in 1961 and the following year joined the renowned Cioch CC based at Stoney Middleton where I was introduced to climbing on limestone and new routing; initially with Jack Street on the first ascent of Jasper. Jack developed into a leading figure of the 60s and was a major influence on my outlook, which was passionately new routing. I subsequently had the privilege of climbing with people such as Joe Brown and Pete Crew and developed long-standing climbing partnerships with Tom Proctor and Ron Fawcett. I climbed in the Dolomites and the Western Alps which I thought was very dangerous and with Tom had the honour of representing the UK in France on an International rock climbing meet. I also went to Cerro Torre, Patagonia and Yosemite, two of the special places in the world. I also discovered new caves and was an early pioneer of paragliding, representing Britain in the first World Championships in Switzerland where we got trounced. I published and edited 'Crags and High Magazine' *for twenty years, which involved dealing with the best climbers of all types on a global scale. This wonderful job came with perks such as meeting the Queen and going to the Himalaya with his nibs Chris Bonington. I suppose one of the highlights of all this was burning off Brown and Crew on a new route on Gogarth which, gratefully, Joe has never let me forget.'*

Andy Cave

Andy left school at 16 with no qualifications and followed family tradition starting work as miner at Grimethorpe Pit in Yorkshire.

At 17, he did his first rock climb and was instantly hooked. He soon began dreaming of scaling the world's most difficult mountain climbs, though many laughed at the ambition in one so new to the sport. Just three years later, he succeeded on the infamous north face of the Eiger.

After four years as a miner, Andy quit his job so he could dedicate himself to climbing. He also returned to education, eventually studying for a degree in English, then a PhD in Linguistics.

He has led expeditions around the world. In the Alps he has completed many climbs considered to be amongst the most difficult of their genre. In the Himalayas he made the first ascent of one of the 20th Century's greatest climbs on the north face of Changabang, a climb that was tragically marred by the death of Brendan Murphy during their epic descent. In 2000 he travelled to Alaska to tackle Mount Kennedy's North Face with Mick Fowler, and succeeded where many others had failed.

Andy's story has been read by tens of thousands in his two award winning books, *Learning to Breathe* and *Thin White Line*. He has appeared in documentaries on radio and TV, as both presenter and subject, and has inspired many with his journey of an ordinary boy growing up to achieve remarkable things. He continues to climb at the highest standards.

John Cleare

John Cleare is a professional photographer who has been climbing since his early teens. After many years in editorial, industrial and fashion photography, he found himself specialising in mountaineering, adventure travel and landscape, and has published more than thirty books since the classic *Rock Climbers in Action in Snowdonia* in 1966.

With the BBC TV climbing circus of the 1960s, John was instrumental in such programmes as *Matterhorn Centenary*, the *Old Man of Hoy* and *Spiders Web*, and his film credits include Clint Eastwood's *Eiger Sanction*; *Surrender to Everest*, BBC's *Last Blue Mountain* and several TV commercials. Expeditions and photographic commissions have taken him all over the world including the Arctic, North and South America, Australia and New Zealand, Africa, Borneo, China and frequently to the ultimate mountains - the Himalayas of Nepal, India and Pakistan. He led the 1978 British Himalchuli attempt, the highly successful American ski ascent of Muztagh Ata in 1982 and the British Kedar Ski Expedition of 1994. Now semi-retired, he lives in Wiltshire.

Ian Cooksey

Ian Cooksey started climbing in the Lake District with his father. In his early teens he teamed up with a group of like-minded individuals of a similar age and started to repeat some of the harder routes in the area. Moving to West Yorkshire also improved the scope of his climbing experiences and he graduated from Huddersfield University in 1987 with an honours degree in English Language. After a period of working for roped access companies and taking time out to climb in Europe and North America he started a teaching career. Moving back to the Lake District, with his wife Sarah and daughter Maria eleven years ago, re-ignited his passion for mountain routes and he has continued to travel and climb throughout Europe.

Graham Desroy

Graham Desroy, known affectionately as 'Streaky', was one of the original 'Clean Hand Gang' members. He moved from his native Wolverhampton in 1973 to be part of a vibrant Leeds climbing scene, which included people like Martin Berzins, Mike Hammill, Al Manson, Bernard Newman and John Syrett. During an almost thirty-year stint in Yorkshire he made a distinctive mark on the area, not only through his significant climbing accomplishments, but also through the production of several timeless guidebooks. He produced *New Grit*, to update the old *Yorkshire Grit* guide, then compiled *Lime Crime*, which he co authored with Pete Livesey in 1982. The groundbreaking *YMC Limestone Guide* came next in 1985, followed by the definitive *YMC Guide to Yorkshire Grit* in 1989. He is still involved in guidebook work with Ground Up based in Llanberis. Graham's essays and articles have been published in various periodicals. He continues to climb at a high standard and has re kindled his Alpine roots with new ascents in the Himalayas in recent years.

Jean-Claude Droyer

Born in May 1946, Droyer is a French mountaineer, rock climber and guide. He carries the title in France of 'Father of Modern Climbing', which is testimony to his influence. His career as a mountaineer progressed with some of the hardest routes in the Alps such as the West Face of the Dru, *Walker Spur* and South Face of the Fou. He developed a penchant for hard solo climbing in the pre Alps, Dolomites and around Mont Blanc, which culminated in the first solo ascent of the *American Direct* on the Dru (1971). He was influential in opening up the free climbing possibilities of the classic French cliffs of the Verdon and Buoux, and established the country's first 7A on his local cliffs of Le Saussois in 1977. His article defining the rules of free climbing was published in *La Montagne et Alpinism* in 1978. The new 7A grade and Droyer's ground up style (later defined as the red point style by Kurt Albert in Germany) was the inspiration for the circle of talented Parisian youngsters which included Jibè Tribout, Marc and Antoine Le Menestrel and Alain Ghersen; these were part of the new wave who went on to spearhead and popularise sport climbing in France. His passion for free alpine climbing continued with successful free ascents of previously aided routes on the Grand Capucin and the *Cassin Route* on the North Face of the Cima Ovest in1979. Droyer has climbed globally with visits to the UK several times during the early 1970's and trips to the USA, Australia and Eastern Europe. As well as a powerful alpinist, Droyer is a talented boulderer with some fine new additions to the boulders in Fontainebleau, including his namesake route *Le Pillier Droyer* at L'elephant. Since the mid 1990's he has worked as a technical advisor for the sports shop 'Au Vieux Campeur' based in Paris where he also resides.

Jim Eyre 1925 – 2008

Jim Eyre was a legend in the world of cave exploration. After the Second World War he began what became about fifty years of continuous worldwide exploration of limestone caves, becoming internationally respected. Born in Kent, Jim moved to Lancaster as a child. He started exploring caves in 1942, shortly before he was put on destroyers and minesweepers in the Royal Navy. He was prominent in the earliest exploration of the Ease Gill caverns, on the Lancashire-Cumbria border, Britain's longest cave system, now approaching 80km in length and still being extended. He went on to probe whatever was worth doing in the big caves in Europe, particularly in Greece and Spain, and was among the first cavers to venture into Asia, especially India and Iran, with spectacular results, before going on to Mexico and the world's deepest vertical shafts. Jim was also known for his writing, which captured the camaraderie and casual bravery typical of an adventure sport with a degree of risk. His autobiography, *The Cave Explorers*, was a best seller and wittily portrays the caving scene with some comical illustrations of the characters involved including Pete Livesey. He was a character, an organiser, an initiative taker and, above all, an explorer, going where no one had ventured before. In his heyday, Jim was a sharp-end leader skilled at recovering injured cavers from difficult locations, where sheer determination and constant ingenuity were necessary. In 1967, he led the rescue team in one of the worst of all caving accidents, when six explorers died in Mossdale Caverns, beneath the Yorkshire Dales.

(Taken from Jim's Obituary written by John Frankland and published

in the Guardian.)

Ron Fawcett

Ron Fawcett is a British rock climbing legend. He was a close friend and climbing partner of Livesey and shared in many notable first ascents during the 1970s. Inspired by Pete, Ron went on to play a significant part in the ongoing evolution of rock climbing, travelling the globe and producing climbs that pushed the boundaries of the sport and were rated amongst the hardest in the world at that time. Like Livesey before him, Fawcett dominated the UK rock climbing scene for over a decade and became arguably the UK's first professional rock climber attracting sponsorship deals and appearing in a number of climbing films and documentaries. His cutting edge new routes are too numerous to mention here, but many are still regarded as test pieces even by modern standards. His outstanding talent was recognised the world over and he developed friendships with like minded athletes and influential climbers overseas such as John Long from America and German ace, the late Wolfgang Güllich. He has written two books, *Ron Fawcett on Rock* (with photographer John Beatty and writer Mike Harrison) published in 1987. His autobiography, *Rock Athlete* (with Ed Douglas) was published in 2010 and won the Boardman Tasker Prize for Mountain literature. Ron is a keen and talented fell runner achieving top rankings as a super vet and still continues to 'boulder' to a high standard.

Peter Gomersall

At secondary school an early trip took Peter Gomersall to the Lake District where he fell in love with climbing; '*That was the effective end of my dream to become a football star; something infinitely grander was calling!*' Pete was one of the group of talented climbers who emerged from the Bingley College scene during the Livesey era. He quickly developed into an outstanding and bold climber and for a number of years was Livesey's main climbing partner, sharing in their new route honours. When Livesey moved into competitive fell running and orienteering, Gomersall continued to hold the torch for hard traditional rock climbing. He transformed the main wall at Blue Scar in Yorkshire into the arena where climbers could test themselves on bold wall climbs. The quality of these routes is second to none. *Death Wish* E7 6b climbed in 1982 was of a new order of difficulty at the time and was perhaps the UK's first Limestone E7. Gomersall's other routes on this wall like *Hammerhead* E6 6b, *Barracuda* E6 6b and *Stairway to Heaven* E7 6b are exceptional. Pete also embraced sport climbing and produced some fine additions to Yorkshire Limestone, like *The Thumb* F8a at Kilnsey which he climbed in 1987 and is still regarded as a modern and eagerly sought after test piece. Pete now resides in America with his wife and works at Northern Arizona University as the IT Systems Manager. He continues to climb at a high standard.

Dennis Gray

Dennis Gray began climbing on Yorkshire Gritstone as an eleven-year-old in 1947 and achieved notoriety, climbing with the talented members of the Rock and Ice Club including the legendary Joe Brown. He has visited and climbed in over sixty countries, including eight visits to the Himalayas. For eighteen years he was the senior professional officer at the BMC, but took early retirement to travel, write and work as a guide. Two climbing accidents led to a change in direction and in recent times he has directed his energies to academia, in China and Oxford. He has written two autobiographies, *Rope Boy* and *Mountain Lover*, two books of anecdotes/stories, *Tight Rope* and *Slack*, a novel, *Todhra* and a book of poetry, *From the Edge*, a second edition of which was published earlier this year. Another interest is climbing songs and he has produced two CD's of these, *The Legend of*

Joe Brown and *The Bar Room Mountaineers*, singing and playing the banjolele and ukulele badly.

Frank Kew

Frank Kew was a departmental colleague of Pete's at Bingley College and at Ilkley College from 1976 until 1997. His activities with Pete were largely confined to the post-climbing phase of Pete's sporting career, sharing memorable experiences in skiing, fell-running, orienteering, and mountain marathons in Britain and France. Together they took student groups skiing in the Cairngorms and also did a couple of ludicrously hectic trips to the Alps. As for fell-running, they usually did BOFRA (British Open Fell Running Association) races mainly from Dales villages, at a time when the 'professionals' were not allowed to participate in FRA events; an anachronistic distinction which has now thankfully gone. As for orienteering, Pete introduced him to the sport whilst rapidly becoming one of the best M50 and M55 age-group orienteers in the country. He teamed up with Pete for about a dozen Karrimor International Mountain Marathons (KIMM, now re-badged as the Original Mountain Marathon) winning the Veteran's prize twice in the A category, and also competing in two Raid Francital events in France, finishing 3rd and 4th in successive years.

Jill Lawrence

Jill Lawrence climbed extensively with Pete Livesey in the 1970s, having served an early apprenticeship on the gritstone of local edges and quarries. On graduation from Bingley College, she took up a post as an instructor at Bewerley Park Centre for Outdoor Education, during which time her climbing ability and experience rapidly improved and for a time in the 1970s and 1980s she was recognised as Britain's leading female rock climber. She went on to form a number of climbing partnerships with other talented female climbers at a time when it was generally accepted that women would play a minor role as support to their male partners; a role which she was instrumental in changing to that more common today where women play an increasingly independent part in high standard climbing.

In 1982 she decided to go for broke, leaving the security of a job in the UK and setting out for an extensive climbing tour of the States. Further Women's International Meets brought her briefly back to Europe where she made leads of classic hard climbs, including *Resurrection*, *Cream*, *Pippikin*, *Zukator*, and, most notably, *Right Wall* of Dinas Cromlech.

On her return to the States she took up an appointment as instructor, and later, Programme Director with Colorado Outward Bound and, more recently, Director of Operations at Deep Springs College, California.

John Long

Born in 1953, John Long is an acclaimed American rock climber and adventurer. He was part of the Yosemite Valley scene and one of the original members of the elite group of climbers known as the Stonemasters who redefined world rock climbing standards during the 1970s and 1980s. Long's many climbing feats include the first one-day ascent of the most sought after rock climb in the world, the 3,000 foot *Nose* route on El Capitan, on Memorial Day, 1975, with Jim Bridwell and Billy Westbay. The following year, partnered with Dale Bard, Long made the 2nd one-day ascent of El Cap via the West Face, in the remarkable time of five hours. He followed this with blitz ascents of *Leaning Tower*, *Washington Column*, *Half Dome* and *Ribbon Falls*, precipitating the modern speed climbing movement so popular today. Long's 1973 ascent of *Paisano Overhang* (5.12c) at Suicide Rock in Southern California, helped to firmly establish the 5.12 grade and was likely the most technically difficult free climb in the world at that time.

His 1978 ascent of *Hangover* (5.13b), at nearby Tahquitz Rock, was arguably the first climb achieved at that grade. He is an international bestselling and multi award-winning author whose stories, ranging from adventure yarns to literary fiction, have been translated into many languages. He has over forty titles and two million books in print. He has worked extensively in TV and the motion picture industry. His novella *Rogue's Babylon* was the basis for the hit movie *Cliffhanger*.

Nicholas Mailänder

Nicholas Mailänder was born in 1949 of Irish-Swabian parentage in Stuttgart, Germany. His uncle John Crofton, who had left his mark on Scottish rock during the 1930s introduced him to climbing in 1963. Livesey and Mailänder met in Yosemite in 1977 and teamed up two years later to harvest first free ascents in the Dolomites, in the Bavarian Alps and in Switzerland while Jill Lawrence and Nicho's late wife Liz (Klobusicky) did first all-women ascents of high-rated classics like the West Ridge of the Salbitschijen. During the 1990s Mailänder was National Access Officer of the German Alpine Club (DAV). In 2003 he started researching the history of mountaineering in Austria and Germany between 1918 and 1945, publishing the results in several books.

Dan Morgan

Dan Morgan graduated from Ilkley College in 1984 and rather than extend his climbing interests in the outdoor education sector he began a teaching career in colleges and universities in Yorkshire and Lancashire before finally settling in the Scottish Highlands. He continued to climb throughout this period, but his interest in hard climbing began to fade in the late nineties and now he swings between paddling, skiing, biking, mountaineering and climbing when his elbows allow. He struggles to accept the competition, commercialisation and overall sportification of mainstream climbing and though no philosopher himself, the vitality of Pete Livesey and what he stood for resound in his climbing consciousness – *'life is naught without the potential for risk and adventure, but most importantly a laugh with mates.'*

Janine Newman

Attended Bingley College in the mid-Seventies where she studied Physical and Outdoor Education. This led to an obsession with the outdoors and climbing in particular. *'My time at Bingley was magical – I loved the course, the hills and moors, the access to activities and the people'*. Pete was the lecturer in charge of Outdoor Ed, but at the time Jan had no idea of the high level at which Pete operated in all the activities, canoeing, caving, orienteering and, of course, climbing, although this soon became obvious under his tutelage. She became a Physical Education teacher, working in secondary schools, outdoor centres, primary schools and eventually for a health education Charitable Trust. She continued to climb throughout this time with long-time climbing partner, husband and editor of *Mountain* magazine, Bernard Newman. She still loves the hills, mountains, moors and open spaces, a lasting passion that was first instilled during her time at Bingley College.

Sid Perou

Sid Perou is an award winning adventure film-maker with a career spanning over forty years. In 1964 Sid began working in film sound for BBC Ealing. During this period he was regularly spending weekends travelling up to the Yorkshire Dales to explore caves and potholes. Perou was co-opted into working on a film project involving the Cave Rescue Organisation, and filmed an unsuccessful rescue (transmitted as *Sunday at Sunset Pot*, in 1967). Perou decided to quit the BBC and start a career as a freelance film-maker and after a year produced a film for the BBC's *World About Us*, depicting the exploration of Yorkshire's famous Gaping Gill (transmitted as *The Lost River of Gaping Gill* in 1971). The award winning *Speleogenesis* (1983, BBC Leeds) took thirteen years to make. His classic series *Rock Athlete* documented the rise in free climbing standards in the UK and featured Pete Livesey, Ron Fawcett and several other leading lights among its cast. The first instalment of Perou's autobiography *30 Years As An Adventure Cameraman – Light into the Darkness* was published in 2013.

Tom Price 1919 - 2013

During a long and active life, Tom made an important contribution to the outdoor world, both as an educator and explorer. During WWII he was drafted into the Royal Navy as an Able Seaman, and he ended commanding a destroyer at D-Day. After the war, he took over as Warden of Eskdale Outward Bound School succeeding Eric Shipton. In the late 1950s he was one of three mountaineers on an expedition to South Georgia led by explorer and professional broadcaster/actor Duncan Carse (the voice of Special Agent Dick Barton on BBC radio), the other two being Luis Baume and Johnny Cunningham. Tom later moved to Yorkshire as an advisor to the old West Yorkshire Education Authority. He wrote some outstanding essays about climbing and outdoor education, including one that was widely published in the climbing press, *Bridging the Gap*. In 1973 he became the Dean of Bingley Teacher Training College, where he was instrumental in promoting outdoor activities. Over a number of years his students included Pete Livesey, Bonny Masson, Jill Lawrence, Pete Gomersall and Gill Price. Tom accomplished many challenging expeditions; including a ski traverse of the Alps with Swiss mountaineer Andre Roch, and a canoe traverse of Canada with George Spencely. Besides being a keen rock climber, he was a fine water colourist and writer.

Although he was quiet and modest, he had a fine sense of humour, and thus was a good public speaker. In his autobiography *Travail So Gladly Spent*, he missed out writing about his war experiences, because he did not think anyone would be interested in reading about these events. It is a very fine book and typical of the man.
(*Taken from Tom's obituary by Dennis Gray.*)

Mark Radtke

Started rock climbing in the late 1970s and by the mid 1980s was pioneering new routes to a high standard throughout Yorkshire and the Lake District. Radtke came to the attention of Livesey through mutual acquaintances and a shared appreciation of the adventure that Gordale scar provides. He followed in the Livesey tradition climbing some fine new routes at Gordale which culminated in his ascent of *The Good The Bad and The Ugly* E7 6b 6b 6a in 1992, with Dave Barton. Other notable new routes include *A Step in the Light Green* E6 6b at Heptonstall in 1987, *Phoenix in Obsidian* E7 6b at Iron Crag in Cumbria in 1988, and *Lucifers Hammer* E5 6a in the Blue Mountains of Australia in 1988. He has climbed extensively throughout Europe, Australia and North America and embraces climbing in all its forms. He was area correspondent for *On The Edge* magazine for five years where he reported on the latest rock climbing developments in Yorkshire and was Yorkshire area chair for the BMC for four years. He has contributed to numerous climbing guidebooks and his photographs and articles have appeared periodically in climbing magazines since 1984. His autobiography *A Canvas of Rock* was published in 2012 to good acclaim. He remains an active climbing enthusiast.

John Sheard

Started climbing using his mother's washing line on his local Gritstone outcrops when still at school and, with the occasional short break, has pursued his obsession over the past fifty-five years. Climbed with Livesey during the late 1960s and throughout the 1970s, sharing the pursuit of new routes and the overdue escalation of grades, particularly in Yorkshire. Moved further afield in 1974 with an overland journey through Iran and Afghanistan to climb in the Himalayas followed by a more comfortable one to Latok 2 in the Karakorum with Paul Nunn in 1978. A Member of the 1980s exclusive and notorious Piranha Club whose motto was *one too many is quite sufficient* – enough said! Continued to climb in the Western Alps in summer and winter throughout the 1980s and 1990s. Followed the Livesey example of seeking out new destinations with several visits to Yosemite and to European Limestone. Shared, with Livesey, the first tentative explorations of the Verdon Gorge by UK climbers. Introduced to sport climbing in 1990 culminating in a memorable lead of *Zoolook* (8a) at the age of fifty-two. Retired from his lecturing career in Civil and Geotechnical Engineering since when he has discovered the dubious pleasure of ocean sailing, with Atlantic crossings to the British Virgin Islands and to Panama, whilst endeavouring to remain active within climbing, particularly with regular visits to sunny, sport climbing destinations.

John Stanger

Born in 1941 John followed a conventional introduction to climbing on a Mountaineering Association training course in 1962. He joined the Huddersfield based Phoenix Mountaineering Club and rapidly rose to become one of their strongest climbers. By 1965 he was partnering Brian Thompson, a Mountaineering Association Instructor and experienced alpinist of the Brown/Whillans era, and making his first visit to the Alps. He took the young Burgess twins under his wing and together they climbed in the Kaiser and Dolomites; perhaps the start of the ascendency of the twins as world class mountaineers. He partnered Livesey on early repeats of routes in Wales and the Lakes. In 1967 they made the second ascent of the *Rimmon Route* on the Troll Wall in Norway, followed by the first ascents of major routes on the East Face of Kongen. Back in the UK he made an early repeat of *Coronation Street* in 1967, two years after the first ascent. In 1968, climbing with Thompson and Burt, he made the first ascent of the extremely difficult 3700 ft West Diedre of Mongejura. Now aged seventy-two he still enjoys rock-climbing, usually with past members of the Phoenix Club.

Raymond Stoyles 1945 – 2012

Ray (Farmer) Stoyles was a leading member of the Bradford Pothole Club. He led the Karst Hydrology Expedition to Jamaica in 1965. The expedition team also comprised Mike Boon, Pete Livesey and Tich Morris and proved a great success as they pioneered and chartered 29km of cave passage, much of it previously unexplored. This was a significant expedition, unique in its day for its duration (six months) and its exotic location. It set a precedence for British cave exploration to wild and exotic destinations around the globe. Ray continued as a keen caver throughout his life.

Tony Thornley

Tony has been orienteering for over forty years. He was national champion in 1975 and 1997 and still wins the occasional race in his current age class, M65. His most recent success was a bronze medal in the World Masters Sprint, although 'sprint' hardly describes his running nowadays. He has contributed extensively to the sport in the UK through mapping, planning and controlling, and has been the international adviser to World Champs and World Masters' competitions. He worked alongside Pete Livesey and others in developing the Yorkshire Dales as an area for orienteering. As well as orienteering, his love of wild places has been reflected in other outdoor activities. Although never a 'hard' rock climber, he has completed all the Munros, including the Skye ridge with his eyes tight shut, and a few easier Alpine summits.

Professionally, he has worked in education throughout his life. He has been a secondary teacher, head teacher and inspector. He still works part-time providing advice to schools, although he knows he is nearing his sell-by date and is likely to be remaindered fairly soon.

Johnny Walker

Johnny started climbing whilst training as a teacher at Bingley College of Education almost forty-five years ago. It was here that he first met Pete Livesey, not as a lecturer, as he later became, but as a student in the year above him. At this time Pete was setting climbing standards nationally whilst Johnny, in his own words, *'bumbled up gradually through the grades'*. It was during this period that, *'Pete occasionally dragged me out to act as one of his portable belayers and haul me up something hard'*. Johnny climbed extensively throughout the next three decades in Yorkshire, the Peak District and the Lakes, with longer weekend visits to North Wales, his best climbing being in the E2/3 bracket. Teaching allowed longer climbing holidays in Yosemite and later those wonderful family/climbing holidays to the Verdon and many other gems in the South of France, sometimes with Pete's brother Alec. Nowadays, he generally indulges in sport climbing both at home and abroad, although holidays often take him back to the South West trad climbing with his son Ed who lives there.

Bibliography

A Canvas of Rock by **Mark Radtke**
ISBN 9781908098009 / 2QT Publishing

A Century on the Crags by **Alan Hankinson**
ISBN 0460047558 / M Dent and Sons Ltd

Cumbrian Rock: 100 years of Climbing in the Lake District by **Trevor Jones**
ISBN 0951111426 / Pic Publications

Extreme Rock by **Ken Wilson** and **Bernard Newman**
ISBN 0906371368 / Diadem

30 Years as an Adventure Camerman. Book 1 Light into the Darkness by **Sid Perou**
No ISBN / Published by Sid Perou

Jonathon Livingston Seagull by **Richard Bach**
ISBN 9780006490340 / Harper Element

Lakelands Greatest Pioneers by **Bill Birkett**
ISBN 0709005377

Lakeland Rock by **Adrian Bailey**
ISBN 0297786377

Mirrors in the Cliffs by **Jim Perrin**
ISBN 0906371015 / Diadem

On Edge - The Life and Climbs of Henry Barber by **Chip Lee**
ISBN 0910146357 / Appalachian Mountain Club

Peak Rock by **Giles Barker, Phil Kelly, Graham Hoey**
ISBN 9781906148720 / Vertebrate Publishing

Rock Athlete by **Ron Fawcett**
ISBN 9781906148171 / Vertebrate Publishing

The Cave Explorers by **Jim Eyre**
ISBN 0969079028 / The Stalactite Press

The Games Climbers Play by **Ken Wilson**
ISBN 0906371015 / Diadem

The Stone Masters: California Rock Climbers in the Seventies
by **John Long**
ISBN 0984094911, 9780984094912 / Stonemaster Press / T. Adler
Books

Travail So Gladly Spent by **Tom Price**
ISBN 0948153679 / The Ernest Press

Welsh Rock: 100 years of Climbing in North Wales by **Trevor Jones**
ISBN 095111140 / Pic Publications

Index

"*The rot has really set in as regards bolting, now firmly established as a protection technique of British rock. Look at Ben Moon's Statement of Youth with seven bolts for protection. Are we no longer to get routes of character demanding great presence of mind, unforgettable experiences where one feels embarrassingly naked with only the rope dangling uselessly to the ground – reduced to mere technical problems or a series of bouldering moves by the glinting ever-protective bolt, demanding nothing in the way of original thought or mind control?*" **PL 1984**

"*Serious doubt has recently been voiced by several eye witnesses regarding the very impressive 'first free ascents' of previously aided routes in Yorkshire and of some completely new lines with pre-placed protection, usually bolts. It seems that the leading activists of the new wave on Yorkshire Limestone, mainly Derbyshire based, have among themselves adopted a new set of ethics, considered retrograde by most, but practised by sufficient numbers to make the influence of peer group opposition unlikely. It is also a great pity that Mountain Magazine, normally a bastion of ethical priority, dismissed such tactics as 'modern techniques and approach' and described the norm as 'Yorkshire traditionalists'. More sad evidence that climbing is being reduced at top levels from adventure to safe gymnastics.*" **PL 1984**

"*British rock climbing is, like the Norwegian Blue Parrot, dead, deceased, passed on and gone away. We are witnessing the desecration of Malham Cove, a superb piece of rock architecture, one of the largest and finest unbroken pieces of rock in Britain which casts a challenge to climbers.*" **PL 1985**

"*There always were elite climbers, ever since we had grades and new routes, and climbers were*